Why Is Landscape Beautiful?

Lucius Burckhardt

Why Is Landscape Beautiful?
The Science of Strollology

edited by Markus Ritter and Martin Schmitz

Birkhäuser
Basel

Editors

Markus Ritter
CH-Basel

Martin Schmitz
D-Berlin
martin-schmitz.de
lucius-burckhardt.org

Translation from German into English: Jill Denton, D-Berlin
Copyediting: Andreas Müller, D-Berlin
Layout, cover design and typography: Ekke Wolf
Typesetting: Sven Schrape, D-Berlin
Printing and Binding: Strauss GmbH, D-Mörlenbach

Originally published in German as *Warum ist Landschaft schön? Die Spaziergangswissenschaft.*
ISBN 978-3-927795-42-6
Copyright © Martin Schmitz Verlag, Berlin 2006

Library of Congress Cataloging-in-Publication data
A CIP catalog record for this book has been applied for at the Library of Congress.

Bibliographic information published by the German National Library
The German National Library lists this publication in the Deutsche Nationalbibliografie;
detailed bibliographic data is available on the Internet at http://dnb.dnb.de.
This publication is also available as an e-book (ISBN PDF 978-3-0356-0413-9;
ISBN EPUB 978-3-0356-0415-3).

© 2015 Birkhäuser Verlag GmbH, Basel
P.O. Box 44, 4009 Basel, Switzerland
Part of Walter de Gruyter GmbH, Berlin/Boston

Printed on acid-free paper produced from chlorine-free pulp. TCF ∞

Printed in Germany

ISBN 978-3-0356-0407-8

9 8 7 6 5 4 3 2 1   www.birkhauser.com

Content

[Square brackets in the text indicate a translator's note]

Strollology. A Minor Subject.
In Conversation with Hans Ulrich Obrist

During a taxi ride through Bordeaux in the year 2000, on the occasion of the exhibition "Mutations," Hans Ulrich Obrist talked with Annemarie and Lucius Burckhardt about an emergent new science, the questions it poses, its methodology, and its cultural and historical background.

Hans Ulrich Obrist: Can you tell me how the science of walking began?
Annemarie Burckhardt: It began very gradually…
Lucius Burckhardt: We held a seminar on the subject of how language conveys the look of the landscape. Six months later we examined texts in the available literature. We looked at descriptions of the "Isola Bella" and asked ourselves what kind of impressions their language conveyed.

HUO: Did the seminar take place in Kassel?
LB: Yes, and it was there too that we came up with the idea of doing our "Walk to Tahiti:" a reconstruction of the hike Captain Cook and Georg Forster took across Tahiti in 1773. We asked ourselves, what do explorers discover and how can one convey impressions of Tahiti? The perception of landscape must be learned—by each historical epoch as well as by each individual.
AB: "The Trip to Tahiti" took place in 1987, in parallel to the documenta 8.
LB: You have to imagine Alexander von Humboldt, for example, traveling the globe and then arriving back [in Europe] with a ship full of stones, impaled insects and notes on barometric pressure, and realizing that no one was listening to him, that no one could

even begin to imagine what the Amazon region looks like. And Humboldt accordingly asked himself, how he might give people an idea of it. Even a stuffed crocodile and an impaled mosquito cannot really convey how the Amazonas looks. When Humboldt realized that, he began to write also about art in his book *On the Cosmos.* He had understood that, although he was able to convey the chemical composition of stone, he was unable to show the decaying layer with its humus, which is that which one actually experiences.

HUO: Have you taken any other walks?

LB: The most impressive walk was the one we did with car windshields along Frankfurter Straße in Kassel. We'd registered it with the police as "an assembly on the move." We aimed to reproduce the motorists' perspective and so the students bore car windshields before them. A long column of us walked like that into the city. There is a Windscreen Society in the UK that still emulates our model. It addresses the major theme of the Kassel walk: What do we experience through a windshield? We are no longer really conscious of how windshields limit our perception. I remember how incredibly dangerous the action was—because we were not enclosed by the sheet metal of a car.

HUO: Do photos of the action exist?

LB: Hessian TV was there but didn't really get what the action was about. Some dismal commentary was made, along the lines of: "the nonsense people get up to."

HUO: So when was "Spaziergangswissenschaft"—which literally means, the science of walking—actually established as such? And was it called that from the get-go or only later?

LB: The President of Kassel University became involved in it against his will. The issue at the time was whether the University should be incorporated in the German Research Foundation. Research priorities had to be specified on the application form. That was in 1990 and in my application I mentioned *"Spaziergangswissenschaft."* The President said this made things very difficult for him. Nevertheless, it was acknowledged to be a valid research focus.

HUO: And the term has been current since then? What is the English translation?
LB: Strollology.

HUO: Has anyone ever graduated in that discipline?
LB: One can take it only as a minor subject.

HUO: You launched the walks because there are certain types of knowledge that books cannot convey…
LB: Certain perspectives can probably be conveyed by art alone, since the human gaze is limited in so many ways nowadays that people are scarcely able to step back and even realize it. Art alone is able to communicate this without being preachy or hurtful. With our walks we switch off people's fear of the unknown. And we have fun, too.

[Taxi ride comes to an end]

HUO: This morning, Lucius, you had the idea of using aircraft stairs in Rome. Aircraft stairs would work wonderfully here, too, in this parking lot in Bordeaux.

[In the mall]

LB: People only see crazy stuff when you do something completely crazy. They'd instantly think you crazy, if you were to draw up in a taxi and install aircraft stairs here.

Of course, aircraft stairs provide an interesting perspective that one doesn't otherwise have. Seen from above, people look like ants. And one would wonder: What on earth are they up to, those people down there?

HOU: The idea of having the aircraft stairs drive through the city and then park somewhere is rather fine.
AB: You have to be incredibly fit to shop here. I would end up searching forever.

HOU: Have you ever used this kind of consumer landscape for your science of walking?
LB: Yes. We made another experiment. We went around town with three mobile gardens. At various locations we unpacked a garden. We unpacked the Italian garden in a mall, in front of an Italian's store. We thought it would cause a stir. That was not the case. The image never really took shape. In this environment, the effect is completely lost. Because everything here is simulation and so you can simulate all you like but it goes unnoticed. It's like pouring blue ink into blue water. Not even aircraft stairs would raise an eyebrow in these surroundings. People would say: "Oh, there's an advertisement for the airport."

HOU: Are your walks in the tradition of taking a stroll on the boardwalk?
LB: The science of strollology addresses something completely different from the traditional stroll. It is a caricature of that role model. It has inherited the leisurely *flâneur's* distance from reality but has nonetheless lost its nostalgic tenor. Strollology was created out of our sense of irony—because there are many things today one can regard only with irony.

HOU: Then what other types of walk have existed—historically speaking?
LB: The walk beginning either on the city margins or outside one's own front door was common in the late eighteenth and the nineteenth centuries. People used to leave the city and make a round trip covering various points. Then there was the walk by rail: one rode to one station then walked to the next. Today, we take a walk by car.

HOU: In listing the various types of walk, I think we have overlooked to mention the walk by taxi that we did today.
LB: Yes, that was our first walk by taxi. Of course, a walk by taxi makes sense only if we thereby manage to reflect on its own particular qualities. That is, we need to get out and walk a bit. We decided we could ensure that happens by offering visitors to the "Mutations" exhibition the following option: they can buy a ticket that allows them a short taxi ride, after which they get out and go for a walk. Then the taxi picks them up again at the end of their walk. In that way, they experience the taxi perspective then leave it behind then re-experience it. Alvar Aalto, who also deals with urban planning, never goes anywhere on foot, but only by taxi. And some theorists claim this is the reason that cities in Finland look so strange.

Everything is relative. One mainly looks straight ahead when driving a car. One is compelled to take that perspective. But one doesn't even realize it until one begins to think about perspectivism. That was actually the purpose of our "0 m [Point Zero] Walk" with Paul-Armand Gette in the Wilhelmshöhe landscape park. We asked, where does landscape begin?

Why is landscape beautiful? It was with this question in mind that students of the University of Applied Arts in Basel set out with Lucius Burckhardt in summer 1979 for the village of Vrin in the Lumnezia Valley in Graubünden Canton, to take part in a special sort of drawing and painting course. For the aim here, for once, was not to portray the beauty of the landscape but rather to understand what makes landscape beautiful. Students turned up at the final meeting bearing a landscape made of cake. Photo: Annemarie Burckhardt

Where does the landscape begin? In 1985, the Parisian artist Paul-Armand Gette used the "0m mark" in Kassel's Wilhelmshöhe landscape park to put this question to the public. Whatever we see lying or growing or crawling in front of us is not landscape, but a stone, a plant or a bug, one more precisely defined by attributing to it a scientific, mineralogical or zoological name. But these days, everything's becoming a part of a landscape... Photo: Monika Nikolić

Of course, what a landscape looks like depends on who is doing the looking. Annemarie and Lucius Burckhardt on the Furka Pass in 1987.

Participants in the "0m [Point Zero] Walk" were able to view and critique the garden in the Wilhelmshöhe landscape park in Kassel through ten metal frames installed there beforehand and hence as if it were a number of paintings. It was therefore possible to criticize certain aspects of the garden in the same way an art connoisseur might criticize works of art. The discussion and critiques of the garden encompassed various levels of meaning. The garden when viewed through certain frames looked just as it must have done when first laid out by a landscape artist in the eighteenth century. Other views attested to a number of eras and might thus be said to evince stylistic inconsistencies, although these too were interpreted here as relevant signs. The first picture frame, once the drape was removed from it, revealed a landscape of antiquity. Photo: Monika Nikolić

During this same walk in the Wilhelmshöhe landscape park, Bernard Lassus gave a talk in front of the House of Socrates on "Heterodite," a term he coined as a positive alternative to the aforementioned notion of "stylistic inconsistency." At the end of his talk, Lassus presented Lucius Burckhardt with a ballpoint pen in the camouflage look—the look used for military operations but which also resembles an abstract landscape. Photo: Annemarie Burckhardt

In building the "Gothic" Löwenburg in Kassel, the landgrave of Hessen reduced the Hercules monument built there by his grandfather to simply one garden ruin among many and simultaneously lent an S-shaped asymmetry to a garden originally designed in the Baroque style. Thus the Wilhelmshöhe landscape park was turned into an English landscape garden without its original features being destroyed. Photo: Monika Nikolić

In 1983, on the sheer and craggy slopes of the Furka Pass, James Lee Byars donned a golden robe then placed a drop of black perfume on a rock: an apparently meaningless gesture in stormy weather, in the company of loyal friends and silvery yarrow. Yet for those who witnessed it, the landscape of the Furka Pass was changed forever. The most minimal intervention in the landscape triggers a shift in meaning and in consciousness. Photos: Annemarie Burckhardt

LANDSCAPE

Landscape Development and the Structure of Society (1977)

The landscape appears to be an everyday thing, something we encounter whenever we glance out of a train window and the image of which adorns those travel brochures printed in great numbers to promote our tourist destinations. But the fact that we perceive as a single entity, as a "landscape," those many and various things that surround us—the tops of fence posts dotting a snow-covered field, the smoke rising gradually from a factory chimney amid the evening clouds, and the group of workers in blue flat caps, returning home—the fact that we calmly pack the blanket term "landscape" around the sum of such diverse phenomena and the wealth of information they convey, just as we'd use a net to capture all kinds of small animals, is an artistic feat with an ideological dimension. For "landscape" is to be found not in the nature of things but in our mind's eye; it is a construct that serves as a means of perception for any society that no longer lives directly from the land. Such perception may have an impact on the environment, may shape and disfigure it, whenever society begins to translate the image it has acquired into actual plans.

When considering the landscape as a social phenomenon it is necessary to trace how landscape is reflected in popular consciousness and thus to somehow express the social meaning or the "language" of landscape. Like any semiotic system this language is subject to the evolution and wear and tear that go hand in hand with structural changes in society. In intervening in or configuring the landscape we ourselves influence how its meaning develops, that is, what it says; and if we fail to take this fact into account when devising plans, our plans may well be mistaken or in vain. Helmut

Krauch reports thus from Japan that when the popular tourist area around Fujiyama proved unable to accommodate the hordes of tourists arriving there, the government built the necessary infrastructure—roads, restaurants, and other facilities—and thus put an end to the popularity of the place among the younger generation.

Like the meaning of any semiotic system, the social message expressed by landscape must be learned. No naïve relationship exists between the landscape and society, except possibly that between the exploiter and the exploited. A naïve person is unable to see the landscape, for he has not learned its language. Or, to cite this in the profound words of media scholar Marshall McLuhan, "environments are invisible." The landscape is as invisible as language is inaudible; colors and sounds alone are visible or audible, but the apparitions they evoke through the senses of the "human receptor" remain still to be fathomed. Is it a coincidence that Homer, the first person to portray landscape, was blind?

Thus when we consider the landscape as a semiotic system, as a language—not in an allegorical but in a literal sense—we immediately run into difficulties regarding the question as to which is the performative factor and which the performed? The claim that landscape is natural, not man-made, does not stand up in our present environments. Yet it would be equally wrong to claim that the artifact "landscape" was consciously created for the purpose of expressing some particular message. Thus, the landscape can be neither the object nor the motif nor the subject of that which it expresses.

This precisely is what determines the social character of the meaning of landscape: that the message it conveys lies not in the object itself, but in its interpretation in cultural terms, in the cultural context through the prism of which we see the landscape and learn to understand it. This cultural context consists without any doubt in such cultural accomplishments as have been made in poetry and painting but also and to an overwhelming extent in those fields accessible to the broader masses: in travel brochures, in naive or sentimental reading matter, and in the portrayals of landscape found both in the trivial novel and in the cheap reproductions hung on hotel room walls.

If we are to endeavor now to see the landscape literally and not just paradigmatically as a language, we must immediately mention an insight of modern semiotics, namely that there is no lexicon. A lexicon—as in: cypresses are sad, birch trees cheerful, cliffs heroic, fruit trees in blossom peaceful, etc.—would not only be pedantic and absurd but also rapidly consumed. Think, for example, how rapidly the meaning of rock and ice in all their awesomeness has been reduced to tatters and diffused in the general merriment of winter holidays in a ski resort!

The grammar and vocabulary of the landscape derive from the poetic origins of our culture. The poetry of Imperial Rome took the canon established by Homer then transported the Sicilian cultural landscape to a semi-divine nowhere: to Arcadia. The Middle Ages adopted the well ordered treasure trove thus established and consolidated the role of its requisites: the deep well and the shade of a tree; the reeds from which the shepherd carves his flute; and the flock sleeping so peacefully at noon that not even a lion would wish to do it harm. What we have described here in modern terms, such as "language" or "semiotic system," etc., was well known to all earlier generations of readers, in particular to the authors of medieval poetics, topics and rhetoric—but in another form. This awareness, that the portrayed and perceived landscape is not a natural phenomenon but one born of scholarship and poetry, began to diminish only when the modern age mistook landscape for nature and vice versa. People tend to attribute this error to Jean-Jacques Rousseau—mistakenly, as we shall see. For in the following, we shall take a look at the evolution of modern society's relationship to the landscape.

In England, traditional relationships were turned on their heads in the seventeenth and eighteenth centuries: the city, hitherto a place for the consumption of wealth generated by agriculture, itself became a place to make money. Country estates that previously had had to provide an income to cover their respective lord and master's pleasures in the city now became pleasure gardens in which lucre gained in the city was spent on leisurely pastimes. The basis of this development was enclosure, which excluded peasants from country estates and turned them into cheap labor for urban industries. Hence any rustic landscape found thereafter on the estates was only for show. However, in order that this show, this illusion, might be distinguished from that which it represented, or indeed, might be recognized at all, it required a certain style, namely Arcadian Classicism. It is not my intention here to sketch the history of the English garden, which extends from the first ventures of Lord Burlington and his designer William Kent to such highlights as Colt Hoare (Stourhead House) and Child (Osterley Park), and also gained a literary complement courtesy of Alexander Pope and Horace Walpole. Noteworthy is the prolific scholarship expended on it: the rural landscape of England was rendered manifest by allusion to the Arcadian paradise of Ancient Italy. Horace Walpole struggled to make clear to his aristocratic friends the economic foundation of this shift: a half-acre in the City of London is the manor and the city palace is located in the countryside ... This is how he described the situation of the banker Child.

We mentioned that the blame for mistaking the man-made landscape for nature is often laid at Jean-Jacques Rousseau's door. No one who reads his *the New Héloise* will approve this accusation. The eleventh letter in the fourth part of that novel apparently spread the fashion for English gardens to French-speaking regions and prompted the owners of Ermenonville to create a natural garden. Yet a careful reading reveals the subtle dialectics that Rousseau developed between ornament and utility, artfulness and naturalness. The garden in front of the palace is the domain of the master: here, the Baroness's husband has converted the monumental garden he inherited into a kitchen garden: in place of the horse chestnut—a "useless" tree but one easily pruned to make a large sculpture—the young gentleman has planted mulberry trees and so encouraged local farmers to breed silkworms. Enjoyment of a beautiful location was thus enhanced by the notion of having philanthropically provided the local populace with a new source of income. The reader is thus led to believe that he is looking at the truly ideal garden Rousseau had in mind until, that is, the Baroness leads him through a narrow wicket gate behind the palace and into the former kitchen garden. Here, the opposite has happened: the kitchen garden has been transformed into an ornamental garden. The artful wilderness is described in all its detail: forest vines were planted such as to clamber over fruit trees; the course of a distant brook was altered so that it would babble through the garden; the fruit, despite being ripe, could not be harvested but served rather to entice the birds to stay. And in order to completely dispel any doubt as to the artificiality of this natural idyll, mention is made even of the high cost of creating it.

Above all, it was the very lack of purpose in this apparent purposiveness that occupied Goethe especially; he saw it as one of the causes of the revolution. True, his political drama *Die Aufgeregten* [The Agitated] does not show the revolutionary party in the best light: but civic pride is attributed nonetheless to Louise, the governess, who looks disapprovingly upon the Baroness's natural garden. It is the sight of true purposiveness that delights the gaze of the bourgeoisie, a class that, as Louise ambiguously notes, "must think of necessities;" these being either whatever the financially beleaguered class requires or the basis of a livelihood for all classes ...

Goethe addressed this paradox of the man-made naturalness of the landscape garden in a burlesque manner. The two heterogeneous parts of his drama *Triumph der Empfindsamkeit* (Triumph of Sensibility) were presumably intended for distinct purposes; yet Goethe ultimately combined them to create an entertaining charade. The central figure in one part, the Goddess of Hell, is persuaded by a deceased English lord to transform hell into a landscape garden. Predominant in the other part is a sensitive prince reputed to be a friend of nature. A picnic in the woods is arranged in honor of the prince's visit but he actually finds the idea in rather poor taste. He is inclined instead to take nature with him wherever he goes, in his myriad boxes and suitcases packed with effervescent springs, birdsong and moonlight—thus with all the requisites of the charming place.

The bourgeois philosophy of Immanuel Kant finally succeeded in identifying the dialectic between that which is unnecessary and that which is useful as the foundation of aesthetics. Among the arts on which Kant draws in his *Kritik der Urteilskraft* [Critique of Judgment] "pleasure gardening" is top of the list: it alone most consummately meets the criterion of being purposive yet simultaneously without purpose. It alone may, to put it in more modern terms, represent purpose without having any. The artistic product insofar became alienated from its admirers. While, in *Die Aufgeregten,* the Baroness's daughter was bent on nothing so much as to kill a rabbit in the newly created nature reserve, the path to that purely administrative approach to property, which would later characterize the heroes of Stifter's novel *Nachsommer,* had now begun to be paved.

Now, after having pointed out some foundations of the Western understanding of landscape, we shall next touch upon a few less harmless chapters in its further development throughout the nineteenth century. Striking here, first and foremost, is how dialectics ceased to play a role in this period, as well as the growing confusion between that which has come into being organically and that which is man-made, i.e. the artifact.

We could head the first chapter "The Ideologization of Nature." Here, "unspoiled" nature and mankind stand in opposition to each other; or, in other words, man is no longer taken to be part of the natural world and is able thus to look upon it from outside, as "the other." A most instructive example of such development is the discovery of the Alps. For centuries, the Alps instilled fear and terror in unwilling visitors but now they are not only being made gradually more easily accessible but also acclaimed as the ultimate in rural beauty. This development is making strides like the annual rings in a tree trunk and may be perused in the brochures and engravings it leaves in its wake. It started with the deep mountain lakes—Lake Lucerne, Lake Thun and Lake Brienz—then reached the lower slopes a few years later. There followed a string of waterfalls, such as the Staubbach and Griessbach; then came the ravines and, after them, the higher valleys of the Alpine foothills. Scaling the major highland valleys of the Alps accomplished the next step: Davos first—reluctantly, but on doctor's orders; then, shortly afterwards, and voluntarily, the Upper Engadine. All that remained then was the zone above the timberline, the actual Alp, and the rock and ice above it. And once these had been scaled and then integrated in the European ideal of beauty, nothing more stood in the way of marketing the winter.

The relevant literature provided a backdrop to this development. Darwin taught us about the origins and survival of the species under conditions shaped by the cruelty of nature; Nietzsche linked heroism to the landscape of Sils; the heroism of Swiss and Tyrolean mountain farmers inspired patriotism and nationalism; a bourgeoisie alienated from its industrial foundations preached the simple life in accordance with such clichés. The national parks established in Switzerland ensued from this confusion of landscape with nature, from demands for the unspoiled cruelty of the natural world. In the high alpine regions, it was said, the forces of nature ought to be protected from mankind and left to wrestle with each other undisturbed, so that storms might fell trees and chamois be abandoned to death by avalanche. Unfortunately, nature let loose in this way does not do mankind the favor of establishing a natural balance and thus "nature" has been endangered for years, not by mankind but by recently migrated deer.

The second chapter, "Manipulating Nature's Image," is based on the paradox that nature must also be visited and hence developed to that end. Man cannot approach nature without changing it. Somewhere between the farmhouse and the castle, "Grand Hotel architecture" is gaining a foothold in the Alps. Each location, each particular spa resort determines what should be on offer there as "nature" and the respective canons of the charming place define which postcard goes on sale; thus, at any one time, the Grand Hotel and the postcard engender the current language of nature as well as novel symbols to give it expression: the Alpine rose and edelweiss, for instance. Sympathy is diverted from the victorious species to the endangered one; the tourist causes the extinction of edelweiss yet simultaneously seeks to preserve it.

This gives rise to the dialectics of tourism as identified by Enzensberger. The presence of the tourist destroys the very solitude he seeks. Tourism persistently wears itself out: one place after another is sought out by the fashionable avant-garde, swamped by great hordes of tagalongs and then abandoned, finally, to economic slump. Tourism becomes a speculative business affair. Whoever manages to discover an up-and-coming location has got it made. The private weekend retreat is an open invitation to get in on the act. Anyone who buys at the right time can earn a second income from his vacation hobby. Perhaps it will prove possible in the future to find a healthy core in this frenzy of activity, namely holiday-home owners' interest in and commitment to landscapes that will otherwise at some point be deserted by their indigenous populations ...

While the discovery of the Alps was not exactly free of nationalism, the "Politicization of Nature" only really got into gear after the

First World War. Each of the nationalist movements that paved the way to Nazism—the "völkische," the "Bündische" and the "country folk" varieties—offered its particular interpretation of nature and of the German people's relationship to it. Franz von Wendrin declared in 1924 that the Old Testament's vision of paradise had been stolen from a Germanic tradition and that true paradise lay in Mecklenburg, and he thereby named Rügen and Usedom "the Islands of the Blessed."[1] The ground on which these monstrous fruits and figments of pedantic minds thrived was German cultural criticism in the style of Langbehn, Lagarde and Moeller van den Bruck. As to literary phenomena symptomatic of the same, there is, on the one hand, Ernst Wiechert's *The Simple Life,* which provided the bourgeois class compromised by National Socialism the comfortable illusion that spending time in the great outdoors remained apolitical even under those circumstances; and, on the other, Ernst Jünger's symbolist tendency to collect beetles, the connection of which to cruelty the author himself pointed out. The extent to which the science of race and anti-Semitism are part and parcel of this ideological complex may be read in the prescient Countess zu Reventlow's *Memoirs of Mr. Lady.*

The simple life in this second edition, i.e. the German people's roots in earth and clay, demanded space; and ideology consequently proved apt also to engender a people without space. Heirs to German cultural criticism, Alfred Rosenberg and Paul Schultze-Naumburg in particular, demanded commitment from the National Socialists to a rural settlement program and, in consequence, to territorial expansion in the Eastern territories they claimed were either empty or populated only by inferior races: policy that was bound to end with the loss of the East.

1   Cf. Armin Mohler: *The Conservative Revolution in Germany 1918–1932,* Stuttgart: Friedrich Vorwerck-Verlag, 1950; reprinted 1971.

After the Second World War and not least as a result of the war effort, especially that of the United States, there followed an era of economic expansion that did not shrink from "Rationalizing Agriculture and Rural Landscapes." Following in the Americans' footsteps, centuries-old traditions and farming practices were called into question, and agricultural life and the lifestyle of farmers themselves were radically revised. Monocultures and an end to self-sufficiency were the most far-reaching changes. Nowadays, farmers produce only the one product that thrives best in their locality. Those combinations once so familiar to us are particularly threatened by extinction. The landscape will soon no longer consist of fields and pockets of land in a broad range of tones; the machinery that attests to a mix of hay and fruit farming will likewise vanish. The incidentals too will disappear from the farm: chickens clucking, corncobs drying and hams suspended in a chimney. Whatever the farm no longer produces, the farmer's wife will buy in a shop, just like a city girl. Although we have probably not yet fully realized it, such changes really shake up the traditional world. Children are still being raised on books in which horses are shod, grain is threshed on the threshing room floor, and cattle are driven by herdsmen—but for how much longer? We cannot yet say what impact the loss of familiar symbolism will have on reality. We suggested above that holiday-home owners might under certain circumstances help steer the fate of their chosen location. It is quite possible that the traditional and, for us, meaningful style of agriculture may continue on a hobby basis.

Meanwhile, "Deterioration of the Landscape," such as we have shown occurred in the Alps in nineteenth-century Switzerland, has now reached global proportions. With the help of charter airlines landscapes that can still provide some visual stimulus are being sought in the world's most far-flung corners. Yet the advent of standardized, uniform tourism rapidly dispels the exoticism of any area visited. Neither the Nordic tundra nor the African bush, not even the primitive world of the Galapagos Islands is able to preserve the charm of novelty. And the pace of such deterioration gives rise to the anxious and simultaneously hopeful question: What comes next?

The final chapter would have to be provisionally headed "The Discovery of the Environment." We use the word environment here in the sense it has acquired in recent years, namely to describe the ecosystem that supports us and which our erroneous economic system is currently robbing of its sustainability and hence destroying. It is distressing above all to learn that our Western society has adopted an economy and a standard of living which, were all the earth's inhabitants to adopt them, would instantly exhaust ecological resources. All that remains for us, therefore, is to go "back to nature," to return to the "simple life." And yet to do so would prompt political and economic upheaval of a sort we could barely even have begun to imagine in the 1930s. Or are those who are building new technologies and rectifying the shortcomings of nature rather than those of society simply abusing the discovery of the endangered environment? Or will mankind manage this time to tear down the ideological veils that have been draped before nature and the landscape and develop a rational and yet at the same time ethically underpinned political program?

The interpretation of nature as an environment is based on the idea of an "ecosystem," that is, a system of natural forces capable of sustaining and regenerating itself, if only its equilibrium is maintained. There are two risks inherent to this interpretation of nature as a system, both of which may lead today's society to deceive itself as to the consequences of its actions. The first is the fact that our beautiful natural environment does indeed evince a degree of stability, and especially so in the Alps. The diversity of plants and animals and other factors ensures that disruptions are remedied and equilibrium restored. Habitats outside the temperate zone are far more labile; they can be quickly and permanently damaged if overly burdened by air pollution or buildings. We alone have managed to delude ourselves that nature is not only adaptable, but actually something quite purposive, like a control system that oscillates around a state of normalcy.

The second risk is that nature, whatever that may be, also includes mankind. Yet mankind does not fit into a self-regulating system, for a highly specific reason. Control systems require elements that react reflexively and proportionally to stimuli. Mankind responds "linguistically" however; he perceives stimuli as signs that he must "read," understand and interpret. His behavior is subject to social processes and learning processes, is bound up with its historical context and is therefore political. Man ignores shifts in nature or perceives them under the heading "landscape;" the image of the landscape—an historical construct in the mind's eye—determines man's behavior and actions, which are therefore by no means controlling or even self-regulating, but have an irreversible impact on history—for better or for worse.

Why is Landscape Beautiful? (1979)

This paper begins and closes with a discussion of what exactly "landscape" is. Which parts of our visible environment are included in that which we call landscape, and which other, equally visible phenomena are excluded? For we agree unanimously on this much at least: the cow pats in Vrin[1] belong to the landscape while tin cans tossed aside by a tourist do not.

So the basic idea here is that the landscape is a construct. And what this terrible word, "construct" conveys is nothing other than that the landscape is to be found, not in environmental phenomena but in the mind's eye of those doing the looking. To espy a landscape in our environment is a creative act brought forth by excluding and filtering certain elements and, equally, by rhyming together or integrating all we see in a single image, in a manner that is influenced largely by our educational background. Was our excursion to Vrin therefore nothing more than a mental exercise? Naturally, we had given the matter some thought during the discussions we had prior to the trip. Consequently, we arrived in Vrin with two scenarios in mind. The first went something like this: when we picture a landscape, we draw on the range of phenomena found in our environment—colors, structures, identifiable natural contexts and signs of human intervention. The environment here resembles the artist's palette. Yet this comparison, like all good comparisons, is not altogether steady on its feet. The phenomena that make up this palette are too different from one another to be able to lie side by

---

1   A seminar with Leo Balmer in Vrin in Lugnez in 1979 for students of Basel University of Applied Arts.

side in a single plane. In a sense, it is truer to say that the landscape consists of many different layers: the merely visual layer of colors; a more complex layer comprising the first hints of natural or productive-technological contexts; and a layer in which social aspects and hence, also a temporal dimension can be identified: an abandoned farmhouse, an annoyingly modern building, or—evidence of an era when farmers were still self-sufficient—a field full of a certain variety of grass.

And then our second scenario: the landscape constructed thus from the various phenomena on the palette is oriented to the ideal of the "*locus amoenus,*"[2] the "charming place" upheld by painting and literature since the time of Homer and Horace, through that of Claude Le Lorrain and the Romantics and, finally, by our tourism brochures and cigarette advertisements. To identify a landscape as charming is insofar synonymous with the endeavor to "filter out" whatever we actually do see in the place visited, so as to be able to integrate the outcome in our preconceived, idealized image of the charming place. The more the walker sees that matches his expectations—the fountain at the city gates, the quiet shore of a lake, Conrad Ferdinand Meyer's white peaks[3]—the greater his degree of satisfaction.

Do these two hypotheses—the "palette" and the "charming place" —stand up? They do and they don't. What follows is an attempt to cover the key points in a debate the class held on the final day of its trip to Vrin.

2 [The term has been used traditionally to denote an idealized place of safety or comfort, which incorporates trees, grass and water, lies usually beyond the city limits, and is suggestive hence of a natural paradise untrammelled by the dictates of urban civilization.]

3 [Conrad Ferdinand Meyer (1825–98) was a Swiss poet and historical novelist.]

Does everyone have the same "charming place" in mind? If it is indeed the case that each person viewing a landscape picks out certain elements and filters out others in order to paint his own picture of a charming place, the outcome is doubtless highly individual: every person applies different criteria. To identify a charming place is to rediscover one's past youth, to rediscover impressions garnered from the parental home, from books, from older people's recollections, from pictures on the walls of one's childhood bedroom or classroom, or those inspired by favorite books. None of us is able to look at the landscape through another person's eyes. Yet common ground does exist: the virile thing to do at holiday time is to take to the mountains, the lakes, the high seas; individual variations in taste are therefore subordinate to that collective entity we describe as "culture." And culture in this regard might best be described as the collective memory of anything we perceive as a charming place.

But places that in no way correspond to the conventional image of a charming place are also beautiful. Some tourists find the desert appealing, or the northern tundra, while we, for our part, take pleasure in the scree slopes in the high mountains of the Vorder Rhine Valley. Opinions in our class were divided, so this phenomenon could not be explained unanimously. One group said that the unusual landscape, the desert or scree slope are a source of pleasure to us also because we "rediscover" them; through the books we read as children—tales of Red Indians and other adventure stories, as well as romantic travelogues penned in bygone times by explorers—they have become for us quasi charming places.

Utility and beauty

Other members of the class took a different view, namely that the impression of beauty one has when looking at a desert, factory sites, or scree slopes ensues precisely from the contrast between those places and the conventional, idealized charming place. Any pleasure the viewer takes in such a panorama derives from the great sense of accomplishment he feels after having integrated it in this concept of "charming." Or, in other words: in a truly charming place the viewer need accomplish very little. Aesthetic pleasure is assured him, no doubt, but he learns nothing new. The further removed the place in question is from his ideal—so long as it matches the ideal to some extent—the greater the amount of information he can garner from the situation. And this gives rise to the question we were able to explore experimentally, also through drawing or painting: at which point does an experience of the beauty of a landscape cease? When is a landscape so alien or strange that it is no longer perceived to be a landscape and hence something charming?

One point that preoccupied us for a long while was this: What role do natural objects such as plants, animals and stones play in constructing a landscape for the person who never bothers to acquaint himself with them; to look up their names in a reference work, for example, or find out something or other about them? In other words: Who sees the landscape as landscape—he who breaks it down into identifiable components, or he who simply enjoys its appearance? At this point, we came to discuss the signal effect of certain combinations of natural phenomena. We noted the way we ourselves subconsciously looked to vegetation for orientation. Where might one park a car in the village? Clumps of nettles are the clearest sign of all that nobody has an interest in a field. Where can our group take a seat in the open air without robbing the farmers of something? Where can we make a small fire? The meadows of the Allmende—the commons—clipped short by cattle, the loosely demarcated edges of the forest (which also serve at times as pasture), and the squat hedges of alpine roses all signal the absence of a private land lease and hence, of a potentially aggrieved leaseholder.

A subconscious knowledge of plant societies steers even the urban dweller to an appropriate site for a picnic. Are such places lovely primarily, and accessible only incidentally? Or has our own sense of beauty latched onto places unsuited to production because we are driven off the others? Plant societies also alerted us to changes in the village. It seemed to us that weeds and nettles covered unusually large areas between the houses in these highland communities. Trampled grass indicated paths still taken in the daily round of outdoor labor. Yet many outdoor activities associated with the traditional, multifaceted, collective mode of agricultural production are no longer pursued today. Paths and squares between houses in Vrin are considered private property. A right of passage is assured yet they are not public streets. The trodden paths are as broad as their use demands; and the weeds encroach upon those areas that have fallen into disuse. So, vegetation here informs the viewer not only about the richness of the soil but also about the shifting modes of production and social circumstance.

This led us to the question of the relationship between utility and beauty. Is the abandoned landscape lovely, or the one currently in use? It was clear to all of us that only city residents would ever debate such a matter; only city residents see agricultural land as landscape. Only someone removed from nature and from agricultural production can look upon agricultural production and natural growth, and label them landscape. In Vrin, terraced slopes and certain types of plant community on the alpine pastures attest still to tillage, the former mode of production. For it is only in the last twenty years that our highland economy has shifted from self-sufficiency to a dairy monoculture.

Monoculture was another problem we failed to get to the bottom of in the course of our discussions. Initially we assumed that diversity and hence also self-sufficiency look "more charming." Then images of extensive monocultures cropped up: fields of grain in aerial photographs from the Swissair calendar. Does their beauty lie in the spatial remove? Or in their geometry, revealed most clearly to the pilot? Dairy production in Vrin implies blossoming pastures—so far. Yet pastureland in some areas of Switzerland is no longer allowed to bloom at all, but is mowed incessantly. The result is an impoverished but still green landscape that cannot yet be said to be ugly. Those monocultures developed in countries where the agricultural economy faces stiffer competition on the global market than ours does are quite definitely ugly however. Wherever cows and pigs are housed in huge industrial stalls and fed on hay and grain grown elsewhere, wherever surplus dung is dumped on land formerly used to raise cattle, the marriage of beauty and utility is well and truly over.

Does that mean however, that our sense of beauty yearns for an old-fashioned style of cultivation, for those production modes recently abandoned and no longer viable? By the time Horace wrote his Arcadian pastoral poetry, Arcadia no longer existed but, rather, a Sicily where masses of slaves produced grain to feed metropolitan Rome. Is our quest for a beautiful landscape therefore also a quest for recently abandoned production modes—a quest for fruit trees on a pasture near Basel, for example, a pasture of the type made increasingly rare by the rise of the electric lawnmower?

The role of ruins

This led to questions about human input in general, about technological intervention and "disruption" of the landscape. Of course, potential mischief has the artist just itching to turn the church tower into a cooling tower, to sketch a nuclear power station alongside the sanatorium, and to draw a highway leading to the heart of Vrin. Nobody will ever find this type of disrupted landscape beautiful. And yet such interventions are relative; today we so readily accept older interventions of a violent nature as to enjoy them even, as indispensable landscape features. Or were the military fortresses of Grisons Canton not once perhaps a terrifying sight? Is the windmill on a landscape painted by a Dutch Master not a modern form of energy production, analogous to our power stations? And did not the numerous viaducts built for the Rhaetian Railway aesthetically enhance entire valley formations?

At this point we discussed the passage of time and the role of the ruin. Technological accomplishment in its derelict form has not only become an integral component of the charming landscape but virtually its emblem: wherever a ruin signals past history, the walker's anticipated and actual images are reconciled. Eighteenth-century English gardeners who placed artificial ruins in their artificial landscapes did not do so in vain: ruins symbolized the past and hence, reality. The ruin as a symbol can be read therefore also as dissatisfaction with our contemporary and in a quite other way, ruinous world.

By way of contrast, the actual ruin of the landscape—erosion, in a word—did give us pause for thought. The ruin attests to past usage and, even had no ruined castles existed in the region we were studying, traces enough of earlier husbandry were evident in the abandoned terraced slopes, and enhanced the beauty of the landscape. Admittedly, "wounds" is the word that springs to mind for the region's deserted farmhouses, often razed to their stone foundations. Naturally we gave some thought also to the laborious pursuit of agriculture on high mountain slopes, and in particular to wild haymaking there. Agricultural production and the preservation of alpine flora are closely intertwined here, and the problem of the farmer as "landscape gardener" is one we of course really ought to discuss at length yet will not touch upon here, for the moment. Erosion speaks of the disuse or misuse of nature in a most extreme form, yet one that is not wholly without appeal for tourists, especially in the Vorder Rhine region. Actually, it was at the eroded spots that we—admittedly with a paintbrush and palette, not with words—were best able to pursue the focus of our research: the question as to how far one might distance oneself from the ideal image of the landscape without destroying the message, "This is a landscape."

We painted landscapes, and noted how the very composition and structure of a painting help convey the message "landscape." If we painted a valley in the foreground, and allowed a mountain range to rise against the sky in the background, it was practically impossible to not produce a landscape. No color, no drawing is so far removed from reality as to destroy the impression of a landscape. "Non-landscapes" could be produced in any case, only by departing from conventional ways of composing or framing the image. Landscape in artistic terms appears therefore to be a construct comprised of conventional visual structures. To our astonishment, our experiments failed in one respect: we did not manage to produce a single ugly landscape. That annoyed us very much, for we had undertaken initially to publish the sort of travel brochure that would discourage other groups from following in our footsteps to Vrin.

Ecology—Only A Fashion? (1984)

Of course ecology is only a fashion, but let's drop the "only," straight off. Only someone with no respect for fashion, only someone who fails to recognize that the proliferation of knowledge and advances in human understanding are entirely due to fashion could be irritated by the claim that ecology is a fashion. Of course the concerned parties will never admit that. Scientists believe it is they who steadily and persistently pierce the night of ignorance with their illustrious, enlightened knowledge. In reality, the map of what is known and what is not is full of strange coves and pockets. Also, sciences decline not because they have exhaustively researched their field but because they go out of fashion. This raises a smile only among those who claim there is no connection between science and society. If a field of knowledge goes out of fashion then evidently only because society no longer has need of it.

And planners or in fact, any of us over forty years old, have already lived through several planning fashions. Yet planners have other reasons than scientists to overlook the existence of fashion: while scientists believe they work continuously in order to increase the knowledge base, planners believe they know it all already and are therefore not subject to the whims of fashion.

Our response to the above question is therefore: Yes, planners' fashions do exist and "fashion" here is the opposite not of earnestness, but of petty-mindedness. But that is not to say that petty-minded people, of all people, do not follow fashion. Because fashion also always implies a shift in our frame of perception: we see the same thing we have always seen (or at least might have seen), but under a new aspect, in a new context. The corset, once an expression of the self-assured, elegant, and open-minded lady, thus comes to symbolize the fustiness of an elderly aunt. Nothing about the corset has changed—only our image of it. The only odd thing is how subconscious a process this is, to the point that the corset in literature is regarded retrospectively as outdated and repressive, even in the context of the period when it was nothing less than emancipatory.

One point must be made nonetheless: when discussing ecology, we must distinguish between its objectives and the means by which these may be attained. These two aspects are certainly not independent of each other and may be separated only provisionally. Yet we can say this much, however provisionally: knowledge regarding the ecological means available to us is progressing today by leaps and bounds. The green wave has led researchers everywhere to turn their attention to complex biological processes and the impact of human production on them. Such scientific research is also increasingly enabling us to take action, for ecological research is now morphing into ecological engineering. But this should not give cause for irritation. Let us rejoice, rather, that Sir Colin Buchanan, CBE, the former traffic planning hero and father of countless inner-city highway loops and pedestrian underpasses, now leads a school of ecological engineering. However, the objectives of ecology are another matter altogether and that is the subject of this paper. Here, admittedly, our activity is dictated by fashion in the narrower sense: by aesthetics, to be precise, owing to a shift in our frame of perception. But nor should this give cause for irritation; it is a phenomenon we cannot possibly avoid.

German forests have been dying now for almost two years exactly. Dying of what? Of types of damage that certainly date back more than two years. A forest ranger was praised in a newspaper report for having "pointed out as early as 1980 that forests are severely at risk." Evidently, other rangers were still unable to see the damage at the time, presumably because their frame of reference, their mindset, was differently attuned. In their opinion, the forest was the quintessence of good health and was therefore ... in good health. However, one place where intervention had created a gap in the forest, a place where so-called damages to the landscape had been identified, was indeed sick. For decades, forest rangers have tried to remedy damages to the landscape by planting young trees, whether or not this was viable.

Today, posters showing indications of forest deterioration adorn the walls of foresters' offices: on the left, a photo of a "healthy" spruce; on the right, the same species but here suffering the terrible "Lametta effect." The forest rangers began noticing the latter about two years ago. I can still see myself—it was during the Second World War— at my father's bookcase, an inquisitive boy leafing through his *Grossen Hegi* [Nature Handbook]. I was leafing through the book in consternation, because not even Hegi had distinguished between the two types of spruce I believed I had identified: the one that looked just like the drawing of it one finds in any good encyclopedia; and the one with drooping branches—the Lametta effect.

As late as February 1984, Lord Belstead, then Minister of Agriculture in England, claimed to see no conflict between modern methods of agriculture and the preservation of natural landscapes. The following May, the same Lord Belstead declared that natural landscapes were inadequately protected from the negative impact of agriculture and that appropriate amendments to EEC treaties were therefore urgently required.

Five years ago in Kassel, in the framework of the Federal Garden Show 1981, plans were afoot to turn the wetlands of the River Fulda—an extensive stretch of mostly abandoned agricultural land full of man-made lakes—into a "Wetlands Park." We brought to public attention the fact that this landscape in its present state was perhaps already noteworthy, owing to its highly specific range of flora and fauna. "But there was never anything there until now:" this, the response we received both from the municipal authorities and, more understandably, from those commissioned to produce the

Federal Garden Show. Today, while writing this paper—and I mean quite literally today, 3 November, 1984—I read in the regional newspaper *Hessische Allgemeine* that the last remnants of the old wetlands on the banks of the Fulda have been declared a biotope, owing to their beautiful flora … Evidently, the Federal Garden Show and the Auepark have changed visitors' perceptions, such that these now can at last *see* this landscape—or what remains of it.

None of that should give us cause to feel victorious, or to smile, or to be ashamed. One may nonetheless feel some astonishment at how little people are aware of the fact that their enjoyment of the landscape, as well as the type of enjoyment they choose, and the type of place to which they direct their steps when out for a walk, are also highly philosophical questions. Such choices always clearly reveal how a person feels about nature, what he considers nature to be, whether he thinks it "good," or "bad," whether he sees himself as a part of it, or as its exploiter, whether he thinks such exploitation is sacrilege or a God-given command to rule the earth. And the choices people make are now changing: — Will they take a step forwards or backwards? — Who knows?

I find myself increasingly confronted by friends just returned from vacation, broadly beaming as they report that they spent their vacation off the beaten track of civilization, in untamed countryside and among friendly people who are not yet spoiled by tourism and take great care of their native landscape. Everything there was peaceful and cheap, they say, and souvenirs could be had for next to nothing; which was no wonder given that those people don't really give a hoot about money—in their neck of the woods, man and nature are in perfect harmony. At times when I hear such talk, it seems to me as if philosophy has come full circle and we are back at the start of the Modern Age, when people debated whether indigenous peoples have a soul or are actually a part of the natural world.

Ecology is a fashion therefore—and this is the thesis of this paper—inasmuch as the importance we accord it nowadays is linked with a shift in our frame of perception, our perceptual reference system. How this system changes—how fashions come and go, so to speak—is a chapter unto itself and is not under discussion here. Yet thought must be given nonetheless to the role of the artist or of any other creative minds involved in this process, although it probably cannot be said with any certainty whether the artist really does create opportunities for new ways of seeing or is simply the first to succumb to them. A classic and perennial example in the field of landscape perception is the discovery of [the German village of] Worpswede by an artists' colony: a "beautiful landscape" was conjured there, not by intervening in the actual locality but simply by pronouncing it a subject worth painting—even though the peat bog from which peasants scraped a livelihood had hitherto been regarded as a miserable, depleted landscape. Conjuring a landscape thus, in the visual plane, had such a great impact that Worpswede still today is a sought-after, picture-book example of rural charm, even though its brief history as a center of peat production has long since ceded to a modern agricultural economy.

Two conclusions, the first in the form of a question: What does all this mean for landscape (or garden) artists? Should they refrain from ecological gardening, simply because it is only a fashion? To do so would run contrary to what I meant to say. I am actually rather glad that ecological gardening has made a comeback, that ancient, medieval, and modern horticultural wisdom is being applied, that the things I learned from my mother about pest control, fertilization and achieving a reasonable yield without too much effort are now once again seen as correct—for I may now throw the hideous garden center catalogs I am sent every fall and every spring onto my pile of (recyclable) wastepaper with a clear conscience. However: ecology does not relieve gardeners of the decisions to be made regarding the art of gardening. What gardeners produce today is an illusion of ecology, an image of ecology, just as they produced with their previous designs a semblance of order or of grandeur. To put it crudely: one can use ecological means to create a French-style garden and one can use a bulldozer to create a biotope, and a very good biotope at that. Most biotopes are created using stuff that can be found in the garden center catalogs. So their ecology is thus an image based not on ecological but on artistic choices.

And the second conclusion is a piece of advice for gardeners. Gardeners used to think about roses in terms of their "bloom yield," or whatever it's called; they certainly speak about "mow yield," even though they don't sell the grass they cut. Today they think in ecological terms: center-stage is taken today, not by roses but by toads and salamanders. Success today is managing to get a kingfisher to settle in the city park. — And here's my advice: Think in terms of the users! Frogs will then follow as a matter of course. Certainly, they have always turned up until now, in all your erroneous plans, in long-delayed construction projects, in building sites rendered useless by planning, and in those badly planned and hence oversized "industrial parks." But a gardener's fenced-in biotope is as out of bounds for users as a rose-bed is.

Nature Is Invisible (1989)

Nature is invisible, but: gardens always deal with nature. They convey as an image whatever cannot be seen directly. The history of the art of gardening is the history of society's attitude to nature.

Of course, the statements gardens make are not easy to read and the meaning of works of art—and gardens are works of art—is by no means unambiguous. Gardens are, rather, the great field of experimentation in which each era gropes its way towards those realms on which it has not yet developed thoughts that can easily be put on paper.

The counterpoint to the city and to the cultivated zone under its control—which was resumed, in the distant mists of time, under the political and geographical term "landscape" (as the name Canton Basel-Landschaft still attests)—the counterpoint to this zone dependent on the city is the forest, the primeval forest. The forest covered the world wherever mankind had not yet set about clearing it; and even after man's victory over superior nature the unruly wilds of the forest belonged to the ruler as a hunting ground. For rulers, hunting is a pleasure as well as a persistently replayed ritual of victory over nature; hunting is a drama that deals with nature and was developed before gardens were. For nature is invisible. We can only represent it. The forest likewise cannot be seen. Indeed as the proverb so aptly says: one cannot see the forest for the trees. The message, "the forest begins here" must be conveyed by visual means, must be staged; and the park of Versailles conveys this message.

The park of Versailles looks not at all as we were told it does in our history lessons, *viz.* "that it can be viewed in its entirety from the king's private quarters so the Sun King can say to himself, '*l'état, c'est moi.*'" Looking at the park of Versailles with an unprejudiced eye, one is struck by how it constantly rivets one's gaze, by how one's views of near and far are measured out in careful doses. The large goose's foot of the long axes does not open onto the palace as the history teacher assured us; rather, one must go to the foot of the steps, must take a path on which one finds oneself always enclosed by walls: by rows of statues and walls of more or less well-trimmed hedges. Once at the spot where the goose foot of the axes opens—axes that are likewise enclosed by walls of hedges, each of which conceals a huge triangular intermediate zone—one by no means has a view of the place in its entirety since, on turning around, one can only just about see the parapet walls of the palace while the rest is hidden behind the stepped terraces.

To cut a long story short: what is on show is not the power of the Sun King but rather the relationship between that which could be controlled back then and that which could not, namely the realm of adventure and hunting. This representation of the transition from the city and the royal palace to the primeval forest succeeds thanks to the horticultural means that Bernard Lassus discovered and de-scribed as "the delayed contrast." Like a piece of music, the garden draws on a series of delaying motifs to slow down the otherwise sudden transition from palace to forest. This delay is accomplished in part by reversing the innate properties of the materials used: the stone of the terraces takes organic form as a figure or statue, while organic materials—plants—take an architectural form, insofar as hedges serve as walls. We are prepared thus for the next step be-tween the palace and the forest, for a new transition from the archi-tectonic to the natural. And only thanks to this staged drama do we understand that the forest at the end of the park is truly the primeval forest and will end only when it reaches the Atlantic.

That the English-style garden speaks of nature is a much more familiar idea. But here too: What does "speak of" mean in the case of an artwork? Alone the viewer who endeavors to put its message into words actually ever speaks. Those who created the gardens were apparently not yet able to formulate their message in words. In difference to the French-style garden, the English-style garden's first message is this: that the disorder of nature in its uncultivated state is more orderly than our square fields and fallow land and—now we are already entering the speculative realm—that in a future, better society, the order of disorder will become visible.

The new aristocracy of ship-owners and bankers makes its money in the city, often as much money as the lords who produce grain or wool on their land, on an industrial scale. The lords make their money in the countryside and squander it in the capital; the bankers make their money in the city—and act as the lords do only when they go to the countryside. Not that the lords have any need to produce things there, for their country estates are a form of agricultural economy without a product. The goatherds' agricultural economy is a better one than that of the gentlemen who have driven the peasants from their land or made them their serfs.

The messages are thus noticeable, but far from clear. Two literary sources provide a mirror image of the underlying problem with landscape gardens. It is written: Is it given to mankind, to go back to nature? The first doubts came from the very person to whom the phrase "back to nature" is attributed, namely Jean-Jacques Rousseau. If we now consider Rousseau's description of the new garden ideal (in the eleventh letter in the fourth volume of his novel *the New Héloise*) in the same unbiased way we did Versailles, we will see immediately that Rousseau was under no illusions. Saint-Preux, the hero of the novel, suggests somewhat awkwardly that this garden has doubtless been created simply by neglect, by allowing weeds to run wild and nature to take its course; and he is given an expert and profound reply, first of all in economic terms: the more natural the garden should be, the more complex the care it requires; and then in philosophical terms: it is not given to man to be natural.

Goethe provides the opposite view. In his *Triumph der Empfind-samkeit* [Triumph of Sensibility]—a drama that aims high but which Goethe unfortunately abusively reduced to a charade—a traveling prince reputed to be a friend of nature comes upon a palace. People there have already given much thought to the question of what nature and a love of nature might be and they are planning a merry hunters' breakfast in the forest. But the prince's tutor, who arrives ahead of him, refuses an invitation to attend, since his prince is fond not of nature in its raw state but rather of artful and charming things; and in order to be sure of finding these, he brings them along himself, in crates and boxes. And, as in a parody of our modern garden shows, the prince's carriages now draw up, and servants unload containers on which is written what they contain: waterfalls, birdsong and the rustling of trees in a forest. Neither the hosts with their hunting breakfast nor the guest with his artificial-natural artifacts are able to see nature itself.

While the French-style garden presents "nature" as an exterior world and strives to render it visible by staging it dramatically, nature in the English landscape garden is "inherent." The English landscape garden renders visible the fact that nature lies in the sheer randomness of the place itself. And where is it most natural? — Of course: there, wherever the human foot or, to be precise, the white man's foot has not yet trodden. Explorers sail off in search of nat-ural nature and they discover whatever they already have in mind, namely images of landscape and images of society. The highlight is Tahiti, and Cook returns with a message that implies the final victory of the English-style garden over the French-style garden. Yet this message from the beautiful island with the ideal society is likewise a child of his imagination.

Cook's return also marks a crisis of the art of gardening. Sailing around the world has put a definitive end to the idea that an "exte-rior" world exists. Primeval forests and oceans now differ from the landscapes we inhabit in Europe only quantitatively, not principally.

Transition from the city to the primeval forest hence is qualitatively no different than stepping from one's own front door onto the street.

This is why the late nineteenth and early twentieth centuries no longer thought about nature in terms of horticultural experiments in their entirety. The range of motifs was expanded yet all images were still classified under the now meaningless main subject heading: nature outside of culture. This is not by any means to say that individual achievements should be ignored. Fin de siècle Europe was intently occupied with the Japanese garden wherein miniaturization was a way to bring an image of nature into the garden realm. Let me list a few unrelated points: Foerster's garden, a marriage of the botanical garden and a miniaturized landscape park, seems important to me. The bourgeoisie schooled by Darwin and botanists from de Lachenal to Schröter to Hegi now sought its nature in the Alpineum. Also important, so to speak as the flip side of the coin, is Leberecht Migge, who presents not nature but work. Gardening is a form of agriculture, but without the edible yield.

The crisis that prompted Captain Cook to voyage around the world has continued to the present day. While Cook's message was that the borders between explored and unexplored parts of the globe had melted away, the modern message of our present day is that the city no longer has borders. Everyone is an urban dweller and everyone lives in the countryside. The unifying medium is the motorcar. The forester lives in the city and drives to work in the forest while the bank clerk lives in the countryside and continues to work in the city: the metropolis is ubiquitous. Where is nature in the metropolis? Certainly not in agriculture, for farmers have long since been driven out. But in the city, in any case, because here I discover a plant from time to time—and I need a pretty good plant handbook in order to identify it.

Do you remember the old city nursery in Basel? Yes, yes, that one exactly: the one that's been haunting our newspapers for a good two years. Don't worry, I don't intend to polemicize, politicize or take sides here—only to say this: in Basel's old city nursery lives the long-horned beetle—the last colony of this beetle to be found north of the Alps. The long-horned beetle too is invisible. One can see it possibly in a museum, impaled on a pin. But it is invisible in nature, since its larva lives underground. The beetle itself appears briefly on the earth's surface but lives only as long as it takes for it to copulate and deposit its eggs. — Assuming we were there at the time and saw it do so, would we recognize it? Would we see it, this example of endangered yet embattled nature in the metropolis? Would we ever even come up with the idea of looking for the last colony of a rare breed of insect there, only a stone's throw from Basel's industrial chemical plant?

How then ought we depict nature for inhabitants of the metropolis who do not perceive nature per se? Residents of the city of Basel did see nature one year long, namely for as long as so-called rampaging youths, (but in reality sweet gardeners) squatted the city gardeners' abandoned city nursery. For one of the arguments underpinning their occupation was: We are preserving nature, since we are protecting the long-horned beetle. Gardeners destroy nature, since they exterminate the beetle. And people pointed with pride at the trimmed grass along the sidewalk, which is actually proof of nothing but the fact that nature is invisible.

Anyone who stayed with us up to this point is surely clear as to the fact that nature today, in official gardening terms, is the biotope. And many a gardener really believes that he can create nature in a biotope. And many a biotope really does contain a rare plant or, more seldom, a rare insect or a worm that no longer exists outside of it. But even that which is natural in a biotope is invisible. The biotope is, so to speak, the opposite of the old city nursery: while the latter no longer shows any sign of having a long-horned beetle in residence, the biotope offers living proof of all that has been driven out of the nursery: the long-horned beetle or whatever else would grow, crawl or fly there, had the gardeners not created a biotope.

"Nature has neither core Nor outer rind ..." (1989)

Georg Simmel's phenomenon—of fakes being passed off as genuine—still sounds paradoxical to our ears, although we actually make use of it every day, namely when we pay for purchases with paper money. Fake money, paper money, stands for something genuine yet its genuine counterpart does not actually exist. Of course it does exist, officially. The gold that partially covers our paper currency lies buried somewhere in the bunkers of Fort Knox. Even Goethe, in the scene at the imperial court in *Faust,* put the question as to why one need bother digging up money only then to eventually rebury it. Finally, Lord Keynes proposed that we fill bottles with bank notes and bury them underground, so as to be able to dig them up again in times of unemployment.

Over the last twenty years, fake jewelry has superseded the genuine article. While people used to wear fake diamonds and pearls because they could not afford the real thing, even the richest woman wears fake jewelry nowadays, because the real thing that the fake supposedly imitates does not exist. This phenomenon has been noted to exist before, in the seventeenth and eighteenth centuries. In the churches of southern Germany trompe l'oeil artists created more beautiful types of marble than ever have been hauled from a quarry—and their false marble deceived no one. It is precisely this combination of natural beauty and the certain knowledge that an artist produced it that creates the desired effect. One's eye unconsciously registers that the columns and cornices are lightweight and would be warm to the touch, if ever one were able to reach their lofty heights.

Today, tourism is faced in a similar manner with the counterfeit issue. Guests no longer want hotels of an urban design but rather, hotels that resemble vernacular residences. For of course Alpine valleys and North Sea fishing villages did once have an indigenous architecture, but not yet hotels, swimming pools, bus stations or hockey stadiums. Therefore, whoever wishes to fulfill his guests' wishes must create replicas for which no model ever existed. But anything for which no model exists is necessarily the genuine article. This explains the triumph of international regionalism, which looks the same at all altitudes and in all climates. Constructed regionalism is, however, only one part of what the tourist really wants to see—namely nature—and showing him the latter is increasingly difficult. This paper addresses below two invisible things that falsification alone can render visible; and falsification alone can render them genuine too, because no model for the fakes exists. Nature is invisible and so too is the will of the people. But both have been rendered visible by the strange story of Basel's old city nursery, a location that is about to be remodeled as a public park.

A prologue in heaven: that nature may be regarded solely as a counterfeit was discovered by he who is mistakenly reputed to have wanted to lead us all "back to nature"—by Jean-Jacques Rousseau. His, in the truest sense of the word enlightening text is found in the novel *Julie or The New Héloise* (in the eleventh letter of the fourth book) and describes the garden Julie created for herself. On Lake Geneva, a couple lives in a palace with a representative garden in front of it and a kitchen garden and orchards to its rear. The philanthropic husband, Baron Wolmar, spends his time transforming the avenues and flowerbeds in the representative garden in front of the palace into a kitchen garden: it is an *ornamental farm* of sorts, where he wishes to replace the useless horse chestnuts with mulberry trees, so as to promote silkworm production throughout the region. Julie, meanwhile, is likewise very busy. With the help of her gardeners she is returning the kitchen garden behind the house to its natural state: forest vines trail over the apple trees, starlings nest in the cherry trees, and a wild brook babbles through the idyll, forming a pond at its lowest point. Saint-Preux, a friend, says in all innocence to the lady of the house that all these effects ensued solely from her negligence: "You merely closed the gates; water somehow came by itself; nature did the rest; and you could never have done it as well as she." "It is true that nature did everything," she replies, "but it was all done under my direction. There is nothing here that I did not order." — And the exchange ultimately becomes simultaneously profound and petty-minded. Nature, it is said, cannot be had for free; the more natural a garden is to look, the greater the effort and the higher the sums to be expended on it. To return to our original point: the more genuine it is, the more it is a fake.

Now let's look at the garden in Basel, the former city nursery that the city gardeners abandoned yet then proved unwilling to actually relinquish. For they wish to turn their former workplace into a product, into a public park. It is to be especially wonderful, this park, and thus no motif that might conjure for visitors an impression of "the charming place" should be overlooked. Even topographical factors in Basel, such as the high banks that contain the Rhine and define its course, were initially to be erased so as to cede place to a sweet brook. The planners realized just in time that this little brook would look ridiculous alongside the Rhine and so decided in favor of ecologically invaluable wetlands. But concerns were then raised that it is impossible to play on wetlands and the area had, after all, been designated a public park. So the ecologists, who are always willing to compromise, proposed a dry meadow instead, which can serve both as a playground and as a substrate for rare pioneering plants. Is that a laugh I hear? Incidentally, the park site cannot be tackled for the moment, since the civil defense force is still using half of it, namely the former slaughterhouse next door; and the defense force, as we all know, is indispensable to national security. Such a pity, that the population no longer believes the civil defense force keeps danger at bay.

In the meantime, anyhow, everything has turned out differently. First, local young people then young people from all over the city and, finally, a section of the population that one might best describe as young-at-heart proved unwilling to wait for this open space to be put at their disposal as a public park and so simply took possession of the land and buildings there and settled in. Thus for two years this garden, the old city nursery, served as a community garden. But the government had eventually had enough of seeing people give other people joy, the joy of a new public park, and so it used the police force to drive away the fake genuine, that is, the real wrong people.

But let us first return to the squatters' garden. How does it look? You must consider that a city nursery is not an ornamental garden but a place of work, comprising buildings, garages, workshops, greenhouses, brick storage bins for humus, manure, gravel and stones, hotbeds and nurseries framed by concrete, as well as space enough for trucks to drive in and out, and turn. When the squatters came marching in, the whole place had been standing vacant for a good while already and was quite derelict. Panes of greenhouse glass were smashed and the iron profiles rusty while, in the nutritious soil of the greenhouses and hotbeds, the last crop plants were fighting off the invasive mighty weeds thronging through the broken panes. The squatters' goodwill and technical resources were inadequate to restore the damaged infrastructure. The garden they set up had to adapt to prevailing conditions. And so it became a largely invisible garden, one that existed only in the mind's eye of its users. The good citizens who wanted to see what the young people were getting up to each Sunday saw: no garden. This, they said, is disorderly—and it cannot possibly remain in such a state.

Did Saint-Preux see Julie's garden? Did the citizens of Weimar, Dessau or Potsdam ever see the gardens of their prince-electors? Were Stowe and Stourhead visible to those people in the eighteenth century who had not yet read the relevant literature of Pope, Walpole, Hirschfeld or Von Sckell? Did not Goethe aptly describe in *Die Aufgeregten* [The Agitated] how the Baroness's daughter wished to shoot a rabbit in the newly created natural garden? She too failed see the garden.

And now to the five gardens the squatters themselves created in those parts of the site they worked on and also saw. But first this one point: Children too saw these invisible gardens, or at least one child did. In front of the nursery's concrete water tank, a kid knee-high to a grasshopper told me, "Look! This is a biotope!" "Oh, really," I replied, somewhat embarrassed. "And do animals live in it too?" "There, in that yoghurt pot, is a young frog." Fake is the real thing.

"Under the cobblestones, a beach"—The first picture shows spontaneous and adventive vegetation sprouting from cracks in the pavement and concrete borders and especially lushly from fertilized flower beds, proving thus that even under the city, or in the city, eternal nature lurks: she who will overgrow everything once humanity has destroyed itself.

The second picture shows nature become rare: the old city nursery was also a sort of National Park. For on the strip of land between the city nursery and the banks of the Rhine lives the last colony of long-horned beetles to survive north of the Alps, only a few hundred creatures in all. The gardeners, if ever they complete their "ecological nature reserve" with wet or dry meadows, will render this species of insect completely extinct in Switzerland. The long-horned beetle is invisible. It spends only three weeks of its life in daylight on the earth's surface. Who recognizes it in those three weeks? It was alone the squatters' knowledge of the site that turned the city nursery into a nature reserve.

The third picture shows a farm. The squatters and workers at the old city nursery acquired some chickens, geese and even two piglets; and they invited local residents to feed the animals with their kitchen waste. Even urban dwellers can be farmers. And while professional farmers are now arming themselves to play animal-factory owner, urban dwellers are becoming farmers who handle animals.

The fourth image shows an emergency. The more vehemently the government declared its intention to meet the true needs of the people, the more eagerly the squatters worked on their garden. Never did one see so many busy people as on the day a false rumor was spread, the rumor that professional gardeners with bulldozers were on the warpath. The "Dig for Victory" campaign of 1940 was propagated with just such images as these.

The fifth and most impressive picture shows a utopia: the utopia of the unity of art and life. Everyone is a worker, everyone is an artist, and everyone makes a contribution to the whole, either alone or as part of a group, whether by making a sculpture, making music, cooking for everyone, or even by sweeping up crumbling asphalt so as to make the grass a little greener.

Citizens lured by newspaper articles and the invitations of the squatters themselves did not see these images. All they saw was an inner-city site in indefensible disorder. The squatters, for their part, could not grasp the fact that citizens did not see what they saw. If they do not understand us here, they thought, then we shall go to them. And so the squatters donned their craziest gladrags, dyed their hair green and purple and went to the marketplace. There too, they created an image: *The Arcadian Shepherds Come to Rome*. But passers-by saw something they simply had to label: "Oh, they are that sort of people!"

Arcadian Shepherds make bad politicians. It is easy for the Romans to trick them. Arcadians rely on democratic rules of play—and also on their garden, their mainspring, remaining visible. But democratic rules of play are not enough; one must also be an experienced player. The "city gardeners" collected signatures for an initiative that they hoped would secure the city nursery for its users, the people. The government cited an earlier initiative, however, which had called for a public park on the site of the former city nursery and adjacent slaughterhouse. The people rose against the people: the people that really existed and were taking action versus the real people, the invisible people. Finally, I realized what I had never understood in history lessons, namely that the difference between the *volonté générale* and the *volonté de tous* is the ballot box. Of course, the people lost; of course, the people won. The people carried the vote against the people. However: the civil defense force has still not handed over the slaughterhouse, so at the moment, respect for the will of the people goes only halfway. Incidentally, it was the people themselves who then refused to loan money enough to accommodate the civil defense force elsewhere—relocation being a prerequisite of the public park's realization. Today, the old city nursery site is a bigger mess than it ever was at the time when squatters were still there, shocking decent citizens. And: the use of police force to evict them has left a wound in the heart of the city, one that will not heal. I dare say even that the people would vote differently today.

Epilog on the PdA [*Partei der Arbeiter,* Workers' Party]: The oldest section of the PdA originated in Basel, as did its name, "Partei der Arbeiter." And it kept the name until the nationwide Swiss PdA took it over. So this is the story of how the only real PdA, namely the Basel section, lost its real name—on account of the old city nursery. The Basel PdA is always right, since it toes the party line. It also knows what the people want—it isn't a sucker for just any kind of people. Hundreds may take to the streets of Basel to demonstrate for the preservation of the old city nursery; but the one and only true people holds a backroom council of three and decides that what the people actually want is a public park. And lo and behold, the ballot showed that PdA Basel was right. The people did not vote for the preservation of the city nursery but for a public park. All is not well that ends badly. Meanwhile, PdA Switzerland has thrown off the yoke of PdA Basel—*perestroika* and *glasnost* here too. Did the PdA Basel act properly when it defended the position of the people (an abstract entity) against the "city gardeners"? — To keep this short, PdA Basel was expelled from PdA Switzerland. And, as if that were not enough, a new PdA Basel was founded and affiliated with PdA Switzerland. So that PdA Basel, the originator of this name, then had to fight for its name. But it had previously ceded the name to PdA Switzerland. A court therefore ruled that the old PdA Basel should look for a new name! The one and only true PdA has hence been living under a false name ever since—because it stood up for the real people and for the wrong people.

So much virtue! And so many weeds! Perhaps we must introduce a second epilog now, on the theme of deceptive appearances? — In his *Falschheit menschlicher Tugend [The Duplicity of Human Virtues]*, first published in Bern in 1732, Albrecht von Haller wrote to Stähelin:

[Yet what good comes of exiling oneself from this world?
In vain, O Stähelin, does one become a tyrant,
If the vice one abhors flees in the face of greater vice
And ryegrass and brome now bloom where one wiped
out the poppy.]

Does nature too deceive? For not even knowledge of nature reveals whether a thing is false or *real*. Haller writes also about faith, superstition and unfaith:[1]

A Newton exceeds the limits of created minds,
Finds nature at work and appears as master of the universe;

1   [LB is presumably referring here to *"Gedanken über Vernunft, Aberglaube und Unglauben"* (Thoughts on Reason, Superstition and Unfaith), the poem Haller wrote for Stähelin in 1729.]

[…] And he breaks open the tables of the eternal laws,
Once made by God and never broken.[2] [Yet your science is still
a child of wisdom
And clever pastimes, a comfort to proud blindness!
You do not reflect on what is false and what is true,
Or on what any man and God may be …]

And now, again in *Falschheit menschlicher Tugenden,* about Newton
this time, who upon discovering certain laws of physics believed that
he had lain bare the core of nature:

[Yet seek by the light of arithmetic
The chinks in artful figures and dark traces]
Into inner nature no created mind penetrates.

He is very fortunate when nature shows its outer shell.[3] The core or
outer shell; the outer shell bears dark traces of truth while the core
is unattainable. What is the outer shell's relationship to the core?
— Surely that of appearances to true being, of false to real? That the
relationship of Newton's principles to nature is that of the core to
the outer shell would be just about acceptable. But Haller maintains
the very opposite: of all the arts, he says, the art of writing offers
barely a glimpse of the outer shell. Haller's metaphor is evidently
ill chosen. Goethe was much irritated by Haller's poem, so much

2 [Cited in Shirley A. Roe, "Anatomia animata: The Newtonian Physiology of
   Albrecht von Haller" in Everett Mendelsohn (ed.) *Transformation and Tradition
   in the Sciences,* Cambridge University Press, 1983, p. 273–299).]
3 [Cited in Hubert Steinke, *Irritating Experiments: Haller's Concept and the
   European Controversy on Irritability and Sensibility, 1750–90,* Amsterdam and
   New York: Rodopi, 2005, p. 95]

so that he added a few ironic lines to his poem *Allerdings—dem Physiker* [Even So—To the Physician]:

Into the core of Nature
O Philistine—
No earthly mind can enter.
[...]
Nature has neither core
Nor outer rind,
Being all things at once.[4]

A manual of ecological urban gardening was published recently in the German Federal Republic, full of instructions that city gardeners should follow in order to produce nature in an urban context. Since nature itself changes yet our image of nature remains unchanged, the book also offers instructions on how to tend a plot of land such that it looks unkempt. Of course, this whole operation is complicated. Once again, we find ourselves back in the company of *the New Héloise*. Nature here does not have a core and an outer shell but rather, a face for show and the opposite of that. Its face for show is the mass of flowers in the city center. The opposite of that is the new equipment in the machine park, which is designed to enhance aeration by gently breaking up the soil; and let's not even mention the new seed-breeding farms. One cannot yet say whether citizens will ever see this new nature. But in any case it appears to require such intensive maintenance that even a doubtful citizen must realize that intentions here are good and that non-subversive urban gardeners are now creating invisible gardens.

4   [Cited in Christopher Middleton (ed.), *Band I von Works, Johann Wolfgang von Goethe*, Virginia: John Calder, 1983, trans. Michael Hamburger.]

Aesthetics and Ecology (1990)

I do not know about you but certainly, I meet plenty of people who tell me they just spent their holidays some place where there are no vacationers. Of course, they got along well with those locals who sell their authentic handicrafts as cheap-at-the-price souvenirs yet who remain unspoiled. For these fortunate people actually get by without money. They live on and can make a good livelihood from this—and here comes the decisive term—from this intact landscape.

Now, before we return to our humanitarian vacationers, let me explain the premise of my remarks. Nowadays, under the catch-phrase "ecology," we discuss the various strategies deployed to save resources, preserve species and protect natural cycles from destruction yet, ultimately, the objectives we pursue do not derive from ecology but are of an aesthetic nature. To sum them up we use the magic phrase "intact landscape." And the definition of what landscape is, is aesthetic. And it is about the aesthetics of the landscape that we will talk today.

To return now to our tourist: he is not unlike theologians in the Age of Discovery who discussed whether the soul of the "native born" resembled our own, or whether a border like the one separating mankind—the master of nature—from nature itself might exist between us and the native born. In any case, our tourist imagines that landscape is natural and intact, so long as the locals till it for their livelihood, but that it is doomed to destruction the moment colonialists or tourists set foot on it—with the exception of our tourist, of course, who gets along so well with the locals.

My geography teacher—he is long since deceased—went one step further. Of course, he too was of the opinion that the land-scape and the farmers who cultivate it belong together, and that urbanization, industry and the hotel trade mar this landscape. Yet suddenly areas opened up where his argument changed to include both industry and the industrial population in the landscape too. I still remember the day he gave me a bad grade because, for the life of me, I could not grasp how smoke-belching chimney stacks, winding towers, slag heaps glowing in the dark, the Bessemer converter's yellow dust clouds, and miners in blue peaked caps, heading home on push-bikes from a shift, might ever add up to a landscape. Neither spruce nor fir trees grew in the Ruhr District at the time; only pine and deciduous trees could survive the constant swirl of dust; and large parts of the region were—and are still today—characterized by plant communities that indicate pollution by heavy metal salts. Yet, in my geography teacher's eyes, this is precisely what made it a "typical Ruhr District landscape."

Let us return now to my opening premise, namely that ecology, insofar as it is oriented to the landscape, pursues an objective rooted not in ecology itself but in an aesthetic dimension. The word "landscape" is without doubt one of our more ingenious linguistic inventions: were we philosophers in scholastic medieval times we might use it to open a debate on the problem of universals. What comes first, the individual item—or the generic term; the myriad of plants, animals, stones, mountains and clouds—or the landscape?

Without the concept of "landscape" we, or at least we urban dwellers, would be unable to see and categorize our environment. To see does not alone suffice for perception—a babe in arms sees, but he does not perceive. Gradually he learns to distinguish significant objects from among the thousands of impressions he is exposed to: he recognizes foodstuffs, potential playthings and possible obstacles. Yet most of it leaves him indifferent. A person whose livelihood derives from agriculture creates a similar cognitive model: the fruit here is ripe, there it is not; this is good soil, that is poor; the neighbor's corn is higher than mine, but his vines have not taken as well as ours have. It is a form of perception based on vested interests.

The urban dweller's perception is accordingly "disinterested," which is to say, he does not expect any profit; he moves around the countryside like a tourist in search of confirmation that the landscape looks either as he imagines it to look or as his schooling and tourism propaganda have prefabricated it in his mind's eye. His enjoyment of landscape lies in the sense that those images and turns of phrase acquired in the course of our cultural history—from poetry and painting as well as from more lowbrow forms of culture such as cinema, TV, travel brochures and the covers of cheap novels—are made manifest. A culturally coded pattern—the landscape—is vital to the urban dweller or to anyone else alienated from agricultural labor, for it facilitates his ability to read an unfamiliar rural environment.

So we see now that the term landscape includes everything within any given environment. On the one hand, it takes a certain agrarian economic system that can put its stamp on a place and, beyond that, it requires that this singular phenomenon born of economic and natural circumstance be rendered visible by literature and art.

Worpswede[1] provides us with an historical example of that which I caricatured in my opening words: the intact landscape and the native born that work it, plus those pioneering tourists who tend to blend their own presence out of the landscape, and who even kick up a fuss at the mere sight of other tourists who (they claim) are bound to drive away the locals, or at the least turn them into waitresses and kiosk-keepers. Worpswede still thrives today on this image created in 1890, an image that now barely corresponds to reality, for not only

---

1 [A small town in Lower Saxony, Germany, popular in the late nineteenth century among artists such as Paula Modersohn Becker and Rainer Maria Rilke. It is a popular artists' retreat to this day.]

has tourism come to dominate the local economy but the entire local economy has changed: peat is no longer in demand, the swamps have been drained, and intensive agriculture geared to EEC[2] demands has won the upper hand. For instance, substantial areas of heath are used now to soak up hen dung from local poultry factories.

The question as to what landscape is, and which guidelines one might best follow in order to keep a landscape "intact" is historically determined. We know that the origins of landscape lie in classical poetry: in the charming place, the imaginary Arcadia, where a shepherd cups a handful of water from a fresh spring, in the shade of a bush. Greek and Roman poets peddled this image to the people of Athens and Rome at a time when the latter's only remaining connection to the countryside was the fact that the state had slaves cultivate grain there, then transport it to the city.

A revival of precisely these forms of landscape set in the moment English capitalists began to create mock-Arcadian landscapes in their actual parks and gardens. Nevertheless, these eighteenth-century Englishmen and likewise their continental prophet Rousseau differed from our modern-day tourist in that they were well aware of the artificiality of their interventions. We cite in this regard the scene in Rousseau's novel *Julie; or the New Héloise,* in which Julie tells her Saint-Preux of the efforts to be countenanced when undertaking to create nature—which is to say, our imagined intact landscape—artificially. Today, when people talk of their desire to maintain landscapes by artificial means—and landscape here always denotes agrarian modes of production—then one must bear in mind this point in Rousseau's work, at which he gives the lie to his much quoted, superficial "Back to nature."

2 [The European Economic Community (now European Union / EU) established by the Treaty of Rome in 1957.]

Let us take another look at an epoch marked by a quite different perception of the landscape, namely the late nineteenth and early twentieth centuries, when preservation of "truly natural landscapes" became something of a rallying cry. National parks came into existence at this time, possibly the most extreme example of which was the Swiss National Park of Grisons Canton. Such parks encompassed areas no longer cultivated by mankind but abandoned instead to the elements and to natural processes. Yet even an area left in its "natural" state is by nature a highly artificial construct. The point of departure here is a concept unlikely to have dawned on eighteenth-century landscape gardeners, namely Darwin's concept of free selection and the survival of the fittest. While a landscaped park offers a picture of seemingly natural harmony, the national park offers a picture of seemingly natural struggle. There on the tree line stand lonely warriors, battling with the wind; there the avalanche roars into the valley, tearing a herd of chamois along with it; and there is where the valiant, hardy alpine flora is meant to prove its strength, unharmed by haymaking and grazing. — Yet that is precisely what it fails to do. The much-proclaimed diversity of alpine flora is part of a system of husbandry based on seasonal grazing and wild haymaking. When this type of agricultural activity ceases—be it by order of conservationists; or on account of the use of more modern production techniques, such as fertilizers and combine harvesters; or simply because the cultivation of alpine slopes eventually proves unviable—alpine flora vanishes with it. The valiant alpine flowers prove not to be the fittest after all, and are vanquished first by grasses, then by shrubs. Total protection serves in this case neither to preserve biodiversity nor to preserve the typical alpine landscape, but leads instead to plant successions with which natural scientists of the day had never reckoned.

So where are these reflections leading? I come now to three points by which I hope to demonstrate that aesthetics and ecology are more closely connected than one thinks; and that two things suffer whenever this connection is not considered, namely the natural regeneration of resources and the fulfillment of the observer's expectations of the landscape. Each example revolves around the production of alleged naturalness.

I begin with a critique of conventional gardening, in particular of that undertaken by the city parks department. A basic premise here, in this era of total agriculture under EEC constraints, is that little of the countryside remains available for spontaneous vegetation. It is therefore not really far-fetched to assert that "natural nature" momentarily needs the city in order to survive. So-called weeds number among the biological reserves with which we might later manage to re-cultivate abandoned agricultural land. Yet our city parks department treats weeds as the enemy. It goes about its business of flowers and lawns as if compelled to imitate modern agricultural practice: true, anything it harvests is cast aside as waste yet, prior to that, it is optimized. Now, this used to be a fairly harmless matter given that city gardening was limited to only a few parks. Planning and speculation, in particular on the city margins, assured that tracts of land—derelict buildings, designated building lots awaiting a buyer, and land lying around unsold because it had been overvalued so as to boost the market—were always available for spontaneous vegetation. Bad planning and real estate speculation insofar make great conservationists: they guarantee the dysfunctionalism that is indispensable to the preservation of healthy weeds. Today, however, city gardeners find all of that disorderly and seek thus to extend the scope of their influence far beyond the parks, to the entire urban area; they mow, lay asphalt, and sow seed in zones where toddlers and teenagers previously would have played on empty lots. Naturalness here seems to be understood as a continuum of unused and unusable areas, as endless lawns and roses that garnish traffic with a touch of green.

The bad thing about this development, and this brings me to my second point, is how gardening wreaks destruction on the information conveyed by a landscape. Children—and hence tomorrow's adults—speak the language of natural vegetation. Hoary plaintain, wall barley, chicory and nettles alert them to whether they can play undisturbed in a place, climb over the fence and make a fire, or expect an angry owner to arrive and instantly lay claim to the land as his own. Vegetation is information; gardening, hence the act of putting vegetation in order, is consequently the destruction of information. It clouds issues of authority and responsibility.

This destruction of information swept through villages for many years in its most virulent form under the watchword, "Unser Dorf soll schöner werden."[3] The titivation of our villages was achieved by ticking boxes. Accordingly, whatever was unique disappeared; generalities ran rife. A prize jury knew exactly how a beautiful village should look: the village fountain is shut down, its basin is planted with begonias and geraniums, and a lawn on which stand two park benches is set around it. The lawn is perfectly manicured, so no path is ever trodden to the benches. No villager or occasional visitor ever dares take a seat on the benches because they emit an aura of having never been used. Trampled paths are frowned on anyhow. The children now cannot tell whether or not they may step on the grass, and therefore don't—or at least not when an adult is watching—simply to be on the safe side. Naturalness is understood here as the obliteration of all traces of human existence by means of perfect gardening.

3   [The national competition "Our Village: Growing Lovelier By The Day" was launched in 1961. Villages with a maximum population of 3,000 could compete for the title "Loveliest Village." In 1997, the competition was renamed "Unser Dorf hat Zukunft" (Our Village Has A Future).]

The destruction of information also plagues entire branches of the tourism industry. The creation of so-called nature reserves, which nowadays have little in common with the National Park's Darwinist approach, consists primarily in establishing a network of hiking trails. These trails are marked out in such a way as to render redundant any natural sense of orientation vis-à-vis prominent features of the landscape: the objective is quite clearly to make the urban dweller forget how to find his way around a place on his own. Today, there are regions of the Federal Republic of Germany in which the Forestry Commission itself creates a dysfunctional landscape: it propagates landscape images that actually reduce the viability of forestry yet somehow correspond to the images of forests allegedly entertained by hikers. Naturalness is to be read therefore in this context both as the illusory absence of an agriculture economy, and as the introduction into this "wilderness" of human beings who must be constantly informed and instructed.

So one asks oneself: what is the true objective when endeavoring to manufacture so-called naturalness? The National Park concept has been downsized to the biotope: the tiniest lots are fenced off and left to their own allegedly natural devices. The result is possibly a reduction in species diversity and the emergence of plant successions that arouse little interest. Yet, as our example from the city margins has shown, biodiversity thrives best on disruption and change. And thus the question arises as to the true objective of so-called ecology. If the objective is to preserve biodiversity then one would have to create an artificial disruption wherever peat-cutting and real estate speculation disappear—which is ridiculous.

If the objective is to preserve certain species then interventions are called for, yet the "naturalness" of such interventions is rather doubtful. Today, many kinds of animal are marooned; the only trout to be found in mountain streams have been stocked there; and zoo parks pride themselves on preserving animals that have become extinct in the wild.

A third objective could be to create stable and typical final states such as steppes, deserts, moors, marshes and forests. Such final states may well be natural yet they generally evince limited biodiversity and are boring. Only outright catastrophes can guarantee the survival of a myriad of species in these final states: forest fires, flash floods, avalanches and the like. The longer we reflect on the ecology and aesthetics issue, the more striking the paradoxes we find ourselves facing, whichever approach we take. Ecology is currently caught up in a debate about its objectives while the aesthetic dimension, namely how nature is perceived and represented, is in deep crisis, the crisis of the modern-day art of gardening. What triggered this development? What has changed in our world, our society, and caused such seemingly normal concepts as naturalness and horticultural beauty to be shaken to their roots?

Historically, society has operated on the premise that nature is there to be exploited. Society understands itself as a productive force and furthers its productiveness namely by exploiting natural raw materials and processes for the manufacture of commodities. The natural sciences are also geared to production and harness all types of knowledge in order to improve methods of mining, methods of breeding—methods of exploitation, in brief. A clear border used to run between the exploiter and the exploited natural world: here is society with its production and distribution processes, and there is nature, the arena of exploitation. Nobody ever suspected that nature in turn would have an impact on society. Yet the buzz words "environment" and "environmental hazard" now herald this precisely.

We are the first generation to witness the natural world, hitherto our arena of exploitation, now rise up in turn and seriously menace we exploiters. And this means not only that we must exploit resources more sparingly, as we did at times in the past, but also that the absolute limits of exploitation are now etched so clearly on the horizon as to effect social change. Society and exploited nature today comprise an intricately networked system of effects and counter-effects: human impact on nature, formerly a one-way street, today runs smack up against nature's impact on mankind. As Ulrich Beck explains graphically in his book *Risk Society*,[4] nature is no longer something external but rather, an integral part of the networked society. So our society is the first to have to come to grips with the idea that nature is part of the social process, and not an object to be exploited.

Nature as such is invisible; it is perceived only when served up in some way—in the form of an arbitrary representation as landscape, in the form of artificial representations as a garden. In this respect too, our generation is the first to find itself in a novel situation.

Our perception of landscape has rested traditionally on the opposition of the city and the countryside. The landscape, as we have noted, denotes the picture that the urban dweller—he who will never soil his fingers with soil—has concocted of the agricultural realm beyond the city walls. Today, this distinction no longer holds true. We live in the metropolis. The metropolis is, on the one hand, the geographical dispersion in space of an endless succession of fragments of both the city and the countryside; and, on the other, an inextricable tangle of urban and rural functions. Where does the urban dweller live? In the countryside preferably, if he can afford to—from whence he drives daily to work in the city. Where does the farmer live? Here in Switzerland, most farmers still live in the countryside yet in Holland, for instance, that need no longer be the case. Someone who cultivates vegetables or tulips can just as easily commute every morning from his urban home to his agrarian workplace. Our forest dwellings are also a thing of the past. The forester does not live in the forest; he

---

4 [Ulrich Beck, *Risk Society: Towards a New Modernity*, Sage, London 1992. First published in German in 1986.]

just visits it occasionally when not at work in his office. Hence our society is on the threshold of a new way of perceiving its physical environment, one that no longer rests on the opposition of the city and the countryside. The city is everywhere, and the countryside is everywhere; and for the planner it is increasingly a matter of rendering this or that more or less urban or more or less rural component of a settlement somehow typical and identifiable.

Just how do we render visible the fact that something like nature still exists in the middle of our metropolis? Today, city parks departments attempt to save the image of nature by transposing traffic-garnish greenery from the slip roads to the city center: through pedestrian zones, right up to City Hall and the courthouse, and along hospital corridors, they present indifferent foliage in an endless succession of uniform concrete tubs. This careful distribution of greenery provokes a creeping sense that the city is becoming ever more unnatural, and ever more stony. It is precisely in this respect that the art of gardening has lessons to learn—or perhaps it must relearn the lessons of the historical art of gardening, with which designers of the French or the English garden were still familiar.

The French garden was a well-staged exposition of the contrast between the city (or the palace) and the surrounding forest. Thanks to a sophisticated system by which materials and meanings were reversed—trimmed hedges represented walls, avenues full of statues represented vegetation—the observer became attuned to the fact that he was progressing from the palace to the forest, a forest where the duke rode to hounds and slew the deer and hence in which the principle of man's struggle against nature, and man's exploitation of nature were given ritualized expression. At a time when the infinite reaches of the forest had been curtailed by agrarian workers' clearance of land and introduction of crops such as cereals and wool, there emerged among this rationalized and "geometricized" agricultural terrain a patch of natural wilderness: the English garden. It too, is rooted in a paradoxical transition, namely from the exploited landscape to a purely symbolic representation of its archaic function as the realm of shepherds. — We see that both styles of garden, the formal French and the natural English, are rooted in a paradox. They are in dialogue with the environment: here, with the forest, and there, with enclosed agricultural land. Here, therefore, is our lesson for the gardener: greenery becomes visible only when it is discussed; when it raises and renders tangible the issue of the hazards that greenery faces.

That we pursue ecological gardening today seems to me a matter of course. However, ecological gardening is not yet a means to represent nature, or to render it perceptible. The ways and means of this new art of gardening must first be developed. I presume artists will drive this development rather more forcefully than professional gardeners or landscape architects will. And I can draw on the example of an actual landscape intervention undertaken by Joseph Beuys in the city of Kassel in the period 1982–87: his renowned work "7,000 Oaks."[5]

"One cannot see the forest for the trees" is a proverb that holds more than a grain of truth. It really is not at all easy to see a forest; for, if we are standing within it, we see the trees that surround us, some tree trunks, a few crowns swaying above our heads—but we do not see the forest as such. So let us therefore leave the forest and take to the open fields. Doubtless we now see something of the forest, its edges; but we cannot tell whether it consists only of a line of trees or continues within, whether or not we are on the edge of a really large forest. It takes several thousand trees to make a forest, but can one

5 [The full work title is "7000 Eichen—Stadtverwaldung statt Stadtverwaltung" (7,000 Oaks—City Forestation instead of City Administration). It was developed in the framework of documenta 7.]

see them? Can one see 7,000 trees? The forest is evidently an idea, a concept we must construct in our mind's eye. Only with the aid of a map can we establish whether we are on the edge of a forest or faced simply with a strip of woodland only a few meters deep. How, therefore, Beuys presumably asked himself, does one ever see 7,000 trees? And in a city moreover, where a forest between the streets, houses and gardens is inconceivable. And yet Beuys called his work "The Forestation of Kassel." It is well known that Beuys had a basalt block half-buried alongside each of his 7,000 trees. Before the action began, all 7,000 basalt blocks were piled up on Friedrichplatz in Kassel. Every resident of Kassel saw them. Then the blocks were gradually taken away, to join the 7,000 oaks being planted. So now, whenever we see a tree accompanied by a basalt block, near our apartment or workplace in Kassel, we know there are 7,000 such trees. And 7,000 trees make a whole forest. So there is a whole forest in Kassel—but the forest was made visible, not by planting 7,000 trees alongside one another, which in any case would never have been perceived as a forest, but rather, by encouraging us to put two and two together in our mind's eye and hence to deduce the number of trees. It is an intellectual, artificial and artistic forest—and yet it is a forest rendered visible in the environment in which modern man is destined to live: the metropolis.

Aesthetics of the Landscape (1991)

We sit in the grass and see the things in front of us: blades of grass, flowers, some small stones among them and, here or there, a black beetle, aimlessly scuttling about. We also see meadows and green hills in the distance and we know that these too, consist of blades of grass interspersed with herbs, and that there too, the same flies, bumblebees, and black beetles are scavenging for their food. Nevertheless, we call only that which we see in the distance a landscape.

However, the concept "landscape" neither consists in the fact that details cannot be named nor results from our myopia. Rather, it allows us some level of abstraction. It allows us to omit certain information and yet also to combine heterogeneous elements in a single "image." Thus we include in landscape by no means only natural things, such as meadows, trees and hills, but also the various artifacts common to the landscape in question—farms, certainly, but technical installations too: windmills in Holland, of course, and even pit-head frames in the Ruhr District; and many a resident of a port city takes pride in a sweeping view of his technological landscape of docks and oil refineries.

The landscape is thus a trick of our perception, one that makes it possible to synthesize certain heterogeneous elements in an image and to exclude others. Undoubtedly, this requires a certain detachment: it is, so to speak, the first degree of abstraction. Beyond a mysterious point—one that the French artist Paul-Armand Gette has so aptly used the "0 m" symbol to address—identifiable details, such as stones, blades of grass and dung beetles are transformed into a landscape.

But there is a second level of abstraction too, besides this distant landscape, namely the "typical" landscape. We take a walk somewhere not far from our city, on Mount Lägern near Zurich or in the Black Forest near Basel—each city has its own particular hikers' landscape. We leave the city, pass through fields, cross a stream, meander through a grove of trees then, after that, we walk beyond the village, mount a hill and take a detour through a picturesque little valley, before returning to our home in the city. — And what do we talk about when we get there? — We describe the landscape: in the Black Forest near Basel it is like this; on Mount Lägern it is like that. Nowhere on our walk were things exactly as we later describe them. We accomplish in our narrative a double abstraction. We adapt the landscape in the distance, the one we have actually seen, to the "typical landscape" that can be found only in books about the region, in travel brochures or in paintings. And when, at the end of our tale, we claim that we enjoyed our walk and that the landscape in the Black Forest is beautiful, our pleasure lies in the fact that we have succeeded in abstracting some of the elements perceived on our walk—the bridge over the river, the edge of the forest, the view from the hill—such that they correspond to a certain extent to our anticipated image of the landscape. We thereby necessarily suppress some details. We do not report that a gray cat crossed our path, that the village church is hidden behind scaffolding, or that a refrigerator factory has set up its storage depot alongside the village. Had we seen too many such deviant details we would probably not have managed to abstract the landscape. We would have reported back home that the Black Forest actually doesn't start just outside Basel, or that the Black Forest is no longer what it used to be. But I'll say more about that later.

As the landscape is very often no longer what it used to be—or so we believe in any case—we are more than happy to agree when someone proposes that we should protect the landscape. But how is one to protect a thing if one doesn't know exactly what it is?

Without a doubt a science of the landscape that can say what it is does exist, namely geography. But the way geography creates or defines its landscape is not very scientific, or at least not comprehensible in terms of experimental science.

Let's take styles by way of comparison. The art-historical styles are a child of the nineteenth century. At the beginning of that century there existed only "classic" works of art and "barbarian" ones. The "Gothic" style gradually evolved from the barbarian one and then the whole sequence of styles we now regard as matter-of-fact. Today, however, people act as if styles were not constructs but rather, characteristics of works of art. They debate whether a particular church is Ottonian or early Romanesque, as if this might be established by reference to the church alone, rather than to the conceptual framework.

Humboldt created landscapes in similar manner and called them "realms." After his trip around the world he had to face the fact that his material was too abundant to be dealt with. Certainly, one might specify rocks, plants and animals and apply the sciences of mineralogy, geology, botany and zoology to them. Yet the many images Humboldt had seen eluded such science and it is quite touching and at the same time instructive to read that he suddenly remembered an integrative method—art—and tried to apply it instead. Humboldt's "realms" are intuitively created reductions of cosmic abundance and what is so remarkable about them and what distinguishes Humboldt from later geographers is that Humboldt was conscious of the "artificiality" of the tools and methods he chose to use.

And now here is another difficulty that distinguishes the conceptual framework of landscape from that of styles. We discuss the styles by referring to the treasure trove of art created in the past, a treasure trove that remains unchanged. We can always return to the controversial early Romanesque or Ottonian church. We can shift the conceptual framework yet the objects described remain the same. But let me quickly correct that: they do not remain completely unchanged. Conservation and restoration, which serve to preserve historical artworks, are oriented to style concepts and allow the artworks in question to come to resemble—more than they ever ought to—the respective prevailing ideal style.

However, the landscape quite patently changes. So when we decide to protect the landscape, we do not always know what we ought to preserve. Not even historical maps or old photographs may be trusted. Perhaps people used only to photograph whatever was considered typical at the time. We are dealing with two shifting phenomena: reality is changing, and so too is the conceptual framework that supposedly defines it.

So we are looking for "intact landscapes" but do not know exactly what this means. Certainly we don't mean by it the untouched, pristine landscape—which is one we might like to reflect on but can surely never hold on to. "Intact landscapes" is used rather to denote landscapes that have evolved from those particular forms of agricultural economy that seem to us authentic. We then often reach an overhasty conclusion. Farming practices of the past seem to us organic, or at least more ecological or sustainable than contemporary practices. We think to ourselves that old farmers of yore had their personal survival at heart and no interest in ruining their livelihoods. Yet this hypothesis must be put to debate. No doubt historical evidence of overexploitation could also be found.

The problem of the intact landscape therefore does not consist in our inability to define primeval landscapes: for however unattainable these may be for us, they remain conceivable and describable. The problem, rather, is that we have become accustomed to regarding grandma's farm as an ahistorical and authentic an artifact as the primeval landscape is. We experience a landscape as intact when we see, to our great delight, wild flowers in the meadows, cornflowers and poppies among the grain, and a poor farmer harnessing an old nag to his manure cart. But grandma's farm was never "eternal." It too represented only one moment in a long history: the history of the emergence then the abandonment of the three-field system; the history of the replacement of oxen by the horse as a beast of burden; the introduction of the potato, fodder plants, and fertilization. Surely, grandma's agricultural methods never polluted the waters as much as ours do; no doubt the maybug and butterflies still flew around her place and the red-backed shrike nesting in the hedges ensured pests didn't get out of hand. But other animals and plants had already been driven off her farm too while others previously not in existence there had arrived, sometimes from even as far afield as the New World.

So what does the preservation of intact landscapes now imply? Strategies depend on definitions, depend on whatever we understand "intact landscapes" to mean, on our aesthetic goals, and on whatever ecological cycles we wish to support or prohibit. The sympathy we feel towards all manner of preservation campaigns must not prevent us from bearing also these aspects clearly in mind.

Naming such species as one wishes to retain is thereby still relatively straightforward. But we must not delude ourselves that we proceed rationally in this matter. Even scientists have pronounced preferences. It is striking how often mention of orchids is made during nature preservation planning, and in particular of the lady's slipper. Many people are aware of the decline of the stork and would like to re-introduce this beautiful and sympathetic bird. In the meantime, hundreds of plant and animal species are completely disappearing, unnoticed. Everyone regards the so-called gourmet fish as a sensitive natural phenomenon—so to speak, as an indicator of the purity of water. On the other hand, anyone who has ever looked on as an eel is killed at the fish market considers this a tenacious creature. It was eels that suffered most from the chemical disaster on the Rhine near Basel. Gourmet fish were also decimated but a major intervention financed by the guilty company, Sandoz, served to quickly replenish stocks. Once gourmet fish were happily swimming again in the Rhine, both the public and experts were satisfied. People mostly not only neglected to ask about eels but also failed to consider those countless living creatures—the freshwater limpet, for instance—which are the true indicators of water purity and have now been absent from the Rhine for ages. But who wants to build a sewage treatment plant just to save the freshwater limpet?

When it comes to preserving farming practices that ensure the continued existence of certain species, things become more problematic. The so-called alpine flora we all love so much is not a product of purely natural processes, but of wild hay harvesting, which is part and parcel of the "primitive" agricultural economy. When long grasses on the alpine meadows are mowed once each year, short-stemmed species such as the gentian, the prairie crocus, and the houseleek thrive better than ever. "Grandma's farm" should therefore be preserved artificially, which is to say by the allocation of subsidies. The debate about "farmers' role as custodians of the countryside" took place in Switzerland several years ago—but it is not yet over.

The previous remarks relate to the preservation of species or plant and animal communities. They remain thus in the realm of classical science. Yet we were actually talking about the preservation of something quite different, namely landscapes. They alone are perceptible to the layman and essential to keeping our country attractive. The lady's slipper orchid is perceptible to whoever seeks it and can identify it. The landscape is perceptible insofar as it is recognizable. To preserve landscapes therefore entails maintaining them in a recognizable form. The strategies required to do so must therefore attend not only to the environment itself, but also to those who regard it—the onlookers. A forest that landscape conservationists succeed in preserving may naturally thrive, sustainably regenerate itself, and evince flora that is typical of the region; yet it may be considered part of the intact landscape only if all these aspects of it are clearly visible, perceptible to the onlooker.

In conclusion, therefore, two questions and then three attempts at hypothetical answers: Why can we no longer accustom ourselves to progress in the agricultural economy? Why are our agriculturally exploited landscapes not beautiful?

Firstly, previous landscape aesthetics in grandma's era ensued from the contrast between the city and the countryside. Anyone taking a walk used to leave the city and look at the landscape. Once back in the city, he would tell how things looked "outside." Today, we live in a continuum that we call the metropolis. The country has become urban and, whether you believe it or not, the city has become rural. Never before were cities as green as they are today.

Secondly, our ability, when taking a walk, to integrate all we see is now vastly reduced by our use of the motorcar. On our "walks" we wander through regions the size of Tuscany, Burgundy or the Alps. Our perceptive faculties are overwhelmed by the challenge of recognizing what is "typical" about these landscapes. Therefore, we return from our weekend trips and tell everyone at home that the Alps are no longer what they used to be.

And, thirdly, our relationship with the landscape is marred. On the one hand, we know that we ourselves are the cause of environmental catastrophes. We accelerate the forests' demise with our vehicles and oil-fired central heating. On the other hand, we know that the fertilizers used in agriculture backfire on our urban systems: the groundwater poisoned by farmers is our drinking water too. This puts an end to the classic view of the indifferent urban dweller. We are now party to a large system and no longer simply onlookers. Changes in the aesthetics of landscape occur in pace with our growing awareness of ourselves as an integral part of the system.

Landscape Is Transitory (1994)

A new science has come about in recent years: environmental history. Initially, this sounds quite simple and logical: that which we now call our environment has a past of its own. But environmental history immediately raises the matter of methodology.

In earlier days, we suppose, there existed animal species that are now extinct: not only bears and wolves, but also inconspicuous mollusks, insects and ostracods. There was less nitrogen in the water, back then, less carbon and sulfur dioxide in the air, and less of lots more besides, for all I know. In any case, environmental history is the history of the environment as seen—or assessed—by people today. People back then did not notice the presence of ostracods however, or the low sulfur levels in the air, at least not as factors relevant to their own lifeworld. In this sense, environmental history is a chimera, a story without a subject. This environmental history cannot be written, except by the dear Lord himself.

The further we go back in time the rarer the statements by those contemporary witnesses who observed and judged an environmental factor—or that which we name as such today—become. Did people even notice that plants and animals were becoming extinct? Doubtless they were glad to be rid of the wolf and the bear while regretting the disappearance of the Waldrapp ibis—but what about those small, seemingly insignificant creatures that do neither harm nor good? Will we ever know whether a species name once denoted the same animal or the same plant for Linnaeus as it does for us today? Certain old generic terms have now been differentiated for individual species. On the other hand, when the passion for zoological collections was at its height around 1850, far more species of worm and beetle existed than today. The joy of discovery was such that any slight variation gave occasion to define a new species.

All of this brings us to another environmental history, for environmental history is also the history of any environment as perceived in its own day. It is the history of synchronous analysis. What did our ancestors perceive at any given time? What was important to them? When did they begin to notice that springs do not bubble endlessly, that wild game can be decimated and thus hunting must be regulated, or that the forest must continue to grow? Environment is always relative to its historical condition. Certain actions by ruling authorities, the enclosure of Epping Forest for example, may be regarded now in retrospect as environmental protection. Exploitation and the fact that exploitation was the prerogative of the few gave rise to the cultural landscape.

Cultural landscape—beware! This term too is a chimera. It suggests eternity. We are tempted to see landscape as something a-historical. The farms and rice fields of the Po Valley, the vineyards of Bordeaux, the buffalo herds of the Roman Campagna feign to show us the seemingly cyclical production and reproduction of timeless societies. The phrase "old cultural landscapes" sounds a bit like "the cradle of mankind." How we love to describe these beautiful, ancient landscapes as eternal: the Tiber plain, Mesopotamia, and the flood plains of the Nile! And yet the whole thing is a paradox: culture implies activity, invention and progress. The cultural landscape is therefore anything but eternal. It is truer to say it corresponds to the historical snapshot. The primal cultural landscape, itself a contradiction in terms, is symbolized by Poussin's painting of Arcadia: and even in Arcadia we come across history, the sarcophagus, and war and death. Images of ancient cultural landscapes say nothing else but how things used to be, back when man plowed with oxen, used the three-field system of farming, and learned to preserve milk by curdling it for cheese …

The Dutch have depicted various types of cultural landscape ever since they began producing realistic landscape paintings. We know, however, that we today do not interpret such images in the same way as their contemporary audience. For us, Dutch windmills symbolize a suspended era, the era of an unplanned energy supply, the era of a still tentative approach to resources. Yet historians of technology tell us that the windmills in the Dutch paintings were the latest models at the time and thus must have had the same effect on contemporary viewers as the image of a dam or a nuclear power plant has on us today. And what about the hilltop castles? How we love them, especially those in ruins. But should someone want to erect such a castle on a hill today, the local authority would intervene, and so would the Society for Preservation of the Landscape. For us, castles in beautiful rural locations conjure images of a still "unaware" era. We imagine that the builder —a knight, a lord or an abbot—had no idea he was creating a beautiful scenic landscape for the future. His concerns were security, provision, and domination. — Is that true? Probably not. — In any case, people in the nineteenth century quite pointedly set the castles' legitimate successors—elegant hotels—in landscapes that were much admired; in fact, hotels were built for the very purpose of admiring landscapes. But such hotels as those could not be built today at those locations—so let us rejoice that they still exist! In conclusion, one may say that the cultural landscape can be up-to-date, contemporary and progressive. But that is no longer permissible today.

All this needed to be said, because the cultural landscape is now gone forever. Cultural landscape is any landscape in which one arrives too late. Its charm lies in the fact that one can, just about, make out how it used to look. And the way it used to look is the way we generally imagine it *really should* look: as it did once, long ago, when gentlemen arrived from the city and, on their way to the hunt, paid a visit to the farmers, those "happy People of the Fields, not yet Waken'd to freedom!" Nothing flatters us more than that which I call the aesthetics of the leopard (You surely remember reading the highly enjoyable novel *Il Gattopardo* [The Leopard] by Prince Giuseppe Tomasi di Lampedusa?) The aesthetics of the leopard say: I am the last person to have experienced all that, to have experienced how the world actually should be. Each of us feels like a leopard. Each of us loves to tell of how his mother with her own fair hands planted and harvested all the vegetables eaten at home; whereas now, we all run to the supermarket and carry home a pound of tomatoes and two pounds of potatoes... One often heard said, in my parents' house: "before the First World War, because we had only..." In exactly the same way my parents had heard from their parents how happy people used to be each fall, when farmers brought nuts, apples and firewood to the city.

The cultural landscape feigns thus to be an eternally regenerative cycle whereas in reality it represents a historic moment and gains in beauty whenever we experience its transitory nature. The existing landscape enables us to recognize traces of past conditions in agriculture and husbandry and in turn to gain a sense of our own historicity, of our position as leopard vis-à-vis the younger ones.

The specific location of this transitory cultural landscape is the city outskirts, which is to say, the place where urban dwellers take a walk. We still have the old image in our mind's eye: we leave the city thinking about "Il Buon Governo," the fresco in Siena's City Hall, and we are the citizens looking out over land that is ruled by the city. The tension inherent to this transition from the city to the countryside engenders our image of the landscape. Countryside becomes a landscape owing to the urban dwellers' Easter Walk while the city is the city thanks alone to wide-eyed market wenches and kindling hawkers—but only, of course, whenever this is actually no longer so in reality. So we experience the outskirts twice over nowadays, as the place where tension builds and tension melts away as well as as the continuation of all things metropolitan. We experience a new sense of space there, one that urban dwellers in earlier times either never had or experienced in part as trauma, namely when the walls of the city were razed. In the past, the city gates were closed to keep the mob outside, in the forest, so that citizens could sleep soundly in their beds; but since the walls were razed the mob resides first and foremost in the city. But our present experience is to view the outskirts as a place of transparency on the diachrony: here, grandmother can show us where she flew her kite as a child, although we can barely imagine it, since all we can see today is train tracks and freight depots. But soon we too are able to play leopard, since the current reduction in freight cargo means this site will be redeveloped at some point as a housing scheme…

Where are all these deliberations leading? — We never mention it, but we are always wondering how the cultural landscape might be preserved. But if we ever ask ourselves precisely what is so special about the cultural landscape we catch ourselves red-handed, wielding ambiguous answers. We confuse grandmother's farm with eternity and we believe that the ways, now vanished, in which the landscape was exploited in our youth is precisely what made it so beautiful. The radical changes that we ourselves have witnessed, if we have reached a certain age, leave us feeling that we alone could ever have had such an experience.

In fact, I myself have trouble imagining that an earlier generation ever experienced such change as I, who saw my home transition from a subsistence economy to a dairy industry monoculture. In the course of ten years, countless small plots of land, gardens and orchards disappeared in favor of the endless green carpet of sod, which itself in turn probably looks to the younger generation like the eternal agricultural landscape—because it too is now falling victim to stall-feeding. Only I, the leopard, can prove to them how things here *really should* look. Only I, the leopard, can see those signs that make the "real" landscape visible still behind the veil of the present one:

a few neglected apple trees the farmer left standing; and there, where once he had his vegetable field, horseradish leaves still sprouting in the grass; and the land the young farmer calls Calves' Meadow is actually Steeds' Pasture.

So is it possible to preserve cultural landscapes? — Certainly not, if one doesn't know exactly what they are. And this matter of what they are is neither a factual nor historical issue, but an aesthetic one.

It is a matter of how we perceive it. I believe that, in these deliberations and those made elsewhere, I have now sufficiently expounded my view of the landscape. I consider the landscape to be a construct of the senses, one that ensues from comparisons, which is to say, in the temporal terms of the diachrony, as well as from spatial awareness, whenever one takes a stroll. I leave the city and see the countryside—the Easter Walk is the simplest example—and I see the countryside historically and diachronically as a place in flux, a place whose "real" appearance I reconstruct from the traces the past left on its current appearance: the aesthetics of the leopard. This is why I don't put my faith in the effectiveness of preserving exemplary landscapes—or at least I won't for as long as we only ever get to see them without paths and without traces of their evolution. Does the preserved heath have a parking lot? Does the rescued jungle have a parking lot? Do the Alps have a parking lot? All of them have one—but what on earth can be seen from their parking lots? Inevitably, having returned home, the visitors say: "the heath is no longer what it was." The cultural landscape as such does not exist. It is always on the go between the past and the future and thus is also a snapshot of the present—and it is on the go from the city to the primal jungle, in an intermediate state somewhere between landscape maintenance and landscape exploitation.

To restore the cultural landscape hence means to engender perception of it by creating paths that traverse all eras—and that is the science of strollology.

Wasteland As Context.
Is There Any Such Thing As The
Postmodern Landscape? (1998)

Everything is growing more ugly by the day—on that we all agree. We discovered a beach three years ago, on a remote rocky bay, and we went there time after time with the children. We swam, they searched for seashells, and we never saw a soul all day long. But we returned there last year, and what did we find but a half-built hotel. And in the Alps, two summers ago, we discovered a sunny slope with a whole range of alpine flora: gentians, alpine asters and lobelia. But this year, the struts for a cable lift have been installed, so all the flora will soon be crushed beneath skis and snow ploughs. Don't we all have similar stories to tell when we return home from a vacation? Is the "uglyfication" of our landscape a one-way street? Our grandparents had a much better time of it. When they left the city they found themselves in a beautiful rural landscape and, if they traveled even further a-field, could enjoy magnificent beaches or mountain vistas. Yet we too still have it good, for we manage now and then to discover a lovely spot, and we keep quiet about it; and even when that spot has gone to the dogs, there is a good chance we will find a new one. But how will things look for our offspring? Will a thing of beauty be lost to them forever?

Strong and influential movements protest the "uglyfication" of our environment. There are lobby groups for the protection of local identity, the protection of the landscape, the protection of the natural environment and the protection of cultural heritage. Remarkably, all these lobby groups were founded, not recently, but by our grandparents: "protection of" lobby groups were invented sometime between 1900 and 1910. Evidently, the impression that everything is increasingly ugly was even stronger then than it is today. Yet we like to think that everything in those days was still lovely, and that there was probably little need for the "protection of" lobby groups. Will our grandchildren think the same about us? Will they say: "Our grandparents still had it so good. There were still so many beautiful places, back then; and is it not strange, how upset they all were about environmental degradation?"

Today, we will consider these changes, this apparently one-way development. Without doubt, that thing we describe generally as the landscape is changing. Whether or how one might pinpoint the nature of this change is hard to say, for landscape is a quite tricky word, an interpretation of our surroundings. That which is changing might better be described as "tangible space." Evidently, tangible space used to be in a state such that we called it a beautiful landscape, but we no longer rate it so highly owing to its present alteration. Or do we? Perhaps there are changes now underway that make tangible space look lovelier than ever. It must have been beautiful at some time or other, on its way from primeval Germanic forest to the present-day pig and chicken factories. The decision to describe a certain stage of agricultural development as "beautiful" and as "landscape" is, therefore, historically determined, which is to say, it is a construct created by past generations and one hence presumably subject to change and development. That the more remote and extreme instances of agricultural economy, such as one finds in the Alps, say, are more beautiful than charming, sheltered places in the countryside around Rome attests to specific historical shifts in our interpretation of landscape. Evidently—and this rather complicates the matter—we are dealing with two developments: firstly, with changes in tangible space, however quantifiable or representable this may be; and, secondly, with the ongoing shifts in our perception of landscape—and this brings us now to ask: Could it be that our concept of landscape is outdated insofar as it has failed to keep pace with changes in the modern landscape?

Let us begin by reviewing the classic, traditional view of a beautiful landscape. This rests, for one, on the distinction between the city and the countryside. The construct "landscape" is the urban dweller's invention; it is he—and not the farmer working the land—who finds the landscape beyond the city limits so appealing. He also fulfills the second premise posited by Immanuel Kant: he has no "vested interest" in the countryside; he visits it, not to buy cheap potatoes or to collect rent from leaseholders, but as a "disinterested" onlooker. He admires the golden ears of corn and the industrious laborers bringing in the harvest, but he has no gain from them and nor does he want any. That his existence as an urban dweller actually depends on the agricultural economy is another story altogether. In addition to the opposition of the city and the countryside, and the passing urban dweller's lack of involvement, there is a third premise: it is short distances covered on foot or, in the past, on horseback or, today, by bicycle, that make it possible to construct an image of the local landscape and to label it "typical." Every city has, or at least used to have, a landscape it considers somehow typical: Berliners have their lakes in Brandenburg, Frankfurters the Taunus or the Wetterau, the people of Strasbourg their Vosges, those in Zurich their Lägern, and the Viennese their Vienna Woods. And way beyond the typical charming features of a hike through the local landscape lies the heroic, sublime landscape where we take a vacation: the Curonian Spit, Helgoland, the White Cliffs of Dover, Lake Lucerne or the Matterhorn. These heroic, sublime landscapes are also integrated in the local-typical schema, however, for the simple reason that, having arrived at our vacation destination, we need walk only a short way to see them—perhaps not even that, if the Matterhorn, say, is visible from our hotel window. In this respect we evidently still share the aesthetics of the Golden Age of railroads, with its vacation destinations and hotels.

I would like now to demonstrate the extent to which our situation has changed in objective terms, i.e. with regard to that which I call tangible space, as well as in terms of our subjective attitudes and hence our perceptions.

Certainly, the contrast between the city and the countryside still exists yet it has become much less pronounced. The urban dweller no longer necessarily lives in the city and even someone who works the land may now choose not to live on it. All Forestry Commission properties in Germany have been closed down, for if ever a forester is required to see the forest and happens not to be at work in his office, he travels by car to the point at which his patrol route begins. Nor do farmers need live alongside their fields and stalls these days. They may just as well conduct their business from the city. Whoever toils in Holland in the famous tulip farms can arrive there each morning on his motorbike, and likewise the vintners and cattle farmers in the South of France. The majority population in the countryside, in the villages, is no longer tied to the land for its livelihood. Many commute to work in the city. Others have urban jobs in rural areas, or they simply work at home. This has repercussions also for architecture. The old marketplaces and villages no longer have a distinctly rural appearance, and their smart mayors have no greater ambition than to find an investor for a high-rise. The cities meanwhile, are falling apart. Fast means of transport have made high densities and walking distances redundant. The pride of urban mayors is more likely to be urban parks, urban expansion, and to fill every street and square with so-called urban-garnish greenery. Patches of green therefore envelop the motorist at every turn, before releasing him into the underground parking lot, from where he makes his way to the pedestrian zone, once again surrounded by shrubs.

The motorcar made it possible for urban dwellers to settle in the countryside. So the settlement structures that evolved there can now be reached and explored solely by car. Reasonably enough, anyone who lives in the city or the countryside therefore now gets about by car. This has an impact on the distance he walks. Even the very first step into the classical experience of landscape is denied him, for he no longer experiences a transition from urban to rural architecture. He will therefore travel great distances in search of the greatest contrast, the most "unspoiled" place imaginable. The effect of such overly long trips is that he can no longer manage to integrate all he sees in a local-typical landscape schema. A walk in the immediate vicinity therefore no longer guarantees he will find a familiar and hence preferable landscape.

Every motorist has read somewhere, at some time, that exhaust fumes are partly responsible for so-called forest dieback. Individuals deal with this information in different ways: one can continue to use the car and suffer a guilty conscience; or one can join an association that relieves the feelings of guilt and fosters a "So what?" attitude. Everyone is also aware that the work farmers do in their fields is no longer totally harmless. Farmers sit on grotesque machines that spread indefinable substances on the fields, substances likely to seep into the groundwater and come gushing out of our faucets the very next day. Our complicity in crime and our awareness of such risks sweep away all traditional notions of the disinterested onlooker on the sidelines. Whatever we do has an impact on the landscape—on forest dieback—and whatever the "happy People of the Fields"[1] do implies a menace for us. This destroys Kant's premise, that aesthetic perception requires a "disinterested" relationship to the object observed.

And now comes the third point I wish to emphasize here, namely the impact of wasteland. Wasteland in its narrower sense, meaning

---

1 [The reference is to Friedrich Schiller's poem *The Walk* (1795), in which he discusses the development of human civilization and the fundamental question of man's relationship to Nature.]

land that is available for cultivation yet left to lie fallow, is a modern phenomenon, a result of surplus production in the agricultural sector. A farmer who does not till his fields can register them as wasteland and is awarded compensation accordingly. Many farmers therefore deduce that their product sales do not cover their labor costs: they do equally well or even better to spare themselves the effort and the raw materials and simply pocket the compensation. This is true above all for regions with less fertile ground, so it is there that we most frequently come across the wasteland phenomenon. Initially, wasteland may be a welcome addition to the landscape, since we find wild vegetation there, instead of extensive potato or cereal acreage. First of all, grasses run rife then, after two or three years, thistles and shrubs and, eventually, bushes and saplings. Wherever farmers mow wasteland, which they do as a rule, one finds nothing more than shrubs and thistles. Many hikers enjoy this new type of vegetation and look on with pleasure as their dogs chase though fields of thistles. And yet, in my opinion, wasteland contributes crucially to changing the look of the landscape.

The layout of the historical landscape has its own logic. We leave the city and cross a zone full of the market gardens that supply the city with vegetables and flowers; then come fields of grain, pastures for milk production and, finally, the forest. Forest margins are perhaps the most refreshing type of landscape setting for the urban walker, either on account of their diversity and rich vegetation, or because neither farmers nor foresters patrol them. This layout also has a narrative dimension; it reflects how the city is nourished; it reproduces what has come to be known as Von Thünen's rings,[2] a model of agricultural land use that regarded feeding the city as a

2   [A model created by farmer and amateur economist J.H. von Thünen (1783–1850), which was translated into English only in 1966.]

matter of distance and as the basis of ground rent. Our walker, to whom I shall return in more detail later, also traverses this narrative, this story; and this lends significance to the landscape he sees. To the charming or spectacular image—the well-situated farm or the forest margins—it adds now an explanatory footnote, a narration of historical processes on the basis of which a particular type of agriculture has been deemed sensible and logical for this "green belt" around the city. The narrative also addresses developments and processes, for example the fact that a grain silo or perhaps even a mill wheel can still be found alongside a farm that evidently now restricts its business to dairy produce and raising cattle. Yet while an occasional patch of wasteland may look pretty, the point I wish to make is that wasteland on the whole interrupts or disrupts the narration of a logically structured landscape and thereby hinders the integration of our experience of taking a walk in the local-typical schema of beauty.

So far, we have described wasteland in the narrower sense. In the broader sense, we could say wasteland is the area within the new urban/rural spillover zone in which individual elements are not logically arranged. The conglomerate of newly built housing estates, lots standing empty owing to speculation, abandoned commercial sites, and the scattered vestiges of farmers' existence amounts to a "wasteland," metaphorically speaking; to an illogical wasteland that leaves us in the lurch when it comes to interpreting what we see. In order to describe this phenomenon more precisely, I would like to return once again to that which I have called the charm of the local-typical schema. And in order to understood that, it is essential to reflect briefly on my strollology theory. — We believe we perceive the landscape as an "image;" we learn from pastoral novels and travel brochures how this or that region looks. When we take a walk we seek confirmation of these images. And we are delighted to discover similarities or variations on a theme we can interpret. In reality, however, we see something else on our walks: we cross a field, ford a stream, pass a village, go through a valley or over a hill, feel ourselves hemmed in or come upon a panoramic vista; and we thereby see a thousand details—a gray cat or a burned-down barn—and we substantiate what we see by drawing on our memory or on our oblivion. Whatever we have seen is merged—in our mind's eye, of course—in one image and this we then call "our landscape experience." Once back home, therefore, we do not speak in detail of the narrow valley or the gray cat but instead describe the Wetterau, the Jura by Basel, the Vienna Woods or the lakes of Brandenburg. This artificial image created in our mind's eye and underpinned by travel brochures is feasible thanks solely to the narrative order, to inner logic and to the context in which we have seen these visual sequences. The less logically such image sequences can be classified, the harder it becomes for us to read the landscape and the more clamorous the demands made on us to explain what we see. When I come across objects such as a windmill in Holland, a pithead frame in the Ruhr District or a dung heap in the Black Forest, I can easily classify them. If I came across a pithead in the Black Forest, however, I would condemn it to oblivion or perhaps become annoyed, depending on my mood. I would possibly call the local office for protection of the landscape and demand that it be removed forthwith! And I would probably then discover that the relevant lobby group already existed for the purpose either of preserving pitheads in the Ruhr District or of removing them from the Black Forest.

Armed with insights derived from the strollology theory, we return now once again to the wasteland: to wasteland in its narrower sense as well as to the metaphorical wasteland of the disorderly urban/rural environment. At the risk of sounding banal, I call this "the postmodern landscape." One of the better-known origins of postmodernism is Robert Venturi's journey to Las Vegas. He discovered there, that gigantic, explanatory icons afflict the buildings he named sheds: a huge illuminated sign on the roadside explains a pleasure palace called "Stardust;" yet turn into the drive and one finds oneself approaching a relatively inconspicuous low building, namely a shed; one of modest size for the simple reason that it must be air-conditioned. For Venturi, the lesson of *Learning from Las Vegas*[3] was that the iconic explanation of a building is distinct from its actual structure or volume, and he pitted this insight against the strict rationalism of modernist architecture. I learn something else from Las Vegas, for Las Vegas lies in the very zone I describe as metaphorical wasteland.

Wasteland requires some explanation: the more established wasteland happens to be, the more the object seen must both introduce and interpret itself. The disorderliness of our urban/rural environment gives rise to the loquacity of postmodernism. Take the city hall in an old, established city: a city hall derelict beyond repair or gutted by fire and consequently in need of refurbishment. What a gratifying task for an architect. The city, given its age, has its own logic, its own narrative. I arrive from the railway station, cross the station forecourt, enter the medieval city center, find myself in a jumble of narrow streets then come upon a wide open space, the central square, at one corner of which stands the main church; but in the architecture along one of its longer sides there is a gaping hole, the gutted city hall. Every design, even the most nondescript, even the most functionalist concept of a new building for this site says: city hall. The historical city context has primed the visitor precisely for this. The architect therefore need do nothing more than reveal his particular interpretation of a city hall on this site. Let's take another example, another city hall. A conglomerate of older and more recent

3 [Robert Venturi (with Denise Scott Brown and Steven Izenour): *Learning from Las Vegas*, MIT Press, Cambridge MA 1972; revised edition 1977.]

settlements, abandoned industrial sites, sports fields and highway slip roads are pronounced to be a city. An extensive green area seems a likely site for a city hall. So, what does the architect now design but a postmodern city hall? Of course he does, naturally: since it must convey two messages to the observer simultaneously. The first is: "I am the urban community's new city hall;" and the second is: "I was designed by the architect X." This is the reason for my hypothesis: the more misinformation wasteland disseminates, the more loquacious architecture must become.

So we find ourselves all of a sudden in the realm of architecture. We actually intended to talk about landscapes. Is there such a thing as the "postmodern landscape?" I believe there is. The postmodern landscape is the attempt to attune the observer—whose route to the place in question cannot be foreseen, and who is consequently ill prepared, in narrative terms, for whatever awaits him—to that which he will see. Landscape elements that have their own logic must therefore be created in the wasteland. I call such landscapes "hyper-typical landscapes."

Yet this type of landscape is precisely what I wish to distinguish from that which lobby groups for the protection of nature, protection of the landscape and so forth reconstruct—under the influence of geographers—as typical landscapes. Let me sketch a brief example. One of Germany's major historical landscapes is the heath. Basically, this denotes an area on which *Caluna vulgaris* grows, a plant that blooms red in the fall. *Caluna vulgaris* is a small bush with a more or less fifteen-year lifespan. One of its properties during this lifespan is to prevent younger plants' seed from sprouting around it. So, the heath dies off over fifteen years respectively is dead by the end of that period, and ready to allow other seeds to sprout. The heath is accordingly an artificial landscape that demands "hard graft." The heath farmer digs up some *Caluna vulgaris* bushes before they reach old age, so that other bushes can seed and regenerate themselves. The heath is a landscape doomed to extinction, on the one hand, because nobody these days is prepared for hard graft and, on the other, because the land—especially since the invention of artificial fertilizer—can now be put to more profitable use. Nowadays, if a landscape advocate or nature conservationist wants to regenerate the heath, the situation goes something like this: a sign on the regional highway directs the motorist to the heath parking lot. There he must leave his car and continue on foot to reach the heath. This greets him in the fall clothed splendidly in red. He also spots a conscientious objector[4] or an unemployed person doing hard graft. The visitor could not be more disappointed. He asks himself: What was it about the heath anyhow, which made it so poetic? And he returns home to reread Hermann Löns'[5] account of a walk on the heath: his essay about the black grouse, for instance. Yes, Löns descends from the narrow-gauge railroad car, surrounded (to his initial annoyance) by other hikers, and walks into a small heath village. But then Löns realizes he knows another path and he disappears between the vegetable plots, beyond which he reaches the orchards, and beyond those, finally, he crosses a sand drift. On the far side everything is green and damp; there are birch and juniper trees, and some famous Heidschnucke sheep. Löns makes his way across a swampy patch, comes at last to the blooming red carpet and spots his black grouse—which does not feed on heath flowers, incidentally, but on juniper berries and cranberries. It is clear now: the "typical" landscape cannot be read as an object but only as one

---

4   [Until 2012, young German conscientious objectors could choose to work for two years in a social or civic project rather than do one year's national service in the army.]

5   [German journalist and writer Hermann Löns (1866–1914) is most famous for his novels and poems celebrating the people and landscape of the North German moors and particularly of the Lüneburg Heath in Lower Saxony.]

component of a narrative sequence, a sequence that attests also to processes: the village defends itself against the sand, the fruit trees encroach on the dunes, the farmer encloses some of the heath, and the heath does battle with juniper and cranberry trees...

This simply as an intermezzo, one that teaches us that the postmodern hyper-typical landscape cannot be solely an image, cannot be a heath attached to a parking lot and maintained by the unemployed. Rather, hyper-typical postmodern landscapes are a consciously designed combination of spectacular (hence tangible) and narrative elements. Löns' experience of the heath, with its underlying narrative, must be reproduced on a small scale at the heart of the global wasteland. What are the hyper-typical landscapes of the modern age? — I identify three types: the supermarket, the theme park (such as Disneyland), and the preserved historical city center. All three are forms of landscape with their own inherent logic. Although I have never visited Disneyland personally, I know perfectly well that I would find my way about it. Everything would be familiar to me, from Vesuvius to the narrow-gauge railway through a Wild West high street; and I would be totally prepared for it, because it would unfold in a logical sequence. By the way, the Euro-Disney hotels in the Marne Valley were not built primarily for European visitors; rather, developers had in mind those Americans who must visit Paris on business and are so bewildered by the capital that they gladly retreat to an orderly landscape that they know and understand, in order to gather their wits in preparation for the day ahead.

The supermarket, the theme park and the preservation of cultural heritage serve to recreate a condition that Kant considered vital to the aesthetic experience: the observer's non-involvement or "lack of a vested interest." My role in all three of these contexts is that of observer/customer: I can either shop or not shop. A third option, namely to assist proceedings, do business myself, or personally offer something to the situation, is not available. One visits Disneyland "without interest." Consequently, it is the recreated aesthetic landscape.

We have described these three landscapes—the supermarket, Disneyland / theme park and the preserved historical city center—as postmodern landscapes. They are characterized by the strict segregation of promoter and consumer, whereby the promoter establishes a rigid order. This order is so logical as to instantly make visitors feel at home and, moreover, to trigger in them the required behavior, namely conspicuous consumerism. One might dispute that this holds true for the historical city center. Yet, there too, one finds a growing tendency to control the range of stores available; to favor the sale of historical and traditional products, to say nothing of antiques; and to integrate real and fake traditions: sales personnel and waiters in traditional regional costumes, wine-tasting, cheese samples accompanied by yet more costumes, and a folk-strumming band. There is little danger, moreover, of foreign visitors being unfamiliar with such folk music or with revivals of various architectural styles and regional traditions. For what is on offer on the whole is a largely artificial, uniform style that I refer to as "ubiquitous regionalism:" motifs derived from Turkish timber architecture, applied to Swiss chalets and lit by Japanese lanterns evoke the motifs on a hot-dog stand in a pseudo-historical pioneer town in distant Canada.

Is there any way out of this post-historical landscape? — For here, the main point is this: to overcome the feeling of total "man-made-ness," of total manipulation. The word "landscape" actually originally denoted selected motifs in a heterogeneous type of environment, motifs of incidental origin. Nobody planned the ruins, shepherds huts and farmers' fields in a picturesque landscape—and it is the chance heterogeneity of this mix that delights our gaze. Can any examples of partly intentional and partly incidental landscapes be found today? Any such configuration beyond the postmodern landscape, I would describe as a "potent landscape."

So now, in conclusion and by way of example, here my endeavor to describe a potent landscape: the setting is the documenta 9 in Kassel in 1992—its outdoor areas, to be precise. One need only read newspaper and art journal reviews of the time to know that the outdoor areas were considered a complete disaster. Commerce and restaurants predominated, the few artworks on the forecourt of the Fridericianum were not shown to their advantage and, worst of all—a barbarity that flabbergasted the *Neue Zürcher Zeitung*—the stone steps leading from Friedrichsplatz to the Aue Park had been squatted by unauthorized vendors dealing in pseudo art. To crown it all, the arrangement of ticket sales, the cloakroom and the exhibition entrances was so unfortunate that visitors were obliged to stand in line three times over. On some days, the whole of Friedrichsplatz was full of people standing in line.

Some time passed before we realized that this was nothing less than a potent landscape. True, it had been planned—yet no one had expected it to turn out quite as it did. It was indeed a disaster. And yet all the visitors, except for the journalists among them, were perfectly satisfied. As our home was in Kassel we did not need to stand in line. So several weeks passed before we realized we were missing out on a major attraction. Interesting people mingled there, helped each other out, took a neighbor's umbrella to the cloakroom then returned it when the skies opened. One person was dispatched to fetch coffee for everyone in line and when caught in a sudden shower, he borrowed the café's huge parasol, before handing it on to the next person upon reaching the Fridericianum. The Nigerian artist Mo Edoga[6]

6 [Mo Edoga used driftwood from the nearby River Fulda and remnants of construction timber to build the "Signal Tower of Hope" on a public square in Kassel during documenta 9 in 1992. Visitors were able to watch the artist in action and ask him about his work.]

was magnificent: for one hundred days he slowly constructed his airy tower, answered every question, and gave the public the feeling that it for once had a genuine opportunity to exchange ideas with an artist. I won't go into more detail. What I wished to show was simply this: a new form of artificial landscape, based neither on the old formula—wasteland plus loquacity—nor on the new one—total definition of the design and the roles to be played—really does exist, has indeed become conceivable. The landscape fusion of human activity, human leisure and chance is still possible.

Landscape (1998)

"Nature, labor and aesthetics" is the subject of our conference; and the theme of "landscape" is one of its contrary offshoots. Man's ability to perceive a patch of land as a landscape depends precisely on the degree of his disinterestedness in that land, i.e. on the fact that he does not work it for a livelihood. Were he to work the patch of land it would perforce become a garden; and gardens are perhaps better suited to Ernst Bloch's notion of utopia than landscapes are.

Anyone who works the land does not see it as a landscape but as fallow land, as wasteland, as forest, as a hunting ground, or as an expression of fruitfulness or meager yield. Landscape therefore does not really exist for those who live from the soil, for farmers. Only urban culture has the potential to regard a terrain as landscape. The first ever, poetic descriptions of landscape known to us date from a time in Rome when the inhabitants of the city no longer had any contact with rural laborers and when landscape from Central Italy to Sicily had ceased to exist in the aesthetic sense. The provision of Rome at the time depended on a rationalized system of agricultural production driven by slave labor. Yet poets began at this point to draw on the image of Arcadia to describe the landscape, hence on the image of a wild yet beautiful area inhabited by only a few goatherds and their flocks. However, a dark shadow hangs over idyllic Arcadia, namely that of possible expulsion by a more highly organized form of agricultural economy; expulsion such as Virgil, the creator of this image of the landscape, had already personally experienced in Mantua.

In Virgil's *Satires* we find the first ever, poetic descriptions of landscapes in our literature. The plot of *Satires* is that two goatherds meet and the younger of them suggests they both withdraw to a quiet place—which he then describes—and spend the day there singing songs about beautiful female goatherds. The older of the two goatherds knows an even better place—which he describes in detail—and they then decide to go there. From these *Satires* prologs ensue the accouterments of the "charming place:" a shady grove, a comfortable seat, and cool waters in which goats may be watered. Ernst Robert Curtius, in his book *European Literature and the Latin Middle Ages,* describes such prologs as the basis of a code that allowed future readers of any literary genre to recognize immediately, that the author was referring to a beautiful but agriculturally still (as we would say today) largely undeveloped landscape.

Our word landscape derives neither directly from poetry nor from the Latin. Rather, landscape was first used to describe something political, namely an agrarian zone under urban domination. The famous Sienese fresco "Il Buon Governo" shows how a landscape—namely the area on which peasants worked, under the legal jurisdiction of a city, to meet all of that city's needs—looked in the late Middle Ages. Although the "Buon Governo" fresco does not depict a specific place, the painting serves quasi as a cadaster entry regarding Siena's possessions at the time. We are familiar with realistic depictions of farm buildings and agricultural land such as Dürer and his circle painted on the outskirts of cities in southern Germany; and such motifs were painted, probably, not so much on account of their scenic beauty but rather, to document land ownership. In any case it resulted in jobs for artists while a further effect was that the word landscape came to describe not only the zone controlled by a city but also any painted image of it. A landscape painter was therefore a painter who was able both to represent existing landscape elements and to design ideal landscapes. This gave rise to idealistic landscape painting in the schools of Caracci and others in Naples, of Nicolas Poussin, Gaspard Dughet-Poussin, Claude le Lorrain and their circles in Rome and, finally, of the Dutch Masters.

I call such landscape painting idealistic because the landscapes depicted are nowhere to be found in reality. It was not as if the painter of yore set up his easel somewhere in the Roman Campagna and began to paint on his canvas whatever he could see. The landscapes were always composed, that is, were pieced together in the studio in line with certain ideals. The numerous painters who carted their easels around the Campagna and the Sabine Hills were only in search of picturesque details: they painted distant views, middle ground views, trees and stones as possible foreground or shrouding motifs; they took all their pencil drawings and oil sketches home with them, composed a large landscape freehand then pinned their collection of sketches to the easel, so as to be able to correctly reproduce certain details. Until well into the nineteenth century, landscape paintings depicted non-existent, ideal landscapes, even if one or another painter was perhaps occasionally commissioned to paint a definitive rendering of an actual real landscape.

The ideal landscape is thus always a painted composition, a clear view of the Tiber plain, or a view from Naples of the island of Capri—beyond a rock sketched, perhaps, when journeying over the Gotthard and shrouded by trees such as one may have painted on Mount Janiculum or in the Alban Hills and then stored in one's portfolio.

This "collect and collage" technique corresponded to the impressions garnered by art lovers on their travels. Traveling at the time was a slow matter and the route followed was just as important as the destination. Anyone coming from the north experienced the mountains, the lakes of northern Italy, the Apennines and, finally, Rome surrounded by the Alban and Sabine Hills and the plains of the Pontine Marshes. With these images in mind he could return to England or to Weimar and say, "Italy is like this or like that." The Italian landscape—such as does not exist but would be nice if it were to—does exist actually, not only in Claude le Lorrain's paintings but also in the mind's eye of any traveler who crosses Italy. His perceptive faculty pieces together charming places to create an overall image of the country where lemon trees bloom.

Landscapes of a quite different sort emerged early on, in part even under Salvator Rosa and his successors at the Neapolitan school. These were no longer charming and no longer smoothed out disharmonious elements within the picture frame. Rather, cliffs reared up without any counterpoint, such as a tree, to balance them; and ruins, ancient trees and misshapen mountains served to make a landscape look "heroic."

In England, people began to wonder why only Lake Alban and Lake Nemi should be considered beautiful but not the waters of the Lake District, why the Pontine Marshes be thought beautiful but the Scottish Highlands ugly. William Gilpin set out armed with an oval, slightly convex mirror blackened with a minimal layer of soot, in order to see whether the Scottish Highlands might not look lovely in it. Once a small image was reflected in the mirror, Gilpin sketched it and later had it engraved in copperplate. Thus the Scottish Highlands—of which Daniel Defoe had written, one cannot imagine why on earth the Good Lord created such a place—was transformed into a connoisseurs' destination. Edmund Burke then drafted the theoretical basis for these aesthetics. In addition to the ideal of "the charming place" there is also the ideal of "the sublime:" the former is at peace with itself and complete within itself while the sublime points beyond itself and stimulates the imagination to strive for perfection. The ruins, the shattered cliff, the strange, cone-shaped mountain allow one's mind to conjure something that is greater than each of these but not (yet) present. A hike, too, serves to concretize this "greater something:" anyone who travels slowly through the Alps sees so many jagged mountains that he can well imagine under what dramatic circumstances the mountains came into being.

While the route traveled by the means of transportation available back then was perforce often more impressive than the destination—and the traveler's sketchbook accordingly packed with more sketches of the Alps and the Italian lakes than of Rome—changes in the means of transportation wrought changes also in aesthetics. Both the railroad and the steamship devalue the route itself while heightening the importance of the destination. Thus we buy a ticket at the very start of the trip to Ostend, Helgoland, Mount Semmering, Lucerne, or Mont Saint-Michel. Vacationers' stations pop up, each with its destination hotel. These destinations have to fulfill certain criteria that were previously demanded of the route: the seaside cove or bay of a lake in the Alpine foothills, the waterfall or mountain pass with a panoramic outlook must each unite in a single image those landscape attributes previously garnered, collage-style, in the course of a journey. The railroad and the steamship were used to seek out typical landscapes and large hotels were built in these typical locations. Let us remind ourselves of the Semmering, then Rigi Summit, Belvedere Rhone Glacier, the Giessbach or Maloja … One traveled there then stayed for two or three weeks; and if one had managed to book a good room, one simply threw open the curtains early each morning and found oneself looking at the very same view one had picked out in the travel brochure. Such views were excerpts from landscapes and summed up the qualities of entire regions: thus the Matterhorn stands for the Alps, Helgoland stands for the entire North Sea, and the view from Stresa to the Isola Bella is an integrated North-South landscape.

Many of these hotels built in extreme locations are now in crisis, stand vacant, are used for other purposes or may even have been demolished. New means of transportation ushered in a new aesthetic. The motorcar created the illusion one was taking a walk. If I myself am in the driver's seat then I can see where I'd like to go, can stop at will, veer off to the left or the right, and once again garner beautiful details of the landscape, such that an image of the whole region takes shape in my mind's eye. Except: this just does not work. When I take a walk in the classic sense of the term, I leave the city, trek through the fields, cross a village, come upon a hill, admire the panorama, then swing through a river valley on a different route back to my city. Once home I can say, this is how it is in Wetterau, in the Vienna Woods, in the Vosges or the Marne Valley. With a car, I set out thinking to myself that I would like for once to see Burgundy, the Pyrenees or Tuscany. And what do I see? Motorways, cities and even parts of the landscape, but the things I see are too far apart, too disparate, for me to be able to describe them back home as "typical Burgundy" or "typical Tuscany." So I return to my folks and sadly declare: "Even Burgundy is no longer what it used to be. The residents have ruined it."

Does the younger generation even visit these regions today? Do they still feature on travel agents' posters? Where would kids go these days after graduating from high school, if they could choose the destination themselves? I'm always hearing stuff like, "The Arctic tundra appeals to me," "The desert appeals to me," or "The polar seas appeal to me." The younger generation's tourism landscape is one of extremes, a landscape that is easily named, on the one hand, yet exudes unbroken melancholy, on the other.

None of these extreme landscapes can be found in Central Europe. The aesthetics of exotic extreme landscapes are nourished by other sources than those we have discussed so far. But the longing to get to know other overseas landscapes has always existed, ever since the aesthetics of landscape first took shape. But how might these other landscapes be recognizable as such? We have seen that the landscape follows a code, that it is a charming place whenever it evinces the accouterments listed by Vergil, or whenever it is heroic as in the work of Claude le Lorrain, or when selected by Gilpin on account of its sublime majesty. Funding for Captain Cook's travels was granted by the kings of England and France, not least in view of the fact that Cook was supposed to return bearing new beautiful specimens that it might prove possible to grow even in local gardens. And this begs the question: What do explorers discover? Certainly they discover exotic plants and animals as well as interesting geological formations, coastlines, mountains and waterfalls. But what they most certainly fail to discover is new landscapes, because any landscape follows a given code, as we have said: it represents a culturally informed way of seeing everything that all of us have already seen. Many descriptions of exotic scenes begin conventionally. Georg Forster is not alone in describing the idyllic island of Tahiti with words such as might equally apply to Lake Maggiore: "It was a morning more beautiful than any poet might say …"

"What distinguishes the exotic landscape?" Humboldt asked himself this same question while sailing back to Europe on a vessel laden with collections of stones, pressed plants, tussled over birds, impaled butterflies, and notebooks full of meteorological data. "Shall I share my experiences with Europeans? Will my objects and data suffice to conjure the landscapes of the Amazon, Popcatepetl and the Andes in their mind's eye?" And he sadly reached the conclusion that neither his abundant material nor the entire scientific spectrum—from physics to chemistry, from mineralogy to biology—could ever convey the charm of the landscape; and so Humboldt thought—and one can read all this in his *Cosmos*—about the Old Masters who had heightened our susceptibility to landscape, and he resolved to accomplish a similar feat but one extending over the entire globe. And what this gave rise to was Humboldt's twenty-six types of landscape, which are classified primarily in terms of their vegetation and reduce his entire, infinitely great knowledge to an Impressionist's impression of a plant community. "The Realm of Mosses and Saxifrages," "The Realm of Eucalyptus," and "The Realm of Agaves and Cacti or de Condolle's Realm:" landscape motifs created by Humboldt which illustrators as well as wallpaper designers snatched up in eager. And the latest travel agency brochures such as are published annually in spring and the fall likewise remind me of Humboldt landscapes: "Tahiti and the Charm of the South Seas for 7,523.00 DM."

The landscape thus proves initially to be a way of seeing. The poet created the code, the painter gave us the images to go with it, and we respond to these available signs and say, "It is beautiful here, because this is a landscape." But we also see that this view of things has its own history. Beautiful landscapes come and go—any hotel operator can tell us a thing or two about that. The places our grandparents used to go are places young people won't ever spend their vacations now, at any price. The most beautiful places—Isola Bella, the Harz region or the island of Helgoland—have ceded to more distinctive, exotic and less culturally charged motifs.

Can one protect the landscape? Probably not, because it does not exist; and it is rather more a case of protecting those people who say in a particular place: "Look! Here is a landscape!" The image of the landscape changes—in our mind's eye. The image of reality changes—on account of economic growth. We cannot steer two disparate developments by mechanical means. We can indeed ensure that certain important elements of the landscape code are not destroyed, that riverbanks, waterfalls, trees and views neither disappear nor become built up. Eventually, however, we have simply to trust that new generations will discover new landscapes in new constellations of natural remains and economic interventions.

In 1982, Paul Armand Gette planted small signs alongside various plants in the Botanical Gardens in Kassel in order to indicate their Latin names. This action "Kassel—A Botanical Garden" was part of a broader initiative launched throughout the city by Lucius Burckhardt in the framework of the "documenta urbana—making things visible" exhibition. *Poa annua* is the Latin name for annual meadow grass. Exoticism can be seen thus to be inherent to everyday things. Why, we ask, do city gardeners so seldom draw on local, diverse and natural resources when greening the city and instead plant highly cultivated special species? Photos: Martin Schmitz

"The Landscape Trap" (1986) was a limited edition Lucius Burckhardt produced for the Galerie Eisenbahnstrasse in Berlin. At the opening, he spoke on a nearby bombsite on the theme of "Landscape Exists in the Mind's Eye." We fall into a trap when we confuse landscape with nature.

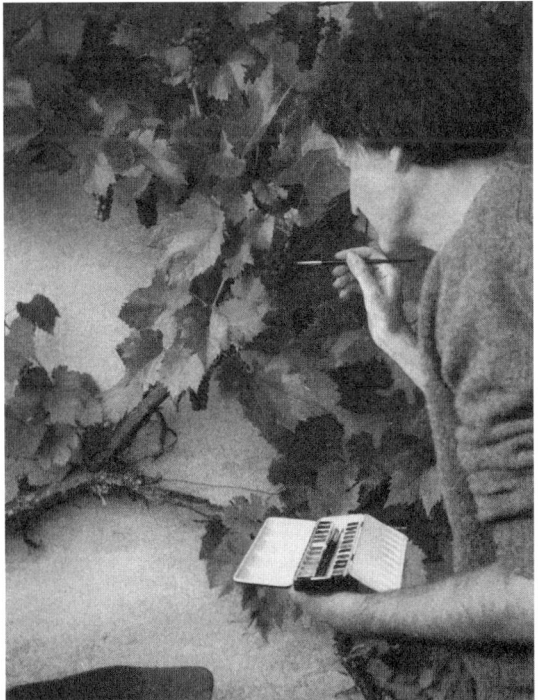

Lucius Burckhardt paints a fly on a grape, in imitation of the artists Apelles. Is a realistic simulation of nature the very best art can do? Photo: Annemarie Burckhardt

Ian Hamilton Finlay has a background in concrete poetry and ultimately focused his whole attention on creating a garden of his own in Scotland, which he initially called "Stonypath" and later "Little Sparta." The garden is quite literally full of meaning, because he created special moods or settings there for various artworks in order to lend it an historical dimension. A stone engraved with Dürer's initials enhances a lawn for us, for example, while another place so clearly evokes a landscape painting by Le Lorrain that we can almost hear Poussin's goatherd playing his flute in the foreground. (Photo on the right.) But such metaphors are drawn not only from Romantic idylls. French battlefields of the Second World War and English naval bases in the Middle East can likewise be found in only slightly encrypted form in different parts of the private garden. From the depths of the ocean to the dark heart of the forest: for the submarine turns the little thuja forest at the end of the garden into a point of transition from orderliness to incalculable infinity. Little Sparta, Stonypath, 1981. Photos: Dave Paterson

In April 1984 Joseph Beuys planted 3,000 trees in the course of his art project "7,000 Oaks for Kassel." In 1982, during the documenta 7, he had deposited 7,000 basalt rocks in a picturesque pile in front of the Fridericianum in Kassel, with the intention of half burying one of them alongside each newly planted tree. By the time documenta 8 opened in 1987, 7,000 new trees had put down roots in Kassel, in keeping with Beuy's project title: "City Forestation instead of City Administration." Photos: Annemarie Burckhardt

GARDENS
AND THE ART OF
GARDENING

Gardening—An Art and a Necessity (1977)

Gardening is an art—and so as to not discourage anyone we must immediately declare that gardening is Everyman's art! Gardening is an art even when the artist is unaware he is making art: in allowing a plant to prosper here, pruning one there, and tearing up that one by the roots in order to plant it elsewhere, or to trash it, he is not merely composting but composing too: composing a three-dimensional image, his garden.

The philosopher Immanuel Kant considered "pleasure gardening," as he called it, the supreme art. For it best fulfilled the demand he made of art: to portray a thing purposively, without purpose. The ostensible need for a well-tended garden—and this includes also any garden kept in meticulous disorder—appears purposive, even if there is no harvest (for, admittedly, Kant was not speaking here of the kitchen garden).

This view of the garden as art instantly poses rather difficult questions, namely as to what a garden actually portrays or, to be more precise: as to what representation is, and as to what is represented? Probably there are as many answers to that as there are epochs. The urban dweller with a yearning for nature today portrays something other in his garden than the urban dweller did in medieval times, for the latter fled nature to seek protection in a walled city. And a French nobleman living off his land at the time of the ancien régime had another sort of garden laid out before his palace than the English banker of today, who makes his money in the City and whose property is sheer luxury. It is this latter "English" Garden that Kant had in mind, probably, when he ascribed to it "purposiveness, without purpose." The English garden represents an agricultural economy without actually being any such thing.

In any case, the major concern seems always to be, how to depict a natural wilderness in its tamed state or to make tamed nature look wild—whereby, generally, a little of both is shown: a mix of artifice and naturalness rather than just the one extreme. Rousseau, who is commonly held to be the prophet of naturalness, also noted how artificial an image of nature *the New Héloise*[1] conjured in her overgrown garden wilderness: "Such great endeavor made to conceal endeavor ..." utters an astonished guest, after being shown the two gardens by the lord and lady of the palace—and this attests Rousseau's mocking yet discerning eye for the paradoxical nature of naturalness. In front of the palace the Baron has transformed a former stately garden into a kitchen garden by replacing chestnut tree-lined avenues with a grove of mulberry bushes. Behind the palace the Baroness has transformed the kitchen garden into a nature garden by allowing clematis to clamber in profusion over the fruit trees and by diverting a natural spring to create a pond. Neither garden bears any trace of the effort its creation had required ...

The official art of gardening is stuck with this same dichotomy still today, although several stories down, in cultural terms. For years, if not decades, all public and otherwise emblematic grounds and gardens have alternated between two styles that commingle in manifold ways: the painterly style, which is a variously blended legacy of the English respectively the Japanese respectively the Romantic garden; and the architectonic style, which is an equally eclectic offspring of the Baroque garden, flowerbeds and the early Romanticism of Art Nouveau gardens, with a dash of the "kidney-form style" of the 1950s, on which Mexican landscape artist Burle-Marx modeled his flowerbeds. In most public parks and grounds, more-

1   [Jean-Jacques Rousseau, *Julie; or the New Héloise*, Marc-Michel Rey, Amsterdam 1761.]

over, one finds elements of two other special gardening genres: the botanical garden with its rare plants and the farmer's garden with its plump, excessively fertilized flowers.

A common characteristic of these two styles of public garden, the painterly and the architectonic, is that they are made for the eye, not the feet. They are not at all user-friendly, and hostile even, if the users happen to be children. This is true not only of those parts too delicate to be walked on: someone taking a stroll often finds no charming spot, even at points where he is permitted to leave the path. A persistent feature of the painterly style, for example, is to plant a ring of bushes around a tree so as to suggest the pseu-do-natural edges of a forest. Yet to be able to sit beneath the tree would be delightful, especially in summertime. An even worse habit is that of planting flowers beneath trees where, shaded and parched, they are bound to perish before the year is out. The modern "art" of gardening has a remedy for that too: at the Federal Garden Show in Mannheim in 1975, the lawn beneath the trees was dotted with flower tubs …

While the display of such primitivisms in representative public grounds and gardens is rather annoying, the true dilettante's primitive garden has a magic all its own. To experience this, one need only stroll past a row of allotment gardens and decipher the different message of each. Bernard Lassus, who is introduced in this issue[2], has taught us the code: the gardens contain symbols of distance, designed to transport their owners from a shuttered existence to a larger landscape with new horizons. One garden dwarf is therefore a captain, his binoculars trained on a flowerbed in the form of a ship;

2   [The article was first published in the *Basler Zeitung* supplement, *Basler Magazin*, Nr. 21, 1977.]

and some birdseed has been scattered on the model of an aircraft carrier lying by the fountain, so that aircraft will land …

Let us now forget for a moment the gardening trade and the official art of gardening pursued in city parks and company headquarters, and consider instead a trend currently emerging in landscape design, that is, in the design of exterior spaces. Admittedly, no examples of this in Switzerland can be named at present.

Lately, a whole string of designs and several completed projects have proposed strict observance of the principles of architectonic gardens. All of them cited the typical features of a classical garden: symmetries, clear borders, terracing and no flowers. Generally, however, an equally monumental disruption was included in order to break the projects' symmetry—a diagonal canal, for instance, at odds with the parallel axes and perspectives of the site. What message does garden art of this sort convey? It reflects an attempt to reify big emotions in a simple form. Elementary symbols of magnificence, gravity, symmetry, grief and joy are instantly clear to everyone. Yet this does not mean the message can be consumed at first glance. The gardens here are ingenious gardens and strolling around them evokes all different kinds of information: memories of gardens in Rome or Paris, certainly, as well as more modern things, such as the way architects in the 1920s laid out their gardens with naivety and optimism, or the way dictators built during the Second World War with the shadow of defeat hanging over them. Should one seek to create gardens ingeniously? — At the least, one should provide an opportunity for experiments to be made and to be judged. Actually, that should be the purpose of any national garden show.

The necessity of dealing with nature

Should we also discuss "land art" here, a discipline in which art is writ large and the garden almost incidental? "Land" here connotes large-scale artistic experiments materialized using earth, sand, vegetation or rock. These initially appear to be the opposite of garden art insofar as they do not depict nature but alienate or, indeed, rape it. Yet they thereby critique and reflect our current approach to the earth or lead us to think about the utopia of a nature fully subjected for better or worse—for this is perhaps how we should read works such as a "Graben, der um die ganze Welt führen könnte."[3] Nature here appears to be misused in order to represent mere ideas; yet these ideas in turn indicate the necessities of dealing with nature.

This leads us a priori to a quite contrary trend in garden art, one born of ecological concerns. Conventional gardening, even when it yields nothing, requires work, plants, soil and, first and foremost, dung, four fifths of which will drain into the groundwater. Yet nature is designed in such a way that large tracts of it, if handled correctly, can be kept in a fine condition without human maintenance, without waste, without polluting the groundwater with dung, without artificial irrigation, simply by allowing natural cross-fertilization and everything else to run wild. The gardener should work with nature, not against it. A major botanical discovery of our day—the discovery of plant communities—put us on to this truth. A single plant must be tended, protected, sown or planted; a plant community, if selected correctly for the site in question, is resistant, robust and wholly self-sufficient. To garden with naturally self-propagating plant communities is a new departure; there are few people special-

3 ["A ditch that might lead around the whole world:" an as yet unidentified reference.]

ized in the field and mixed seeds are still hard to come by. Evidence of this trend at Federal Garden Shows has been puny to date and by no means up to standard on the robustness scale: for the aim is to produce flowers as resilient as the weed families that overrun our railroad embankments, gravel pits and trash heaps.

We can spot a third trend among those garden artists who have taken a leaf out of the farmers' and allotment gardeners' book but have not yet lapsed into the primitivisms of the official gardeners' flower-trimmed battlefields. The art here consists in translating the individual symbolism of a single allotment garden into a universal symbolism, of finding metaphors that have an archetypal impact on everyone. I like to call this type of garden the mysterious garden. The Romantic garden was once mysterious and full of surprises: a stroll would lead one from cheerful symbols, garden houses, panoramic rotundas and glades to sad, mysterious, melancholy spots, stalactite-filled grottos, mock graves, well shafts, natural springs and ruins, all of which invited the beholder to reflect on mortal transience. Such symbolism was for many years the object of derision; it survived only in private gardens, above all in allotment gardens. Today, we have again come to appreciate popular art; at first we had nothing more than a wry smile for garden dwarves, then we came to adore them, and now, once again, we are learning from them the art of creating a garden full of surprises: a truly mysterious garden, in which kids' dreams and distant memories of childhood books revive and render palpable our fear of the deep pond, of seeking refuge in the hollow tree stump, of the fathomless well, as well as of our joy in a dull echo. Admittedly, the official gardening journals make no mention of these trends in garden art—they are too busy discussing new concrete slabs for garden paths; or even larger varieties of tulip and rose, which require more dung than ever; or new chemicals that will at last rid the lawn of weeds.

It appears that the problems of garden art today are too big and too various to be entrusted any longer to gardeners. I can draw on two examples of current and future landscape planning to demonstrate what I mean: when "Grün 80"[4] arrived on the scene in Basel there was much talk of the urban show and of "greening" districts. Today we know that the G 80 essentially comprises a quite literally limited, which is to say enclosed arena on the city's outskirts, where previously a park and a well-tended farm existed. It is evident, therefore, that the aspiration to do gardening in and for the city is by no means being fulfilled.

Consider this analogy: we all are familiar with the green lawns that one finds between apartment buildings. The caretaker mows them regularly. It is not forbidden to step on them, but nobody, at least no adult, does so voluntarily. These areas for leisure and sport, which featured so prominently in the ground plans and were so highly praised on the day the key to your apartment was handed over, serve now only to mark the distance to be maintained between respectable neighbors. There is one way these areas could be utilized at no extra cost, namely by selling them as private lots to sitting tenants. Yet this would create inequalities. Tenants' participation in caring for these areas would require a measure of collective organization—and who on earth has time for that? Certainly not the gardeners, and the landlords won't even give it a thought. For sure, the tenants can do nothing on their own. So here we have a landscape maintenance task of quite a new kind.

A similar problem is posed also beyond the housing estates, in what may properly be called urban public space. The city could be lovelier and greener: yet the effort and expense of having the City

4 [The urban garden development project "Gartenschau der Stadt" or "G 80" was launched in 1980.]

Department of Parks and Recreation make it so would be huge. We know there are people who would love to do a spot of gardening and have been on the waiting list for an allotment garden for years already. Yet not only the law books, but also the unspoken rules of urban co-existence prevent them from shouldering their spades and bedding a few clematis plants on the Heuwaage or casually sowing a few mullein seeds when walking by the trash heap in St. Alban's Valley. Here too, public willingness to participate needs to be revived, organized and intelligently steered.

Creating robust, extensive landscapes

The second, equally grave problem in landscape planning reveals itself beyond the city limits, in the open countryside. So much work and—let's not kid ourselves—such huge subsidies are ploughed into agriculture in Switzerland that undeveloped wasteland is extremely rare. Yet fallow or unused land is virtually characteristic of modern Western Europe, as are monocultures too. If we test our skills in futurology, we quickly come to suppose that fallow land, on the one hand, and ecologically sustainable cultivation on the other, will become a suitable and likely landscape for our densely populated Central European region ... But how do these plots of fallow land look now? For these too, as with our urban parks, the Department of Parks and Recreation has a design style at the ready. — Today, in places where landscape design is applied on a large scale, to the reclamation of disused open cast mines for example, the newly configured, old-fashioned farm is considered a "charming landscape." Whoever plans large-scale landscape design thus plans precisely that which cannot survive elsewhere and will turn into wasteland. There are two things to be learned here: firstly, any available land must be given over to the purpose of leisure, must be dedicated to a culture of leisure that is a source of pleasure and causes no ecological damage; and, secondly, any non-privatized areas should be turned into the kind of landscape on which plant communities can establish themselves solidly and thus stand up to picnics, sports and children's games. On broad expanses of land that were once left fallow as well as on the city's neatly parceled lots, we are awaiting new impulses from gardening, impulses that will, moreover, both in technological and social terms, far exceed the scope of the conventional planning applied to our parks and public spaces.

No Man's Land (1980)

No Man's Land—that's where Schorsch lit his homemade rocket and Anne was given her first kiss. No Man's Land does not exist, at least not in any decently planned city. No Man's Land is a product of planning. Without planning, there is no No Man's Land. But once planners realize they have planned a No Man's Land, its end is already nigh. It is even renamed then—as "a dysfunctional zone." But that is of no concern to either Schorsch or Anne. They get upset only when urban development teams burn down bushes, level the banks of the stream, periodically mow the lawn or set up a public seating area plus barbecue.

The progressive state plans for everyone: it plans sandpits for toddlers, provides benches for their mothers, lays out paths on which to take a stroll, plants and fells shade-giving trees for the elderly, creates a football pitch and sports fields for older children, and parks and playgrounds for families, not to mention roads, which are probably the most important leisure zone of all.

And the state, in planning a No Man's Land, caters also to adolescents. But it is unaware that it does so. No Man's Land comes into being once a zone has been earmarked for property development, because its agricultural exploitation then becomes obsolete yet its urban use is not yet profitable. No Man's Land is the blank space between the city proper and its oversized, tailor-made "planning suit." All of us are grateful to it for that, and adolescents especially.

Of course, planning is also a menace to No Man's Land. This menace is called "green planning." True, green planning has a hard time of it in our cities. Built-up areas cannot be turned into green spaces. So it must strive instead to turn green spaces into green spaces. Ever since city gardeners ceased to restrict themselves to greening only the city park and certain other sites, No Man's Land has been under threat.

Plans to green the city by transforming No Man's Land into disciplined green spaces contribute neither to beautifying the city nor to increasing the availability of recreational zones. Total gardening actually does not give rise to that which city gardeners expect, namely an urban landscape. On the contrary, the more prescribed the visuals presented to the public eye, the less inclined the public is to subsume them under the heading "landscape." Today, the manner and style of city gardening still follows the dictates of the 1930s: to be functional and to promote hygiene. And this goal-oriented greening simply robs open spaces of their freedom to exist as a last refuge, as a place where we—and, above all, adolescents, namely those of an age already tainted with the stigma of unruliness—might stretch our legs and let our minds wander. And we remain adolescents well into old age.

Destroyed By Tender Loving Care (1981)

"To redesign a place also means to replace a landscape that we are not yet capable of recognizing with an identifiable landscape. However, we don't yet know enough about what such replacements take away and what they achieve." (Bernard Lassus)

The Federal Garden Shows are potentially great opportunities for the profession as well as for the host city—and, furthermore, an occasion for the gardening trade to seek to escape the dual bind in which the lovely, popular art of gardening now finds itself: on the one hand, the bind of increased artificiality, which is to say, the demand for ever more highly cultivated flower varieties that must be nursed to good health by administering ever higher doses of chemical fertilizers, insecticides and fungicides; and, on the other, the bind of academic style dictates that draw blindly on one motif after another and empty all designs of their intended content by combining them with their opposites: hence the "natural" lakeshore plus fountain, the hilltops plus ponds, the geometric flower beds plus wannabe-bonsai dwarf shrubs or the desert grasses with rhododendrons.

The host city could seize the opportunity to review its concept of recreational space, to create new, community-oriented facilities and to make a U-turn on urban planning schemes deleterious to the natural environment. This opportunity was available to Kassel. A concept elaborated by a working group of undergraduates foresaw a decentralized Federal Garden Show that would make do without fenced enclosures and entrance fees and balance this by making savings elsewhere: for example, by staging the requisite indoor shows in the fantastic ambiance of disused factory buildings.

The Federal Garden Show in Kassel in 1981 chose a different path. The Show was used to turn a park into a park.

Kassel's Karlsaue, a huge, originally Baroque garden, was turned into a landscaped park at the end of the eighteenth century yet its basic structure was largely retained. The Orangery with its "bowling green" was kept as the centerpiece: a large, practical and barrier-free venue in a beautiful setting, it has since been a fitting backdrop to many a documenta exhibition or other public event.

The Federal Garden Shows occasion considerable and ever-increasing financial outlay. Entrance fee revenue to the tune of circa 9 million Deutschmarks stands against expenditure of between 50 and 60 million Deutschmarks, whereby these latter sums do not include the services provided unremarked by the host federal state or city, which may include preliminary work or putting regular staff temporarily at a Show's disposal. A major example of such preliminary work was the endeavor made by Hessische Schlösser und Gärten (Palaces and Parks of the State of Hessen) to Baroque-ify the Karlsaue. This re-Baroque-ification, which incidentally contravened every principle of modern cultural heritage preservation, was able to be hindered at least in part by a public outcry. But nonetheless, much damage was done. We specify:

– The felling in public parks of trees which should have been conserved as natural monuments on account of their age and size.
– The "tree rehabilitation program" which not only cut back branches and left trees looking wholly god-forsaken but also sealed those hollows in trees in which natural tree rehabilitators had hitherto been able to nest.
– The felling of "rehabilitated" trees subsequent to vocal criticism of the rehabilitation program.
– The replacement of an avenue of oak trees by more ancient oaks, after the former had been transplanted at too great an age and their growth thus stunted.

- Redevelopment of the Karlswiese [meadow] for a rose show, in a way such that heavy bulldozers negatively impacted natural water seepage.
- The use of concrete seepage slabs, concrete grid plates and vertical teak planking for restoration of the banks of all bodies of water in the park, the results of which in every case were aesthetically and ecologically unsatisfactory and hostile to plant and animal communities.
- The ill-considered use of toxins both on the Karlswiese [meadow] site earmarked for rose gardens and on canal banks, the previous neglect of which had enabled the seeds of plants, including weeds, to spread and thrive there.

All the professional errors listed above are man-made and could easily have been avoided by experts. Yet they are nothing compared with the fundamental issue at stake here, namely that an existing, fully functional, easily maintained and widely appreciated public park was quite unnecessarily redesigned and fitted out in such a trim and tidy manner as to require in the future both more public discipline and more maintenance by the local authorities.

Moreover, Kassel was given a further bonus, in addition to the fenced-off part of the Federal Garden Show, for the wetlands on the far banks of the River Fulda were landscaped too. When this aspect of the Federal Garden Show was put up for public debate, the local authorities' response was: "How can you [critics] be so critical when nothing existed there until now?" The "nothing" that had previously existed there comprised the ancient wetlands of the River Fulda with their romantic overgrown banks and a mix of agricultural and fallow land where families, conditions permitting, would camp, build fires, play ball games or even wash the car, which latter activity evidently caused particular offense.

There was an old gravel pit that served as a lake on the site as well as numerous signs forbidding people to bathe, which were an open invitation to jump in; and also a slagheap left over from quarrying and used by many a bold cyclist as a test site. Yet one million cubic meters of material was then displaced to turn this location—a recreational zone in the true sense of the term—into a "real" recreational zone. The lake too was remodeled in the inevitable kidney shape while the typical slagheap profile came to resemble a slack hammock and the site overall an oversized mini-golf course. And once all the natural features of the adjacent Karlsaue wetlands had been obliterated by means of toxins, fertilizers and tree wax, an artificial "biotope" and "eco-island" were created there, on which any creatures that survived the chemical warfare may now settle.

The material excavated from the gravel pit on the Fulda wetlands was used to shore up Kassel's newly built southern bypass road. This "relief road" has promptly helped pollute the southern districts of Kassel with more traffic than ever before. Seen in this light, the Fulda wetlands development is nothing but another step in the destruction of the city's outskirts, that still untamed zone in which the population used to be free to enjoy the fusion of cityscape and open countryside.

Reason Slumbers in the Garden (1988)

The Golden Age—was that in prehistoric times or does it await us still, in a more commonsensical future? Is it irretrievably lost or could action bring it into being, manufacture it? All gardens reflect this question, a question that gained a political dimension in the Age of Reason, in the run-up to the great revolution. In the eighteenth century, the art of gardening was a locus of philosophical inquiry: no man of ideas or action failed at the time to express his opinion on a question that was evidently of universal import, namely whether the formal "French-style" or the landscaped "English-style" garden had the greater merit.

Gardening thereby came to be the most important art form in the Age of Enlightenment. The weltgeist itself appears to have grabbed a spade and modeled this terrain. Nonetheless, its message was not wholly unambiguous. Gardening is an art, not a sermon. Gardens are not political speeches, not even encrypted, i.e. decipherable ones, and when a gardener lays out the long channel as a clear, straight axis rather than lend it a picturesque curve in order to hide its ends from view, he neither takes sides with the parliament rather than the king, nor vice versa. The essence of his at all times and in all eras contemporary art is its capacity to consistently encompass and reflect unknown and unspoken elements even before lexical clarity about the meaning of such symbols has been established. Thus it is superfluous to even naively debate why such a progressive spirit as Mirabeau stood up for the formal garden or why a so behind-the-times ruler as the landgrave of Kassel stood up for the English garden. Even such people as they saw their problems reflected in the most important medium of the day yet they neither wore their politics on their sleeves nor spouted lip service, not even of the encrypted variety.

The biggest problem facing the landgraves of Kassel was without any doubt their own person and its legal and personal legitimacy. The continually self-perpetuating curse of their existence was the need for a prince to be born, legitimately, of an unloved wife. The prince subsequently felt love for his true yet outcast mother as well as hatred for his father the ruler and for his father's mistress. The prince's personal grief over his thus caused repudiation led him in turn into the arms of a mistress and hence to the next procreation of a prince born of a legitimate yet unloved wife for the purpose of dynastic stability and the perpetuation of said curse.

Thus the parks of Kassel are not the works of keen reason but of reasoning on the tricky question as to how a legacy may manifest its legitimacy without giving all the credit to the testator. How can I be unique and a link in a chain, at one and the same time? And, specifically: How can I transform the park of my ancestors without destroying their work? Any attack on the forbears' park may be carried out only on the symbolic level. The Giants' Castle conquered by Hercules, the dominant motif in this Baroque composition of perspective, becomes just one garden monument among others once the Löwenburg and the aqueduct ruins are constructed—and the orderly park therewith to a "landscape with ruins." Likewise the cascade that empties into the dead straight symmetrical axis is outshone by the S-shaped curve of the new English aesthetic, which snakes from Hercules to the Löwenburg to the aqueduct and then through the castle to the lake.

For the benefit of any visitor who may perhaps have not yet fully grasped it, the concept is presented once again in miniature before Pluto's Grotto. Whereas originally eight radial paths leading from the garden's center were foreseen—one of which was to be the main entrance to Pluto's Grotto—the visitor arriving from the aqueduct now follows a diagonal path; and at the point where the path intersects the main axis of the castle, his gaze is drawn sideways by a more arresting image: the Devil's Bridge over the waterfall. At the hub of what was to have become the eight-pointed star, an ostensibly natural body of water into which the cascade falls before flowing onto the aqueduct takes the form of the S-shaped curve so dear to Burke and Hogarth. Grandfather's Grotto is left unchanged and serves as a lateral accessory to the new image, quasi as a prelude to the bridge over the waterfall.

This image tells us a great deal—but, as I already said, it conveys no precise message. Rather it remains imprecise, contradictory even, and this is decisive. Nature when represented as "natural" is just as ambiguous as it used to be when idealized in mathematical terms, terms that are now suddenly being read as "anti-nature." Man can create an area of heightened order, a portico with formulaic symmetries and rhythms, and this "temenos" (to cite the term used by Tzonis/Lefaivre)[1] may point ahead, progressively and optimistically, to a more rational future, free of arbitrariness. Yet such a temenos may equally propel us back to the fiction of primitive, natural arbitrariness, and to the legitimacy of usurped leadership and the will of the leader who has imposed such order by force.

The artist can likewise create a slice of "natural" nature—but only as an image, since the representation of nature also requires a design and, later, permanent care. A border must be drawn between it and the surrounding fallow or agricultural terrain, and an enclosure set up too. The better concealed the latter, the purer the effect of this artificial natural zone—yet its effect would be completely destroyed, were it ever mistaken for genuine nature. Goethe hinted at this fatal prospect in his drama *Die Aufgeregten* [The Agitated], by having an assertive daughter hunt rabbits in the landscaped garden of her

---

1 Alexander Tzonis/Liane Lefaivre: "Das Klassische in der Architektur – die Poetik der Ordnung," *Bauwelt Fundamente* Nr. 72, 1987, p. 202 ff.

mother, the Baroness. May we use the term "temenos" also for such an artificial natural zone?

Such a zone conveys no direct lexical message of its own. As we have seen, it shimmers somewhere between a prehistoric Golden Age and a future in which man will once again live without destructiveness in nature and indeed husband it, between that which is irretrievably lost and such Arcadias as only reason can create. Reflection takes place at the equally ambivalent level of a physiocratism in which progress and reaction are fused. The physiocrats acquired genuine insight into the role of labor and of wealth; to them we owe our image of circulation, the circulation of money from the producers of goods to their masters then to craftsmen and back to agricultural laborers. Thus physiocrats were the first to hold the key to instating a plan-oriented and rationalized modern economy. But they then froze society quasi in a pre-rational state that was simultaneously a child of its era and a nostalgic dream. Immortalizing the class of landowners and masters as part of the natural-given course of things established the regressive utopia of the prince of the peasants, the *Royaume Agricole*.

"What is more valuable, Mentor added, a great city of marble, gold and silver with a neglected and barren landscape or a fruitful, cultivated landscape with a mediocre city, modest in its customs? A large city populated by craftsmen busy with the comforts of life as a means to loosen up local morals and, all about it, a poor and little cultivated kingdom resembling a monster with an overly thick head and a starved body that is wholly out of proportion with the head. The size of the population and the amount of available food mark the power and true wealth of the kingdom. Idomeneus currently has countless, tirelessly toiling people scattered all over the country. His whole country is like a single city. Salante is only the center of it. We have transported people from the city into the landscape because they were lacking there, and because there were too many of them in the city."[2] Telemachus, the future landgrave of Ithaka, had a pretty good grasp of all this.

"Who was right?" the landgrave of Kassel mused perhaps. "That old sycophant who once advised my grandfather to bring Huguenots to Kassel as traders and artisans or the new sycophants who consider alone the prince and his peasants to be productive, and citizens and traders to be mere parasites?"—The landgrave debates this issue with himself through the filter of the landscaped garden. But the beautified look of his own landscaped park provides him with no clear answer. It leaves in limbo the crucial question of whether the Golden Age lies at the beginning or at the end of time, whether it is paradise lost or a reality yet to be forged. The landgrave's reason can continue to slumber as long as he, the ruler, ranks among the eternal instances of a natural order.

A garden cannot solve the problems of its day. But it can certainly articulate a more profound discussion of them than the conventional landscape garden can. This is probably why Rousseau's garden, which is to say, Julie's garden in his work *the New Héloise*,[3] is of the more complex kind. Undoubtedly this too is a temenos, because attention is explicitly drawn both to the trellises surrounding it and to the wicket gate. This meticulously enclosed orchard, which is off-limits for mere mortals yet has been transformed into a sheer paradise for birds, quite explicitly does not prompt discussion of the dream of a natural paradise. Instead, the inaccessibility, extreme futility and so deeply coveted beauty of pure nature in its untrammeled state are revealed there, a state that exaggerated artificiality alone can rep-

2   [François de Salinac de la Mothe Fénelon: *Les aventures de Télémaque*, 1699]

3   Jean-Jacques Rousseau: *Julie ou La Nouvelle Héloise—Lettres de Deux Amants*, vol. 4, 11th letter, 1761

resent. And this artificial nature is likewise financially viable alone thanks to its dialectic mirror image, namely the garden created by Baron Wolmar. For he has turned his father's representative park into a profitable venture by planting mulberry trees as nourishment on which silkworms might thrive. Only in this schizophrenic dual garden in front of and behind the castle—the representative garden made profitable at its front and the kitchen garden turned luxury garden to its rear—does reason become wide awake.

Garden design today is no longer the artistic field of pre-philosophical experiments. In an era marked by congestion of the natural environment, by agrarian surplus, by eutrophication of our groundwater, by the no-holds-barred agricultural chemicals industry and mass breeding on the boundaries of genetic engineering, the official art of gardening indulges itself in an irresponsible paraphrase of this manic agricultural economy. Giant tulips spring up in place of oversized corncobs, disposable plants produce excessive offspring, nurseries supply the treasures of Japan's imperial gardens cheaper by the dozen, and soil preparation and drainage technology ensure that plants of arid origin flourish in moist soils and moisture-loving plants in arid soils, that everything can be planted anywhere and that each stylistic device may be beaten to death by the next. Even the biotopes so popular among gardeners in recent times are produced by means of plastic films and the accouterments necessary to permanently maintain their unstable status are already in the production pipeline. In other words, professionals have already figured out how to make as much money from supposedly untamed nature as from rose beds.

On the sidelines of the profession, however, some gardeners/non-gardeners are debating garden types more appropriate to the current era. We have spoken elsewhere about Kurt Brägger, Louis

Le Roy, Bernard Lassus and Ian Hamilton Finlay.[4] Here, I would like to comment briefly on a garden that appears to reflect in a very particular way the situation we face in our era. The garden in question is a former city nursery abandoned by the profession. A city nursery is basically a place of work comprising concrete-framed flowerbeds, seedbeds, greenhouses and other hotbeds of cultivation, interspersed with driveways so that trucks can deliver fertilizer and pick up plants. The city gardeners originally moved out owing to the city's plans to convert their old workplace into a "real" garden. The events described below unfold in Basel, one year after the Sandoz disaster in Schweizerhalle.

The garden, the old city nursery, is currently being squatted by young people who have lived and worked there since the early summer of 1987. They are firmly convinced that the garden they have created is both beautiful and useful. They invite the citizens of Basel to come and view their work, since they believe they will succeed thus in mobilizing public opinion against the city's plans to build a "public park" on the site. — Does it not go without saying that the official plans for this future park evince every sign of that lack of taste so characteristic of the more modern art of gardening and, also, that they have the effrontery to propose, on account of the course of the Rhine and its steep banks, that some 200,000 cubic meters of earth be displaced in order to create a "natural wetland?"

Well, the citizens of Basel who come with goodwill to view the garden, to judge whether it might be left to the young squatters in its present form, all have a bit of a fright. "Oh no," they say, "this is not at all what we had imagined—the site cannot possibly be left in such a state." Huge weeds are thriving in the still over-fertilized

4   Lucius Burckhardt: Garden Design—New Trends (1981), in this book:
    p. 177–185

hotbeds, some panes of glass in the hotbeds are shattered, rust is corroding the reinforced concrete frames, and thistles are sprouting from the cracks in the asphalt-covered turning bay … The older visitors cannot see the garden the young people claim to have created here. They are completely blind to it—or it is invisible …

Did earlier citizens of Kassel or Weimar immediately recognize their ruling princes' landscaped gardens as gardens? Probably only once these had cropped up in paintings, been commented upon at length in writing or depicted in copperplate engravings specifically as landscape gardens. — Likewise in the former city nursery in Basel, images had first to be interpreted. Through the veil of its former disorder or new order, I discovered five such images: five images of the new garden, of the garden of the new risk society, of the society of nature destroyed, of limits attained, of the garden of the society obliged to rethink its concepts of production and environmental exploitation. These five images are:

– "Under the cobblestones, the beach." This first image shows spontaneous and adventive vegetation sprouting from cracks in the asphalt and the concrete borders and, especially lushly, from the over-fertilized flowerbeds and greenhouses: living proof of the fact that eternal nature lurks even beneath the city and in the city, and will one day overrun everything, if mankind ever destroys itself.

– The second image shows nature become rare. It is a fact that the strip of land between the city nursery and the banks of the Rhine is home to a colony of rare long-horned beetles, the last few hundred surviving examples of this species on Swiss soil. The former city gardeners, if ever they finish building their proposed public park and regardless of whether or not it includes wetlands, will inevitably hasten the complete extinction of this species from Switzerland.

– The third image shows a farm. The young resident-workers at the old city nursery have acquired chickens, geese and even piglets; neighborhood residents are invited to feed these creatures with

their kitchen waste. The message behind this image is: even urban dwellers can be farmers.
- The fourth image shows an emergency. The more vehemently the government declared its intention to realize the true needs of the people, the more eagerly the squatters worked. Never could so many people be seen busily at work as on the day it was rumored former city gardeners were about to roll up on bulldozers.
- And the fifth, most impressive image shows a utopia: the utopia of the unity of art and life. Everyone is a worker, everyone is an artist, and everyone makes a contribution to the wider community, either alone or as part of a group, either by making a sculpture, making music, cooking a meal for everyone or even by sweeping up the crumbling asphalt so as to make the grass a little greener.

Let me emphasize once again that the visitor lured there by newspaper articles and the squatters' invitations saw none of these images. He saw only an inner-city zone in a dysfunctional state and indefensible disorder. The young people, for their part, could not comprehend how older people could fail to see their images. Well, if they do not understand us here, they thought, we shall go to them. And so the squatters donned their craziest clothes, dyed their hair green and violet, tuned their guitars and went to the marketplace. There too, they presented an image: "We are the good guys!" Unfortunately, passers-by perceived something else altogether and thought to themselves: "Oh dear, they are that sort." And this teaches us something about the enlightened-enlightening garden, namely that it needs to be enclosed, fenced-off. Outside its fence, its symbols are incomprehensible.

If there is no "shift," ordinary things remain ordinary; and then Wilhelmshöhe is once again located in Northern Hessen, not in the Roman Campagna, and talk is neither of the Golden Age at the beginning of time nor of the realm of reason at the end of history but only of the vagaries of the here and now.

Gardens Are Images (1989)

Since gardens are experienced on a scale of 1:1, it is easily overlooked that they are not a reality but only represent potential realities. Since the eighteenth century they have drawn on two languages in order to do so: the formal, so-called French-style garden demonstrates how the orderly man-made world should relate to the chaotic natural environment and the so-called English landscape garden, by contrast, asserts that the chaos of nature is an order in its own right, one in which a harmonious society can live and earn a livelihood.

These two basic formulas define the art of gardening to this day. Both of them first became banal in the nineteenth century then were given a new lease of life through the use either of both sets of contrasting motifs in the same garden or of borrowed motifs and real innovations, such as Japanese impulses, Foerster-style perennial gardens, cottage gardens or the Alpineum inspired by botanical gardens. However, all such innovations served only to perpetuate the old dialectic—cultivated order versus natural chaos—on a broader scale.

The decline of the art of gardening in more recent times set in owing to pressure on it to perform and be commercially successful. Anything goes—and powerful companies are just waiting to prove it. You want marsh plants set amid dry grasses? — We can deliver. You'd like giant tulips between the dwarf shrubs? — Just tick the box on the order form. — You want a fountain in that pond of yours with the naturally designed banks? — Our experts will advise you. — Yet the meaning of such increasingly spectacular displays goes by the board. The loud tones of musical instruments drown out the concert while the perpetual combination of contrasting motifs annuls their alleged impact. Moreover, the art of gardening of this sort, if one can still call it an art, leads to a kind of professionalization that reduces the amateur gardener to a fool, one who spends his time trying desperately to catch up with such successes as are shown at garden shows and in catalogs. However, despite record attendance at the Federal Garden Shows, the views of large sections of their audience have undergone a paradigm shift and the end is nigh for this era of instant gardening and disposable plants. As we saw in the opening lines of this paper, vibrant and meaningful gardening is always a means both to represent society's relationship to nature and to put it up for debate. And much has changed in this regard. The exploitation of nature has reached its limits. Modern technologies are becoming a menace. Our trash is poisoning the environment and will ultimately poison us. Countless species have been eradicated or are menaced by imminent extinction. Contemporary garden design is expected to take a clear position on nature's altered circumstances. Gardening which does nothing but perpetuate such exploitation by continuing to depend on over-cultivation, over-fertilization and disposable plants is unable to provide any new guidelines.

Mind you, even professional nurseries have now noted this. So they have added a new motif, the biotope, to their already too broad product range. The biotope is the new "must-have" for any garden show worth its salt. And the biotope is also an opportunity to disseminate pseudo-professional expertise and demonstrate absolute feasibility. Moreover, it makes full use of the performance capacity built up for other purposes, for a biotope too may require considerable quantities of soil to be displaced as well as complex maintenance. True, the kingfishers that the pilot project people anticipated would nest at the Federal Garden Show have yet to materialize but, nevertheless: one can use just as many wire fences and prohibition signs in a biotope as in any conventional rose bed.

Yet the biotope we are mocking here does in fact make sense, since it leaves nature to its own devices for a while. For one, it's actually amazing how quickly some of our native flora and fauna can regenerate. Seeds and fertile colonies can evidently still be found at many locations. In the general run of migration and evasion, therefore, the biotope can provide certain species with a niche and a temporary habitat. The biotope is also of pedagogical value, because it shows that our no-holds-barred agricultural economy is a threat to animal and plant life. In general, however, any species protected by the biotope is invisible or unknown to the public. No one notices the larva of a palmate newt or a rare beetle swimming in a pond. In this sense, the biotope too is only an abstract image in our mind's eye.

Gardeners should certainly make good use of this natural motif. Yet building biotopes generally proves far less effective than more economical and ecological forms of gardening. The latter imply not only a reduction in the use of fertilizers but also matters that should have long since become second nature, such as the need to completely renounce herbicides, pesticides and the terrible habit of using so-called "virgin" soils, namely those which have been made completely germ-free by the injection of poisonous gas. Also, things formulated in negative terms—the avoidance of toxins, for example—must be filled with positive content, be filled with such knowledge, skills, and experience of dealing with plants and soil as gardeners—even amateur gardeners—used to possess before professionals' offers of total feasibility systematically pushed them to the brink of oblivion. My mother, for instance, knew how to keep earthworms in check while gardeners today know only how to kill them off in one fell swoop. There is, however, one recent botanical insight that we can add to our established knowledge of gardening, namely the fact that plant communities can be deployed as a landscaping technique.

But we can take the art of gardening seriously as an art form only when it serves, as in historical times, to convey meaning and to articulate problems by visual means. I cannot emphasize enough the fact that both the French-style and the English-style garden are representative: each makes a statement that revolves around mankind's relationship to nature in the age of discoveries, colonization and early industrialization. Arguably, such gardens are indeed "reality;" but they are symbols too, and their arrangement brings new dimensions into play. The fountain at the top of the park at the Villa Lante "is" in the mountains; the group of exotic trees beyond the long channel "is" in America. In both cases, the viewer is presented with a precise problem in symbolic form. In the case of Villa Lante, a natural scientific question that much occupied people at the time: How do the waters of rivers and streams arrive in the mountains? And, in the second case, a social question: What do we make of the New World overseas?

With one exception, the people I wish to mention now are outsiders and artists who have given new momentum to the art of gardening—even if their peers at least in Germany continue to ignore the fact. Louis Le Roy deserves a mention, first and foremost, for he has liberated gardening from compulsive planting and weeding by showing how it might be regarded instead as a technique for dealing with spontaneous vegetation. How his garden came into being is already legendary. Le Roy purchased a meadow from a farmer with the intention of building a studio there for himself. His first move was to allow a contractor to deposit several loads of demolition material on the property. Immediately, spontaneous vegetation began to sprout from the cracks in the blocks of debris, mosses formed humus, and the meadow gradually ceased to be eutrophic and flourished. Five years later, when Le Roy submitted his planning application, the local authority told him his land was the last patch of untouched nature in the community and refused him permission to build ...

The ecological aspect of Le Roy's approach is certainly important yet people are mistaken in thinking it alone is the whole story, since his garden is by no means a biotope. Le Roy is a gardener, not a botanist. He intervenes, sows and prunes in order to create a visual effect. There are two things we can learn from Le Roy's artwork. Firstly, something about how he works—for Le Roy creates without a plan. Planning is a way of giving orders. It imposes certain hierarchies. I give my plan to craftsmen and demand that they carry it out to the letter. Le Roy shows that design does not require a plan. The designer acts directly, on a scale of 1:1. This alone amounts to a radical critique of the profession for it asserts that the gardener, not the person poring over the drawing board, is the one who makes things happen. And whoever adds the finishing touches to a design has the final say, even if he thereby destroys something someone else made the day before. Someone changes a thing, evidently, because its previous form was not quite right.

Secondly we can learn that the "picture" a garden paints differs from a normal image on account of the timescale. While the conventional gardener is proud to create a lasting image—a garden in which he uproots annuals, year after year, then plants the exact same sorts again—Le Roy's garden changes over time, just as the natural world changes owing to mankind's destructive interventions. What Le Roy reveals to us is the biological struggle for survival of the fittest; but it is stylized as a tournament, since Le Roy always ensures when sowing and pruning that the winner does not establish autocratic rule. Photographs of Le Roy's gardens are therefore often misleading because they show only a temporary "as is" state, not a cinematographic process.

And in order to understand the whole story one must consider the fact that Le Roy's gardens are located in Holland, in part on land reclaimed from the sea and in the midst of rectangular canal networks and other infrastructure. They hence prompt discussion of the opposite of that which the French garden—that geometric cultivated spot amid immense forests—hoped to explicate for its viewers.

"Ecology is a trap," Bernard Lassus once said in order to emphasize that he is not afraid to make technical interventions of great
magnitude, if ever the situation demands it. In general, however, the
principle of "minimal intervention" underpins his approach to gardening, namely he arranges things such, that even those which remain unchanged will be seen in a new way. Contrasts and transitions
render things more visible, although the degree of visibility depends
on the context. Anyone in a group of soldiers who wears a cap unlike
all the others is highly conspicuous whereas to be noticed in a group
of elegantly dressed people takes rather more effort. Moreover, there
are different registers of order and comparison. Oranges and tennis
balls are similar in one respect but completely different in another.
Lassus conceived his gardens in the light of theoretical considerations as to how meaning is generated. He gained renown thanks
to his design for a park at Marne-la-Vallée, which was awarded first
prize but never executed. How might one ensure that the residents
of a new settlement in the most densely populated region of Europe acquire a sense of both the history of the city and the natural
environment? Firstly, Lassus demanded a hard transition from the
city to the park since landscape, in his view, is that which the urban
dweller sees when he looks over the city's walls. Thus, contrary to
the planners' intentions, Lassus resisted the obvious but tempting
prospect of greening the entire new urban development by retaining
a few old trees from the forest that had had to be felled to make
way for the development in the first place. For the presence of such
"enslaved Indians," as Lassus called them, "would make the wild
Indians look no longer authentic."

Lassus likewise intended to preserve most of the existing landscape as a basis for the landscaped park. But since he knew that
the meaning of the landscape would not be the same once the new
development had been built, he proposed to overlay its surface with
a network of points that would inspire children, primarily, but also

open up layers of meaning for adults. Certain points marked by a kind of totem pole were intended to convey a sense of an historical or paleontological past. A light that went on briefly at the bottom of a pond at dusk each evening in combination with the sound of distant church bells was meant to revive a sense of the old village now engulfed by the new development. And a fountain so deep it would be impossible to hear the impact of a stone thrown into it—a device was installed to ensure stones would not hit the water—brought an element of the unfathomable into the mundane world of a new residential development.

Of the artists mentioned here, Gustav Lange is a real gardener. He too assumes that perception of all things in existence relies on visual means. His school recreation yard built on the banks of a river with varying water levels is impressive. How easily a quay wall would cope with the changes in water level! But Lange prefers to draw attention to the fact that we live in a world in which everything is not yet wholly regulated and that a river is hence still higher after three days of rain than after a dry spell. He therefore lays out his dams not parallel to the river, as a means of flood prevention, but, rather, at a ninety-degree angle to it. Consequently, children can play on the entire surface of the playground in dry spells but on the dams alone during floods.

A more recent, not yet executed project concerns the site of a factory demolished because it was too close to the city center for production there to continue. An adjacent bank building and a youth club were seen, in the light of conventional planning considerations, as grounds to create a park; yet even before the long-drawn-out decision-making process had been terminated, young people from the neighborhood seized the site and used it "as found," namely as a rubble-strewn place with spontaneous vegetation. Lange's proposal simultaneously and ironically highlights this situation and the desire for a park, without leaving the latter wholly unfulfilled. A wall of rusting iron on the abandoned gravel-strewn wasteland defines "an island," which is to say a concealed, intensely cultivated paradise garden with ornamental plants and a fountain. Even the narrow path leading to the garden is shielded from view by a hedge—although the crowns of trees towering over the wall reveal a part of the mystery.

The poet Ian Hamilton Finlay had nothing less than a complete rethink of the art of gardening in mind. Finlay makes very short poems and, lately, solely poems only one word in length. A word only acquires meaning in a context, in a language, in a sentence, or—as Finlay discovered—in a garden. For example, at Stonypath, his garden in Scotland, a stone engraved with the initials AD (for Albrecht Dürer) can be found on the large lawn. Thus, although our gaze merely sweeps the lawn and instantly blends it out, the pictorial addition heightens our perception of it. This is a truly minimal intervention: changing a situation simply by adding initials!

Finally, I'll mention a design that I personally devised in cooperation with landscape architects and ecologists.[1] It concerns a former barrack yard at an inner-city location. The barracks themselves form a large U and no longer serve their original purpose. Given its location, the site has all the makings of a city square—and yet a park is currently required. The solution outlined in the proposal is to use large sections of the barrack yard as a square, to provide park fans with a seemingly extensive swathe of park and also to keep alive the memory of the barracks' history. At the lower end of the U-shaped courtyard is a large square whose upper limit is demarcated by a moat. One looks across the moat onto a park that is actually nothing more than a strip of green, although the combined arts of gardening—and not least an S-shaped path that snakes its way across the

1   With Martin Josephy, Martin Schaffner, Markus Ritter, inter alia.

green strip then vanishes in the dark of the woods, in the undergrowth—all contrive to lend it depth. In order to emphasize the design's intent, several (camouflaged?) cannons could be aligned on the banks of the moat (on the edge of the square) and aimed at the depths of the enemy territory. Anyone entering the park from the city side, which is to say from the open end of the U, would have no idea that he was encoded from the square as an enemy …

These examples are intended to demonstrate that the art of gardening has moved far beyond the routine professionalism of Federal Garden Shows. They are intended also to show that the general trend, now, is to minimal intervention, hence to a more ecological form of gardening. And, thirdly, they demonstrate that requisite naturalness, if the public is ever to perceive it as relaxing and harmonious, must not only really exist but must also be conveyed by visual means.

In Nature's Garden (1989)

Yale University Press has published a slim volume by John Prest and I intend first to outline the stimulating thesis presented therein before adding a few of the reflections likely to come to mind when reading his inspiring treatise. Prest's thesis is that the botanical garden is the reconstruction of the Garden of Eden.

Of course, there have always been gardens with interesting plants: monastery gardens, medicinal gardens and herb gardens. The actual botanical garden, however, came into being at the moment when explorers returned to Europe with novel plants from the New World on board ship. Even before then, it was common knowledge that there existed in southern climes plants that do not thrive in ours. Such plants therefore came as no great surprise. What did surprise the explorers and their peers, the stay-at-home botanists, was the fact that plants unknown to us exist also in the more temperate climes, and that seeds and cuttings from those New World plants thrive here or even run wild. They asked: Then why had they not existed previously in our climes? Is there another creation that we don't know about? Why does the Bible not speak of it? Do these plants also have names and who gave them their names? — All such considerations gave rise to a theological premise: In the Garden of Eden all plants were still assembled. A division of flora occurred only after Adam and Eve were forced to leave paradise following their fall from grace. A part of creation was given them, but another part was reserved for the New World. We—the explorers and their contemporaries—are therefore the first generation in a position to reassemble the old creation, namely all the plants that once grew in the Garden of Eden. The botanical garden thereby acquires a new significance: it is the systematic restoration of the Garden of Eden.

With this thesis John Prest opens up a myriad of perspectives on related questions. First, an obvious one: And what about animals? Were there any animals in the Garden of Eden? — Animals are the product of a later stage of creation than plants are. It is said that Adam gave them their names—but did he do so in the Garden of Eden? The Bible supplies no precise information and Bible commentators disagree on the matter. Prest presents an illustration of Adam at the gates of the Garden of Eden, preparing to give the animals names. Animals can thus be presumed to have remained outside until then, with the exception of birds, which are able to fly. Other Bible commentators hold a different opinion. And everyone knows the paintings of paradise by Jan Breughel and his imitators, in which animals are grouped together peacefully around Adam and Eve. That the lion and the lamb are grazing peacefully there, side by side, is virtually the epitome of paradise. Only after the fall from grace did some animals become predatory and feed on the flesh of others.

Can one keep lions alive with grass alone? — Probably not, or at least not with the kind of grass that grows in our climes. Then what did lions eat in paradise? — The existence of a wonderful New World answers this question too—for the time being. Perhaps lions became predators only because the plants on which they could live did not leave paradise with them. Perhaps those plants can be found in the New World! Perhaps those plants—the lack of which, in our climes, is the root of all evil—can be found in the New World! Perhaps we are sick because the herbs that would ward off our diseases grow in the New World! — Here, the aims of the ancient medicine garden meet those of the restoration of the Garden of Eden.

But where was or is the Garden of Eden located? Is it in this world or another? —According to Prest, the early explorers assumed Eden was to be found on earth, in the east. But does not ancient tradition maintain that Eden is the source of the four streams of paradise? And are these not the Euphrates, the Tigris, the Ganges and the Nile? The more the earth has been explored, the more remote the Garden of Eden has become. Once it became clear that it is not located in Mesopotamia, hopes were focused on the Nile. Anyone who spread his net long enough in the Nile, so the rumor, would find leaves of the Tree of Life in it. If this were true, the Garden of Eden would be in Abyssinia, home of Holy King John and the Queen of Sheba. But voyages and news increasingly cast doubt on this version, too.

The explorers finally came across new rivers as well as clear indications that the Garden of Eden was very close by. And this happened not entirely unexpectedly. Anyone traveling west to east ends up directly in the Far East. And if we take literally the Bible's assertion that the Garden of Eden is located in the east, it stands to reason that anyone travelling west has to drop anchor directly at the Garden of Eden. Columbus had seriously considered whether he might run into people there who spoke Hebrew still, or Chaldean even. And people took parrots to be a sure sign they were close to the Garden of Eden. — Columbus is not one to admit he has not found paradise. Nor does he admit that he hasn't spotted a sea monster or mermaid—he says only that they look quite different from how one imagines. Alone the feasibility of mere mortals entering the Garden of Eden causes him to begin to have doubts. The shift from paradise on earth to the transcendental paradise takes place only gradually.

What do explorers discover? We know from our own travels that we mostly only discover things we have previously seen described in our travel guides. New is new and we tend to recognize only that which we already know. Even Neil Armstrong had trouble seeing the moon as something other than one might see on a trip to the canyons of Colorado. In his book *The Image*, Kenneth Boulding examined how new information affects our minds. How do we process novelties? — Either new information (the new discovery) fits into our "universe," into the personal explanation of the world that we have built up over the course of our lives, and serves thus to confirm what we already know; or the new information proves incompatible with our universe, in which case we are faced with the question of whether we should better ignore the discovery and keep the same world view as before, or take the trouble to reconstruct our world view to accommodate the new discovery. Mostly, we choose the first solution and forget—repress—the new information.

Rainer Specht in his book about discoveries and their consequences discusses a related problem but approaches it not from the individual but from the cultural-sociological perspective. A new discovery can have consequences for one's previous knowledge, such that this must be revised. For example, the discovery that the sun does not orbit the earth and that the earth revolves on its own axis casts a long shadow on the Old Testament description of Gibeon's battle, during which Joshua successfully stopped the sun in its tracks. Rainer Specht calls this type of consequence "subsequent issues." — So, what then are the subsequent issues arising from discovery of the New World? Are there two worlds? Of course not, say the theologians—and yet reveal their own lie through their use of the term "New World." And there are different animals there, after all, and they also have names; and there are people, who give these animals their names. But they are not the names our Adam gave them. Are there two stories of creation or were there once two Adams?

Is the New World a better world? — The question has remained unanswered to this day. The explorers discovered the "Noble Savage" but also experienced bitter disappointments. Captain Cook's new friends struck him dead. Religious movements left the old, sinful Europe and found a better world in the New World. Somewhere one will find as much morality as in the New World but nowhere so many vices: the USA is the land of prohibition and narcotics.

Anyone wishing to create a botanical garden for all plants needs to know how big the garden will be. Is the number of species finite or infinite? Are the species defined or are there transitions, sprawling borders and uncertainty? Anyone who collects animals and plants can tell you a thing or two about all that. And yet the Bible assures us that Adam gave a name to every creature, so sufficient names must be available. — One way out of the dilemma perhaps, is to distinguish between genus and species. Species may be infinite in number, but we can get a grip on the genera. But as Moses already realized, this too has its pitfalls. Those split-hooved ruminants are there to be eaten. But there are non-ruminating, split-hooved creatures as well as ruminants without split hooves and they are unclean. Unclean, as Mary Douglas has shown, is that which constitutes a species in-between genera. The most impure thing of all, uncleanliness personified, is dirt. Dirt consists of things that are no more and therefore no longer have a name.

Padua was the first botanical garden to set about systematically classifying novel, newly arrived plants. Cortusius, its director, bore with pride his moniker "the new Adam." The true new Adam, however, was Linnaeus. Yet he was by no means fond of the nickname Albrecht von Haller gave him. Linnaeus himself gave names to plants, names that were, as we know, binary. They consisted of both genus and species, of certain and uncertain properties. Linnaeus describes his system as natural; he wisely does not further define whether this system corresponds to the nature of nature itself or to the nature of our minds. The human mind classifies everything as either genus or species; but it is debatable whether everything is actually so constituted.

Linnaeus's system is a first step in the process of "scientification." It is also a privation, for the general public's knowledge shrinks in the face of the botanists' new knowledge. Linnaeus declares it unscientific to name a plant after a saint and yet scientific to name them after a man who has proved himself amicably helpful; and he notes with pleasure the name *Linnaea borealis*. Since the time of Linnaeus, the naturalness of nature has been the preserve of scholars. Linnaeus not only considers his system natural but also even believes that he has read in it the mind of God. And, in fact, his system is closer to ancient theology than he thought. Above all, it is hierarchical: the stones, the plants and the animals. It corresponds to the central part of the global hierarchy. The upwards-oriented sequel would be the hierarchy of angels, or so says the statement of Dionysius the Areopagite in the most widely available medieval textbook. One might imagine the devil's cunning to still be at work beneath the stones and mankind between animals and angels. Indeed, late in life Linnaeus wrote a systematic classification of mankind, distinguishing its various degrees of sinfulness.

Linnaeus's system is evidently hierarchical. Indeed, there is something hierarchical in all our dealings with nature. The lion is the king of beasts, the rose the queen of plants, and mankind the pride of creation. Equality as a prerequisite of "neutral" scientific treatment probably first came from another corner entirely, not from systems, but from the Encyclopedia. Diderot and d'Alembert are the first to speak equally of different things. Nor did the French Revolution overlook to abolish the king in the animal world: the lion was expressly stripped of his title.

If everything is the same, does it mean there are no beneficial or harmful plants and animals? Rousseau considered medical doctors' functional mindsets to be a menace to scientific botany. Knowledge of plants, he said, must not degenerate into quackery. — And yet our knowledge serves the production of value as well as the prevention of harm or uselessness. The first scientist of the modern era, Frederick II, was interested in that most useless of all creatures, the bird of prey; but solely on condition that he might make it useful. His book on falconry addresses how to tame the untamable. So, is everything potentially useful? Is the poisonous plant a medicinal plant for an as yet unknown disease? The question of usefulness arose once again during the French Revolution, on account of the starving masses. What good were botanical gardens or the menageries of kings? Did not these rulers keep pointless, useless, silly animals, on a mere whim? Shall we kill their monkeys and let their parrots fly to freedom, to their deaths? In fact it more behooves the virtuous youth to learn from farmers than from botanists, and how to improve the crops' yield can certainly be taught and learned in botanical gardens. — Is that so? Maybe not. Bernardin de Saint-Pierre was commissioned to take over the Jardin du Roi [King's Garden] and the royal menageries, and to endeavor to reconcile the lion with herbivores—this, virtually, is where the new Garden of Eden is made complete. And Bernardin de Saint-Pierre did indeed manage to get a dog and a lion to so befriend each other that they embraced in joy. The Good Lion: it plays its role also in early French socialism. In his first work, Charles Fourier prophesied the advent of the Good Lion in the coming age, a lion that would allow itself to be harnessed to our cars and would transport our wares faster than the fastest horse.

But let's return to the system. Is a system static or dynamic? And if it is dynamic, does it run like a music box, along paths preconceived by God; or does non-essential, random stuff happen? Theology can imagine both. God has already thought everything because bigger than He cannot be thought, or: God already built into his creation the non-essentials and contingency that make the world's course impossible to predict: Anselm of Canterbury or Johannes Scotus Erigena.

Does the system say that everything is connected with everything else? The question alerts Buffon but he is knocked flat by Linnaeus' dry "scientificity." Winckelmann, in his exposition of the history of art, sticks with Buffon rather than with Linnaeus. And Goethe, finally, obsessed with his idea of the archetypal plant and the comparability of vertebrates, clings to the theories of Geoffroy Saint-Hilaire de Saint-Hilaire in his dispute with Cuvier. — And are not we back on similar tracks today, long after Darwin and Heckel? Research can no longer do without the concept of teleology; but we prefer to think in a forward direction, to think about goals rather than sources. We still regard mankind as the crown of creation.

Is the crown of creation destructive? Can man destroy nature and, if so, what would that mean? — In our era, the ecological principle is becoming common knowledge. Other issues are minor by comparison. No one asks nowadays whether an animal or plant is beneficial or harmful. We censure their extinction. And then we let them die out. The desert is growing while the Garden of Eden shrinks. Is this characteristic only of modern times? Certainly not. And nor is it at all clear, whether the desert is a bad thing or beneficial. John the Baptist, Hieronymus and others went into the desert precisely in order to find salvation. But perhaps that desert was not as desolate as we imagine desert to be. In any case there was still food there—locusts at least.

Today, we would call the desert of John the Baptist and Hieronymus a biotope—and we have thus discovered something that—despite being already known not only to ordinary people but also, at the unconscious level, to scientists—actually became a science very late in the day, namely plant sociology. Anyone who goes for a stroll and thereby looks for flowers, berries, insects or fungi can tell from the vegetation where that which he seeks may be found—yet since the days of Braun-Blanquet and Hegi, he makes a science of it. And this science has greatly altered our view of nature, by which I mean, our mental image of nature. Nature no longer communicates itself through species alone but through their socialization. Today, when we want to relax or boost our energy, we seek to see "nature." People used to go into the garden to do so. However, our generation believes nature can be seen only in those places where natural plant communities come into being.

This is why our gardeners have become biotope addicts. Because, to our modern minds, the biotope is a reflection of nature, gardeners believe they can use it to conjure nature forth. What they produce, however, is that which botanists would call a hindered succession. That which looks so natural and timeless is either changing or heading for its end state. The flower-filled meadow, the forest margins and the peat bog: all of these are not just end states but phases of transition. They were stable only as long as they were maintained by labor-intensive, now obsolete farming practices. If they are now to be maintained artificially, interventions will be required, such as the care of a rose bed. The gardeners' biotope insofar matches the image that we have now of nature; but it contributes little to the conservation of nature.

Nature is invisible and in fact anyone wishing to display it must make it visible. Mankind is alienated from nature. He has two ways to approach nature:

through science—Create a botanical garden!

or

through poetry—Sing, paint or design a landscape!

However, it is not given to us to recreate the Garden of Eden.

Nature and the Garden in Classicism (1963)

Once, when in Vicenza on the lookout for traces of cultural zeal, I visited the Villa Capra, the Rotunda, and bought a picture postcard of it as a souvenir. It was a colorful postcard, I must admit, even though its colorfulness overwhelmingly consisted in the unnatural grass green of the meadow on which the Villa stood. An English architecture critic, whom I once showed the card for lack of a better illustration of the place, laughed and said it looked like an English Georgian country house.

I had never fully understood the truth of this quip, until I found myself, years later, standing for the first time in front of Chiswick House, the country estate of Lord Burlington. This was indeed a second Rotunda, a Villa Capra, set in the middle of an English lawn as green as only an English lawn can be. And suddenly it seemed to me as if this English lawn might have a strange double meaning, as if it might with truly English diplomacy be distracting attention from an irresolvable contradiction. In this Thameside area to the southwest of London—the Britannic Brenta, as it has sometimes been called—there are castles and gardens from the Baroque and Classicist eras. The lawn in the English Baroque garden constitutes the so-called parquet (in its original sense of "small park") that in drier climes is composed of flowerbeds or stone. At other sites, such as Syon House, seat of the Dukes of Northumberland, the landscape garden almost reaches the house—the lawn there suggests nature is surging at the walls like waves at a cliff. And now here in Chiswick: How is the lawn intended—as nature or as a garden? The oldest landscaped garden leaves the beholder so strangely in limbo regarding this question that it seems to me worthwhile to meditate for an hour on the topic of "Nature and the Garden in Classicism."

I promise myself several outcomes from this reverie. For one, it will provide me with a chapter for my as yet unwritten book on the history of taste. Friedrich Theodor Vischer described as the antinomy of taste, the fact that both the following statements are true: "one can argue over taste" and "one cannot argue over taste." Difference drowns out antinomy, whether we seek to do away with it in the world of the ancien regime, the nineteenth century or today. Why should matters of taste not be disputed under the ancien regime? The dispute will be settled when the more learned of the interlocutors proves the other's ignorance. Why should matters of taste not be disputed today? "The dispute will reach an inconclusive yet peaceful end. An antinomy can arise only against the backdrop of class, hence when the discussion partner is déclassé."

In socio-historical terms, the rule of taste lasts from the emancipation of the bourgeoisie in the eighteenth century to the latter's demise owing to modern-day phenomena of expropriation; and, in art-historical terms, from the destruction of the formal Classicist-Baroque canon to the destruction of each and every formal canon and the degeneration of style into coexisting currents that no longer dispute each other on grounds of taste.

In this unwritten social history of taste, the chapter on gardens would also provide us with insights into how the new aesthetic relates to nature. The chapter would thereby have to answer two questions, both of which are rather far-reaching. One question is: Why does a new Classicism flourish at the end of the eighteenth century, why does a new and more serious enthusiasm for Classicism as well as a deeper understanding of its forms flourish at the very moment when all the theorists of aesthetics are agreed on the fact that an authoritative canon of beauty, a Classicist aesthetic, cannot possibly exist? And the second question: All classicists—and I mean this in the broadest possible sense, hence also the art theorists of the Renaissance, such as Leone Battista Alberti, Leonardo da Vinci and Giorgio Vasari, as well as the many minor ones whose writings or statements have survived only in part—all classicists name the imitation of nature and the verity of nature as the highest objectives of art. It is conceivable that the Classicist concept of the natural garden may reveal to us what is actually meant by nature and by the verity of nature.

And then I promise myself a third, final outcome, one that points to our own era—for it makes little sense to deal with history that does not concern ourselves. We are horrified by the changes the landscape is undergoing in this, our era. Industrialization, the expansion of the cities we live in and, finally, changes in farming methods are wreaking that which the German Werkbund once called in an appeal "the great destruction of the countryside." The strange helplessness with which we look upon such developments or preserve here and there a small nature reserve, a moor or a heath, can be explained by a romantic relationship to nature, one that is in search of nature as it was before the fall from grace rather than concerned with the only humane option, which is to recognize the landscape as an object of design. Is it not permissible here, to look back on an era that chose landscape design as the noblest expression of its artistic intent?

These questions bring home the fact that we are by no means on esoteric and whimsical ground when we concern ourselves with the art of gardening. I'll speak later once again about Kant, who saw pleasure gardening as equal to painting in the field of visual arts, an equation that appears strange to us only because painting has since continued to develop while the art of gardening has fallen into mannerism. And yet it is virtually a primeval art, maybe not in the historical sense, but in principle. If we consider the act of making something visible as a mainspring of artistic activity, then gardening leads the way: by transforming nature into landscape, it makes visible, i.e. frames or stages that which previously was merely perceived.

Admittedly, it was not always so, historically speaking. Before the advent of landscape gardening there was Claude the painter and, at the start, it was the blind poet Homer who made landscape visible.

But let us return to the green lawn in front of Chiswick House, the lawn that led us to wonder whether it is a remnant of the French garden or a first sign of the English garden, whether it symbolizes culture or nature. Lord Burlington, who commissioned the house and the park, was personally far too ambivalent, far too caught up in images of Classicism and Romanticism to have a very clear view of his lawn's ambiguity. It must be said, however, that the so-called Exedra[1]—an apsis-like arrangement of statues and pyramid-shaped dwarf cedars—may, in his day, have marked a border between the "parquet" lawn and the green park. Today, the pedestals' footing in the disrupted regular arrangement is less than steady given that the cedars, if they have survived at all, are no longer the well-behaved pyramids of Burlington's day but great, hulking, two hundred-year-old veteran warriors, whose lower branches sweep the ground like snakes in Japanese woodcuts and whose roots are undermining the statues.

Thus, the garden today probably makes a far wilder impression than was originally intended, even though we cannot fully trust the somewhat feeble vedute of the period. For where on earth were decent painters supposed to quickly learn how to read and portray this new type of garden? How were they to know it represented something so entirely novel in comparison with that which had gone before? This was especially hard to see given that Burlington's garden still worked with the traditional means of garden design,

1 . [By 1745 a large lawn had been created, lined by alternating cypresses and stone urns and closed at the northern end by a semicircular hedge known as the Exedra, a dark yew hedge which formed a dramatic backdrop to Burlington's collection of eighteenth-century sculpture.]

with arrangements, avenues, scenery and vistas. The new elements of landscape design were yet to be discovered. Not even older gardens evinced purely geometric ornament: the serpentine path had long since been in use as a means of concealment; and likewise the wilderness,[2] such as had long existed at Hampton Court. But the old wilderness—hedgerows cut to create a maze of cryptic passages—by no means only represented a natural wilderness. It also and first and foremost served far more elementary needs than the new landscape garden; for just as Burlington's landscape garden was dedicated to cultural edification, the wilderness was dedicated to the gauche game of courtly love.

It is at the cultural level also, that one must try to resolve the contradiction between the supposed naturalness of the landscape garden and the amount of work that its creation and maintenance actually demand; and, especially, to resolve the amusing paradox that sought to give expression to the peculiar naturalness and absolute solitude of certain places by adding an architectural motif: a tower, a grotto or an artificial ruin. It is repeatedly claimed that people in the eighteenth century never noticed this paradox, that members of court society were too far removed from everyday life to notice how artificial such gardens were; this, despite the great improbability of Lord Burlington, the banker Child or the Weimar privy councilor von Goethe himself ever being unaware of what exactly they had commissioned from their gardeners. That the maintenance of a seemingly natural site depends on artificial means is an issue discussed very extensively in the letters of Saint-Preux to Lord Bomston in Rousseau's *the New Héloise*. How to create naturalness by artificial means: a conundrum not only for the tired taste buds of

2   [LB is referring here to the UK's oldest surviving puzzle maze, which was commissioned around 1700 by William III.]

the late ancien régime's overfed courtiers, but also for the modern world—and one that will perplex us all the more in the future.

The paradox of the naturalness of the landscape garden resolves itself, as I said, at the cultural level. The landscape garden is not natural; it portrays nature. Yet nature cannot be so directly portrayed or depicted. To reiterate what I said earlier, to make visible that which is merely perceived does not happen spontaneously, but always on the basis of schemata that have developed throughout history. In the realm of painting, such schemata lie in iconography; in the literary realm—as we are aware since the time of Ernst Robert Curtius—in topoi. Curtius identified "beautiful nature," the "charming place," as the most important literary topos and traced its passage from Homer and Virgil through the Middle Ages, and up to Ariosto. Then, in the late Renaissance, this topos cropped up in the realm of landscape painting. Salvator Rosa, the Carracci brothers, Nicolas Poussin and Claude le Lorrain developed the iconography of the classical landscape. The English landscape garden was therefore initially nothing more than the continuation of this topos in a third genre: true, nature was represented, but as the nature of Arcadia or of Pedagogy, not of Britain; or, in other words, that which was shown probably was the nature of Britain, but it was represented by philosophical Greece, by pastoral goatherd scenes of antiquity.

Approaching the Villa Capra in Vicenza, one instantly and always feels that it cannot bear to have a neighbor or, at most, one at a considerable remove, beckoning from another hill, perhaps, over an hour's walk away. Thus Villa Capra, though not wholly without urban affiliations even of the contemporary variety, is surely the most non-urban architecture in existence. Did the Greeks of old live like that, and the Biblical patriarchs? Looking at Claude's paintings, one likes to think so. And Palladio certainly believed it was the case. The ancient residence was not handed down to us—and so it was reconstructed from whatever was available, its appearance modeled on the Greek temple, its location on the feudal castle. How bizarre yet how momentous the consequences: a shimmer of this same design can be detected to this day in castles, palaces, institutions, hospitals and institutes. But what of the land in-between? Where is Hagar off to, in Claude's painting? I don't know whether Palladio asked this question. But it must be asked. For sure, there are two things one will not find between these houses: geometric gardens and intersecting avenues; and nor will one find a primeval forest held at bay by the house and its garden. In reality, the care of any in-between space was left to the industrious Italian farmer—without a word being said or much thought given to the matter—namely to he who worked his fields, put his animals out to pasture, drew his wine and kept his farmyard in as best makeshift order as he could—and thereby at least approximated Arcadian conditions. But in Burlington's England, in the England of enclosures and no more than six miles from Charing Cross, to boot, what was to be done there?

Well, human wit had to accomplish that which it finds most difficult of all: it had to create naturalness—not by doing nothing, which is how national parks have been created in the twentieth century, namely by leaving them to their own devices—no: it had to create naturalness by representing it.

Classicism had conquered England in three stages: with Inigo Jones under the Stuarts, with Wren under the House of Orange and then again, in its strictly Palladian form, under Hanoverian rule. Burlington was its advocate at that time. Our opening question today was, how this final triumph of Classicism was possible under the bombardment of contemporary aesthetics that had just broken all the established rules? In any case, both anti-Classicism and Classicism benefited the natural garden. Hogarth shows the secret of beauty on the palette in his profound self-portrait: the S-shaped line. Later, Edmund Burke found the adjective to describe this line: "smooth"—"smoothness" became the ideal of beauty in Burke's aesthetic. "In trees and flowers, smooth leaves are beautiful, smooth slopes of earth in garden, smooth streams in the landscape..." Smoothness for him is "such an important property of beauty that he cannot think of a single beautiful thing that is not smooth." Of course, we find the serpentine line also in Burlington's garden. The long channel, the most important staffage in aristocratic garden art, is S-shaped here and casually embedded in the terrain. Wild ducks dip their beaks into it while shrewish coots chase them, grab at their food and follow them to the end of the pond, where a shell-covered grotto marks the natural spring—the old, Italian shell-covered grotto, repurposed. Is this grotto also one of the backdoors through which Classicism broke into the romantic park?

Lord Burlington had a protégé, a painter, yet a painter of the lowest order, who decorated carriages and furniture: William Kent. A trip to Italy was arranged for Kent and so he saw the south perhaps as it really existed, but above all in terms of how it compared with the ideas of it he had brought along with him from home. It is possible, as Mrs. Gothein spiritedly supposed, that Kent's imaginative landscape garden was inspired by the overgrown Italian garden with its dilapidated garden pavilions and clusters of beech in leaf. More likely, what with its masses of shadow, contrasts, vistas, scenes and surprises, is that it derives from the painter's box of props, one filled in imitation of Claude and Salvator Rosa and permanently in use until the advent of Naturalism. Indeed, the techniques of grouping and staffage survived until the mid nineteenth century: the way the painter collects motifs and incorporates them in his portfolio only then to piece them together in a large composition, suitably dosed and mixed, is clearly described by "Green Henry."[3] Anyone who has

3 [The main character in the eponymous novel (in German: *Der grüne Heinrich*) published in 1855 by the Swiss author Gottfried Keller, a partly autobiographical account of an entire generation's transition from Romanticism to Realism.]

ever had the opportunity to inspect the estate of a landscape painter of this ilk finds proof of an activity and an economy not unlike that of the garden designer, the landscape gardener.

But let us return to Kent and Chiswick Garden, to the well-tended garden masquerading as the neglected garden, to the neglected garden masquerading as the landscape of Arcadia—there is no end to the ambiguity. If one walks in Chiswick Park from the house to the end of the Exedra—to the start of the great forest scenery with its masses of dark green foliage—one comes upon a spot where something wholly un-Arcadian happens, namely the forest opens up, offering three radial sightlines, each oriented to a distant point. One of the sightlines at least is still intact, still offers a view of its original objective, Rustic House; yet the Doric column and the menagerie are no longer part of this stellar constellation. That is perhaps a good thing, because the star with its rays of unequal length does not quite fit into this beautified nature anyhow; and the Deer House, the naked Cubism of which presaged Ledoux, works much better as a recondite surprise, a stray architectural element from the province of Pedagogy. In looking ahead to Ledoux for a moment here, we must be careful not to overlook another genius architect who actually had a concrete connection with Chiswick Park. One gardener's boy in the service of Burlington's heir the Duke of Devonshire was [Joseph] Paxton,[4] the inventor of the cast-iron greenhouse and the architect of Crystal Palace.

So Burlington's garden heralds many things including much that is contradictory and is accordingly itself heterogeneous. Where do things go next? While architectural style becomes more rigid in Classicism under Louis XVI—the English counterparts to which are the light-footed Palladianism of Wood, Wedgwood and Adam,

4   [LB here mistakenly wrote William Paxton.]

as well as the Empire look—garden design loosens up increasingly and moves towards the landscape type of garden. Or am I wrong to frame these as opposites? Do not both perhaps denote such an increase in pathos, earnestness and concentration in garden design that the gaiety of flowers no longer has a place there and must be banished behind the walls of the kitchen garden?

The step from Louis XVI to the Empire style must be read as a sudden deepening and renewal of understanding of the ancient world, as a step from a cosmetic (exterior) type of Classicism to a Classicism from within. Wolfgang Schadewaldt, in his unerring interpretation of Goethe's *Knabenmärchen,* identifies the latter as an encrypted representation of this step and the farce *Gods, Heroes and Wieland* as a more obvious satire on the aristocratic antique view of Rococo from the standpoint of the new educated bourgeoisie. Especially apt for our present topic is the comparison between the castle site and the castle garden in Goethe's *Elective Affinities,* with its description of the province of Pedagogy: here, the step from Louis XVI to the Empire, the step from Perrault and Blondel to Ledoux and Boullée, really does concur with literature.

And yet even the purified landscape garden now, however homogenous it may seem alongside the conglomerate of Burlington's garden, harbors equally strange antagonisms; except these were incorporated in it retrospectively, in a sense, namely at the time when it too began to be mistaken for nature. To all appearances, its initial development was quite consistent—consistent with the English prerequisites, of which there are two. The first is the famous and momentous enclosure, more specifically, the enclosure of that which had hitherto been "the commons," (i.e. the land available to all), in line with a new interpretation of the law favorable to local landowners—and the ensuing pauperization of rural folk assured English manufacturers an incomparably cheap source of labor, which is a chapter unto itself in Western history. The second, more innocuous prerequisite is the Englishman's fondness for taking a walk. Englishmen—quite unlike their foreign peers, who visit their small garden at home on foot but take a carriage to roam larger properties—tend to walk far beyond the domestic garden, out into the surrounding rural landscape. So not only their ornamental gardens, but also their entire estates became parks, became landscaped gardens, not least under the influence of the latter's passionate advocates, important writers such as Shenstone, Walpole and Pope.

But how was the landscape garden supposed to look? Continental imitators were always persuaded that the English had copied a Chinese model. Yet, while the Chinese garden is indeed a small, artfully artificial slice of nature charged with symbolism, it is only a miniature composition, to be looked at but not to be strolled through. Continentals who far underestimate this insular passion for walking tend to mingle the Chinese and English gardens: le *jardin anglo-chinois* thus became the generic term for all asymmetric compositions, even if these were as overfilled and over-embellished with set pieces and artificial ruins as Prince Philip Egalité's Parc Monceau. In any case, the real English garden had three characteristics quite contrary to the Chinese model: it was composed in three dimensions, so that one might enter into it without the landscape image falling apart; it was infinite, thanks to the fact that it shamefully hid that which defined its existence, the enclosure; and it was used.

Expansion of the English garden turned it into an ornamental farm, into an embellished form of agricultural economy. And this, one presumes, is what must have finally saved it from being mistaken for nature. If its owner looked out the window, he saw grazing cows and sheep and so was immediately reminded of the benefits of purposive use. But this distinction between purposive use and unspoiled nature, which is so familiar to us and prompts us to seek out mountains, forests and national parks, was still quite hazy at the time. Nature—at the start of the modern era the term implied the countryside beyond the walled city, where the farmer pulled his plow. Even Cardinal Wolsey inquired at the University of Padua before building Hampton Court, whether country air was harmful. In the meantime people were no longer quite so wary but the choice was still between the city and the countryside, not as now, between culture and nature.

It is at this point that Rousseau steps in with his famous letter from Saint-Preux to Lord Edward Bomston, in which the garden of *the New Héloise* is described. How difficult it must have been for readers to distinguish back then between the three concepts kitchen garden, national park and natural landscape is evident from the following comment. I use an edition of Rousseau from that era and it contains pretty little etchings that are meant to illustrate certain points. The words "parmi les bosquets naturels, qui forment ce lieu charmant" are accompanied by this etching: some trees can be discerned beyond a balustrade spanned by an arch and flanked by a stone urn. This is how the engraver imagined nature's "charming place" to be.

The description of the landscape garden—which is without any doubt the heart of the novel and puts *the New Héloise* on a par with Goethe's *Elective Affinities* and Stifter's *Indian Summer: A Tale*—is very carefully prepared. It is made clear in a few words that Julie's parents' estate consists of a traditional palace and gardens. This stands in stark contrast to the perilous journey across the Walliser Alps embarked on by Saint-Preux, who sends his friend enthusiastic descriptions of the "astonishing fusion of untamed and cultivated nature." The mountain range is indeed one of the few places where pristine nature is always beautiful and, in Switzerland at least, its discovery is a synonym for the discovery of nature overall. There now follows, as a direct introduction to the natural park, a description of its exact opposite, whereby the reader initially believes that this is Rousseau's opinion of garden design: the description of how the young Baron transforms his father's ornamental garden into a practical kitchen garden. Even the horse chestnut trees are felled to this end, those torchbearers of French palace architecture in the enlightened-absolutist era. They cede place to the mulberry tree, an emblem of silk production. The young Baron thereby develops a rather far-sighted theory on intensive cultivation. He is of the opinion that soil becomes more fertile the more intensively it is tilled and that it always feeds as many people as spend time on it. He thus anticipates the brisk expansion of agricultural output over the following hundred years.

However, this beautiful vegetable garden is not the only subject of the description, for the guest is led in conclusion through a small gate and then experiences the reverse of the doctrine just preached. Here, Julie has transformed an old orchard into an artificial wilderness by filling it up with native flora, shrubs and trees and draping the existing fruit trees with tendrils of wild clematis. Julie and the Baron explain to the guest how they used sophisticated gardening methods to produce the effect of untamed nature and regular feeding to convince even the birds that the garden was uninhabited by human beings. There ensues a discussion about the naturalness of this nature. "What do you believe it cost me to put the garden in this state?" Julie asked. "My dear girl," replied Saint-Preux, "it cost you nothing but neglect. This place is adorable, that's true, but rural and abandoned; I see no human work here. You closed the door; the water came somehow; nature did all the rest, and you could never have done it as skillfully as she." Julie then describes the many tasks that were necessary to put the garden in its current state until Saint-Preux admits that: "a place that was so different can have become like this only through effort and hard work; but nowhere do I see the slightest trace of culture … The gardener's touch is not in evidence … and I see no trace of man." "That" replies Baron Wolmar, "is because we took such trouble to erase all traces. I was often a witness, often an accomplice to this fraud." Saint-Preux is astonished that such pains were made to conceal all effort. Julie defends herself: nature flees any visited place; it shows its face only on mountains tops, in the depths of forests and on deserted isles. Those who love it yet cannot seek it so far afield must do violence to it and force it to abide with them; and none of that is possible without a little magic. The conversation—which includes a sharp critique not only of the old French gardens but also of the new Anglo-Chinese ones with their petty and tediously created ruins—ends with a remark from Saint-Preux: "I have only one objection to their Elysium, but one that will seem harsh to them: namely, that this is a superfluous pleasure."

Here, the word "superfluous" has not yet the harsh note it will later acquire. It is Saint-Preux, the plebeian, who utters this reproach. Yet the world of *the New Héloise* is still very firmly embedded in an immutable realm, far beyond worldly concerns. Things sound quite different in Goethe's *Die Aufgeregten* [The Agitated], where a clumsy sequel to the French Revolution unfolds on a country estate. Goethe—who in his *Triumph der Empfindsamkeit* [Triumph of Sensibility] has already mocked the Anglo-Chinese garden by having an English lord foist one onto the gods of hell—now puts the following into the mouths of *Die Aufgeregten:* "It has all grown admirably," says Louise, "the wilderness you have created appears to be natural; it charms everyone who sees it for the first time and even gives me a certain pleasure in a quiet hour. But I must confess I prefer to while among the fruit-bearing trees in the nursery. The idea of purposiveness takes me out of myself and gives me a happiness that I do not otherwise feel…" To which the Baroness replies: "I appreciate your good domestic sentiments." And Louise: "The only [sentiments] befitting the class that must think of necessities and can ill afford itself caprice."

The beauty of utility is purposiveness. I do not know who first discovered the beauty of purposiveness Hogarth knew such beauty and was probably not the first. The purposiveness of a garden would be its yield and the ideal of beauty the ornamental farm. While, in the domestic realm of furnishings and the like, the ideal of the beauty of purposiveness may coincide with the interests of the upcoming class and a critique of the nobility's showy extravagance be rooted in the citizenry's finer sensibilities, things are a little different in the horticultural realm. The nobility has lived from its estates since time immemorial and so always keeps an eye on the yield. The citizen earns his money elsewhere. His park is pure luxury. The banker Child has earned so much money in his small exchange bureau in the City of London that he buys the estate Osterley Park as a summer residence and has Robert Adam build him a palace there. Horace Walpole, Lord Oxford, who visits him, cannot hide his astonishment at this reversal of circumstance. "Oh, palace of palaces," he exclaims, "and yet a palace without a crown, without a title, and what a task, how much taste and what expense—and yet a half acre generates income enough to fund this glory. In short, a shop is the estate, and Osterley Park is the seat." Things have been turned topsy-turvy. Revenue derives from the city and luxury lies in the countryside. Creating gardens becomes an act of purposiveness without purpose.

Purposiveness without purpose—this is the linchpin of Kant's aesthetic and indeed must become the central concept of a bourgeois aesthetic. Gardening for pleasure's sake is a form of painting which expresses a physical extension of the truth, "but only the semblance of use and use for other purposes than just the play of imagination in contemplation of its forms." It is "the adornment of the soil with the same diversity with which nature represents the act of looking, just differently, and compiled in accordance with certain ideas." These ideas are namely a means to render purposiveness visible, but in a "disinterested" way, without purpose.

And so we find ourselves facing once again, but from a different angle, the question of how true to nature a representation of nature may be, a representation held together in this case by the glue of these "certain ideas" that stand between nature and imitations of nature. The painter Joshua Reynolds once observed that the artificially created garden cannot serve the painter as a model, although one is inclined to imagine that the natural park would be the most consummate model of all (and here our thoughts turn secretly to Schirmer's work in Muskau's park.) The problem of how true to nature a thing may be leads us to the broader issue of bourgeois aesthetics and philosophy's inquiry into the relationship of outward appearances and the essence of things. In a rhyme in *The Natural Daughter*, Goethe tried to bridge this gap in one sovereign leap: "What is appearance if it has no substance? Could there be substance if it were not seen?"[5]

But his correspondence with Philipp Hackert shows that this leap is not so easily made in reality. Nor is the knotty problem solved in the essay on the "simple imitation of nature, fashion and style;" indeed, Goethe exclaims with a deep sigh that, "deliberations on the latter would fill entire volumes."

How does Hackert, according to his letters to Goethe, intend to portray the beautiful landscape? "It is namely with the grand ideal style that the verity of nature may be grasped in tone and form. Poussin, Caracci, Dominichino, etc. have great style; alone the objects are often untrue, as if they came from another world."[6] Another part of the correspondence clarifies what is meant here by truth: "that every botanist must be able to instantly recognize" the

5 [Cyrus Hamlin and Frank Ryder (eds.) *Verse Plays and Epic by Johann Wolfgang von Goethe*, trans. Hunter Hannum (Princeton Univ. Press, 1987)]

6 [Philipp Hackert, letter to Goethe of 18.03.1806 (written in Florence), in *Goethe's sämtliche Werke in vierzig Bänden, Bänder 29–30*, J.G. Cotta'scher Verlag 1840, p. 274]

tree the artist paints; if not, the latter's art is too stylized. Certain details may be omitted, he concedes, "because the artist lacks the tools to portray such small objects." Where then, we ask ourselves in the face of these demands, does the border with vapid Naturalism lie?

Answer: The border lies in that which Hackert calls the "grand style" that every landscape should evince. The artist "should not imitate mutilated nature. The artist takes note of beautiful nature, which helps him deal with nature that is lacking."[7] How does beautiful nature, the perfect landscape look? It is "always decked out with beautiful cattle,"[8] "interesting monuments" are to be found on it and it "primarily helps one see that everything is amazing."[9] Hackert describes the artistic task as follows: "If I bring now to the task all my endeavor I may perhaps succeed in portraying, in a painting that conjures the impression of a perfect landscape, a grand style, the silvery light of beautiful nature, the rolling mists and the fine form of trees, without neglecting their character; in short, to portray the most ideal possible image of the beauty that nature affords the landscape. In order to thereby avoid the pitfall of mannerism and of plagiarizing or slightly mocking the Great Masters, as imitators are wont to do, I have chosen to portray for my portfolio regions that already truly bear the stamp of the grand style, in and of themselves. And even if I idealize these, I hope my works retain something of their originality and that viewers find reflected there the truth of nature."[10]

For what purpose have we cited all this? First and foremost, to supply evidence of the fact, that the portrayal of nature and actual

7   [Philipp Hackert, *Über Landschaftsmalerei* p. 258; LB here actually paraphrased the original quote.]
8   [Philipp Hackert, *Rom und Neapel*, p. 71]
9   [Philipp Hackert, *Über Landschaftsmalerei* p. 263]
10 [Hackert, letter to Goethe of 18.03.1806]

nature were not mistaken for each other at the time. The recent statements by a French critic (Louis Hautecoeur)—"The 'English Garden' that considers itself natural is likely to be as deceived in the matter as the society that thought it up" or "Those who invented it fail to notice the contradictions," and so on—are certainly mistaken. The natural garden and likewise the representation of landscape in the Classicist period is nothing more than the three-dimensional or two-dimensional manifestation of that which Ernst Robert Curtius has described to us as the topos of beautiful nature: a form of artificial, artistic design applied to the object landscape.

The question of what landscape is and what role artificiality plays in it has suddenly reared its head again today. Not only does the enormous rate of urban expansion now necessitate the purposive design of all remaining public and private green spaces, but also the face of rural areas is being changed by increasingly rationalized agriculture to a degree Baron Wolmar *in the New Héloise* did not foresee. And a third additional risk is now on the horizon, namely that in those parts of the country where rationalization proves unprofitable, agriculture will cease, the landscape will go to seed and be destroyed, and as many characteristics of the "charming place" will be lost as in cases of excessive exploitation. The total settlement and exploitation—or elsewhere, the leaving fallow—of our land blurs the distinction between "nature" and "garden." And so that which, at the start of the industrial age, was the landed gentry's pleasure is now become a necessity: landscape design.

Garden Design—New Trends (1981)

This paper presents a concise overview of the development of garden design, beginning with its roots in two major stylistic traditions: the geometric-architectural one and the landscape or English garden. Surveys show that the various historical forms of garden design are often used today only schematically, which is to say, that elements of their formal repertoires are drawn on or copied. Historical patterns of meaning are thereby lost, however, and the art of gardening reduced to the meaningless manipulation of form. This increasingly academic approach to garden design, this toying with empty formulas, is facilitated, firstly, by a certain type of professionalization—the garden designers' assumption of the role of expert—but above all by the commercialization of horticulture. The fact that one might now place the wrong plants in the wrong place and create inappropriate plant communities is due solely to chemical methods of cultivation, fertilization and care. But the work of four outsiders in the garden designers' guild evinces some novel, exemplary approaches.

Expressive elements in European garden design bear the stamp of two major stylistic traditions. On the one hand, there is the geometric-architectural garden, such as was developed in the Baroque era. Its elements never disappeared entirely and enjoyed an unexpected renaissance not only in Art Nouveau, but also in the work of certain pioneers of Modernism. On the other hand, there is the legacy of the English garden. Elements of the latter, which was intended to represent a landscape or "natural order," likewise never completely vanished from sight, not even at the time of the aforementioned Art Nouveau and Modernist gardens.

Baroque gardens and landscape gardens

Both garden traditions, the Baroque and the landscape varieties, speak not only of the tastes of a particular era but also of mankind's eternal need for artistic expression. Manifest thus in the Baroque garden is the will to create a non-natural world, the need for boundaries, a bottom line, and safekeeping from the onslaught of any disorder from the far side of the fence. By contrast, the English garden embodies the longing for the earthiness of yesteryear, when man lived as a shepherd among his sheep, drank water from the fresh wellspring and rested in the shade of a tree. The landscape garden too was always a type of design, and neither the great landscape gardeners nor their advocates nor Jean-Jacques Rousseau ever mistook it for nature. Its effect rests precisely in the fact that the landscape gardener draws on artificial means to represent nature.

Each of these two great traditions of garden design stood in a specific direct or dialectical relationship with the building. The order of the Baroque garden responds to certain signs of disintegration in the house or the villa, such as emerged in Mannerism and served to dissolve the boundaries between indoor and outdoor space. The English garden corresponds, however, to the Neoclassical building that may under certain circumstances disrupt the continuity of the artificial pastoral landscape in a deliberate gesture of estrangement and isolation. Therefore, complaints in the rest of this paper about the academicism of present-day garden design and its meaningless manipulation of traditional formulas apply equally to the loss of a distinctive relationship or dialectic between buildings and open space.

Influences in the nineteenth and twentieth centuries

It would be futile to try to list all the elements that came to supplement these two stylistic traditions of garden design in the course of the nineteenth and twentieth centuries. Let us mention here, very summarily, the lawn, which began as a symbol of the pasture but developed into the formal "green carpet" so well suited also to geometric gardens; and, as a second example, the invention (paradoxically by Pückler-Muskau, no less) of a type of flowerbed that brought the art of gardening almost into the pastry chef's realm. We should also mention the advent around 1860 of diverse elements inspired by the Japanese garden, which have since been used in Europe with no regard for their original meaning. Among these number on the one hand, that whole army of evergreen dwarf shrubs originally taken to represent miniature landscapes but which is now the commonest commodity and marshaled around any old building or square. The use of gray-leaved dry plants, often in conjunction with pebbles, is presumably also of Japanese origin. It originally served to represent poetic river landscapes whereas European gardeners used it initially to enliven dry urban locations and now simply anywhere and everywhere, even when most inappropriate. One invention, Foerster's Alpineum—the roots of which lie in the Baroque tuff grotto as well as in the botanical garden—is now frowned upon if used in its unadulterated form and hence has merged with the Japanese dry garden. In the 1950s, Mattern introduced landscape modeling, which initially complemented the trend to Japanese-style gardens but has since become as epigonic an element as those eternal 1950s-style kidney-shaped tables. And, while on the subject of kidney-shaped, we should give a mention also to Burle-Marx's novel use of that form of flowerbed (primarily for non-flowering plants, by the way), which initially had artistic significance but has now become simply one more element in the mundane repertoire of universal urban horticulture. In this respect—given that they combined a high turnover of plant material with rational processing—Burle-Marx's designs accommodated the objectives of present-day gardening.

Ossification in academicism

So there we have a description, albeit a summary one, of the repertoire that is available today to garden designers and which simultaneously serves to define our way(s) of seeing. For the way(s) in which we "read" gardens respectively the elements that compose them is charged with the meanings these had throughout history. This history or, rather, the way history has taught each of us to interpret what we see, constitutes the backdrop to every garden designed today. No one who designs a garden begins with a blank canvas or at point zero, no more than his peer the painter or sculptor does. Rather, he responds through his design to everything that was created before him. Garden design is in crisis today because it constantly draws on almost every design element in existence and perpetually blends contrasting elements, such that their meaning is worn away and the onlooker ultimately presented with nothing but empty formulas.

To use linguistic elements in this way, regardless of their content, is called academicism. To give you an example, at the Federal Garden Show in Mannheim there was an artificial pond, the banks of which had been equipped with elements intended to denote "naturalness:" level sand inlaid with pebbles gradually ceded to a botanically interesting arrangement of plants, including narrow-leaved species, such as the iris, etc. And yet one could also see the nozzle of a powerful fountain jet poking out of the pond—and the nozzle was a constant reminder of the artificiality of the pond's natural appearance.

Such misleading use of semantic elements seems to us to be symptomatic of the state of garden design today. Someone is planting flowers there, beneath the branches of a tree with a rounded crown—but was not that form of crown once used to denote an already grazed pasture? Someone there is installing an artificial spring at the top of a hill—but does not groundwater too flow downhill? In the wetlands of the Rhine near Bonn, streams used to run counter to the course of the Rhine. In the Karlsaue wetlands near Kassel, the very river pebbles that nature had once embedded as a lower drainage terrace now rise up in hill-like mounds. The dry brushes and grasses flourishing in lush village soil are often almost overwhelmed by adventive sunflowers and hollyhocks. Quartzite slabs laid out as "natural" paths cede so suddenly to interlocking paving stones that we are hard put to tell whether the garden designer hoped to put us in mind of the solitary Alps or of an urban space in the south. Since all elements occur everywhere, all differences in meaning are leveled. The many colors of the palette, mixed to a paste, ultimately turn to gray.

The horticultural profession and the nursery business

Academicism in contemporary garden design is no accident. It is closely bound up with the profession's vested business interests. To understand this, one need only leaf through the advertisements in gardening magazines. The product range available there, besides dwarf shrubs and artificial and natural stone, encompasses all the chemical and mechanical means necessary to cultivate the wrong vegetation in the wrong place. This market, which strives always to combine a high turnover of material with minimal labor requirements, dominates the nursery business in its entirety thanks to its various media and institutions, among which numbers the Federal

Garden Show. It can therefore effectively brand contrary trends as dilettantism—and indeed does so, because the profession has a vested interest in devaluing that traditional knowledge of gardening handed down by amateur gardeners from one generation to the next. It thus drains amateurs' self-confidence and delivers them helpless into the hands of the so-called experts.

Where today can one find approaches apt to get the better of academicism? In the following, I very briefly describe the work of four gardeners, each of whom in his own way is developing a regenerative art of gardening based both on traditional perceptions and new thematic content.

Kurt Brägger's "Garden of Illusions"

I call Kurt Brägger's garden the "Garden of Illusions." Its overall style is derived from elements of landscape gardening whereby Brägger draws chiefly on the principles of "infinity" and "chambering." In his major project to date, the redesign of the Zoological Garden in Basel, he sought to turn the relatively small city-center park into an island on which one might instantly forget the city's existence. Brägger thereby worked with elements of concealment and disclosure. He first and foremost concealed borders and that which lay beyond them. Visitors therefore had only a vague idea of where their respective paths would lead. Animals are no longer presented on a plate, so to speak, and the visitor no longer passes between successive enclosures. Rather, his path cuts through bushes and undergrowth, and occasionally offers a "green window" to the left or the right, namely a view of animals in a small clearing.

Kurt Brägger is not picky in his choice of plants. He believes that certain combinations of leaf shapes and leaf colors best symbolize those landscapes we imagine that the exhibited animals come from.

He mixes native and non-native plants and thereby reinstates plants that gardeners often consider worthless, such as the elderberry tree. Yet at the Zoo, Brägger also insisted that geographical features be taken into account. Since Basel Zoo is located on the low terraces of a river valley, Brägger foresaw bodies of still water only for the valley floor and of flowing water solely at those points on the site where a downward flow was natural. Brägger removed both the tuff used when the Zoo was first built as well as the cement walls added in the 1930s. And he used the conglomerate rock and marl of the local geology for any artificial modeling. What one can learn from Brägger, and from the following three gardeners likewise, is that to use a limited range of materials consistently produces sites imbued with meaning whereas to use the complete arsenal of available materials proves as ineffective as it is costly.

The vernacular gardens of Bernard Lassus

Bernard Lassus's position is not so easily defined. His basic premise is that each case is special—and that studying a site will reveal which particular means and materials should be used there. He uses a broad palette, yet sparingly. He draws not only on conventional garden art to enrich this palette but also and especially on motifs derived from amateur and allotment gardeners. He has a special fondness for them and to them he dedicated his book *Jardins imaginaires—les habitants paysagistes* [Imaginary Gardens: Landscape Dwellers, 1977]. Lassus endeavors therein to decipher the private language of the amateur gardener in order to introduce widely recognizable motifs into public gardens and gardening.

Lassus believes that, since our cultures and hence also our perceptive faculties are highly diverse, a public garden must offer different levels of legibility. One and the same garden, therefore, may be reminiscent of an historical garden for the connoisseur, may represent an array of species for the flower lover and, finally, may provide allusions to fairy tales and adventure stories for children. Such motifs, if properly arranged, do not contradict each other but together create a highly complex yet nevertheless coherent picture.

Ian Hamilton Finlay's intelligible garden

Ian Hamilton Finlay has a background in concrete poetry but at some point focused his whole attention on designing a garden of his own in Scotland. The intelligible garden was realized there in its most extreme form insofar as the insertion of an artwork in each specially designed small ambient space lent it an historical dimension. Here, a stretch of meadow becomes a part of Dürer's lawn; there, we are led to believe that we are in the foreground of a landscape painting by Lorrain, listening to the haunting flute of Poussin's shepherd boy. But Hamilton Finlay's meanings tend not only to the idyllic: in other parts of his private garden one finds, in only slightly encrypted form, the French battlefields of the Second World War and English naval bases in the East.

The wild gardens of Louis Le Roy

Probably the most popular new gardener is Louis Le Roy. In the eyes of any superficial observer he is the one who "lets weeds grow willy-nilly." On closer examination, two levels of meaning can be identified. One of them concerns nature, which is presented here in the Darwinian tradition, as the struggle for the survival of the fittest. Le Roy is interested thus in the process, not in the end state of a thing. His gardens are in constant flux. And the very thing one imagines Le Roy would want, namely the easily maintained, self-sustaining plant community, is something he will not tolerate. Rather, he chooses to demonstrate how one group of plants begins to overwhelm another but, just as the first seems poised for victory, he cuts it back and thus redraws the boundaries of combat.

The other level of meaning concerns planning. Le Roy proceeds without giving orders and without information. Work in his gardens is accomplished by whichever casual laborer happens to have the time and inclination to do there whatever he personally at that moment considers right and fitting to do. The work lays no claim to permanency. Perhaps someone tomorrow will take away the stones so carefully stacked today because he has need of them elsewhere; or perhaps the work accomplished today will remain untouched for many years and gradually become part of the natural artifice. Thus human activity too is presented here in processual terms, not as a finished product. Le Roy heralds the most outlandish outpost of a post-professional form of production, where work is accomplished without a chain of command.

These perspectives on the work of four major yet, in professional circles, largely neglected garden designers do not amount to a common trend. They merely give some hints as to how garden design may re-attain a measure of meaning and how our perceptive faculties, which academicism has so worn down they can barely function, may once again be nourished.

A Critique of the Art of Gardening (1983)

One critique of the contemporary art of gardening is generally based on ecological concerns. To pave over or lay concrete on garden paths, to spray weeds out of existence and to treat ornamental plants as disposable goods is indeed both wasteful and harmful. Another critique of the art of gardening, and in particular of city policy on parks and gardens, is based on the presumption of public use. It therefore regards the growing tendency to landscape every last patch of green in urban space as the seizure of public goods quasi, and as a disciplinary measure. Critics here also and rightly point out that merely to alter the style of a garden—to turn an eclectic ornamental garden into a so-called biotope—by no means improves things for users. Neither such type of garden can accommodate children's games, for example. The present critique addresses a third angle by inquiring what the style of a garden signifies—what message a distinctively designed or a neglected area actually conveys—as well as how the viewer or user perceives and interprets that message. This approach ties in with the second aforementioned, user-oriented critique insofar as the potential to use a place must of course be perceived as such—and also be taken advantage of, for opening a door does not automatically mean the public will step through it. This critique is oriented to information issues and addresses three points in particular: the misinformation that ensues from a style of gardening apt to destroy traces of former use; the professionalization that seeks to divest laypersons of their competence in gardening; and finally, academicism, namely the depletion of the codes of landscape and garden design through their excessive and indiscriminate use.

Human behavior in open spaces is governed by two pieces of information: the user must know whether a particular use of a location is physically and legally possible or whether natural obstacles or proprietary rights stand in its way; and he must consider also, whether the general public will tolerate his intended activity. After asking "Can one do this here?" and "May one do this here?" comes the question "Is this done here?" In a village that is striving to become more beautiful, it is not enough just to put two benches on the village square and plant begonias around them; for as long as being idle in full view of village society is subject to sanctions, no one but drunks would ever dream of taking a seat on the benches.

The user gleans messages about how possible or well tolerated an activity may be inter alia from vegetation. To detect either the natural qualities of soil, or proprietorial rights or current use by reading spontaneous (i.e. unplanned) vegetation is a skill we have acquired quite unconsciously since our earliest childhood. So-called plant sociology is, strangely enough, the latest fruit of botany; only after many centuries of studying individual species did botanists "discover" this century that certain species form communities, that such communities succeed one another, and that their socialization patterns tell us something about an area's soil conditions, human use, age and impairment. We all possess this knowledge unconsciously, however, even when we are unable to name the individual plant species. The fact that vegetation one can walk on indicates a right of way, that undergrowth indicates the current absence of agricultural exploitation and that annuals indicate short-term changes is no more foreign to us than our ready interpretation of prohibition and traffic signs.

In essence, city gardening uses this same language. Its motto, "Say it with flowers," signals the behaviors it believes should be tolerated or prohibited in public parks and facilities. A "mute" dialogue thus ensues between the City Department of Parks and Recreation and the public: the first response to people tramping through the newly created flowerbed on Königsplatz is to plant roses. After a row of rose bushes has also been trampled underfoot, the form of the flowerbed is changed and the public's footpath paved over. The language of gardeners differs from the language of spontaneous vegetation, however, insofar as care and maintenance always destroy the past. Landscape or garden designs attempt to lay down new rules whereas the eye of the user scans the condition of existing vegetation—the grass that invites one to walk on it, bedding meadows or waterside shrubs—to glean information about social acceptance or sanction of the regulations in force. The only spontaneous vegetation gardeners foster is weeds. Botanically speaking, weeds are species that thrive in soils prepared and fertilized for ornamental plants and that are able either to produce several generations a year (if their propagation cycle is brief), or to establish themselves rapidly by sprouting deep, tenacious roots.

Our interest here is not the vegetal-sociological dimension of the weed phenomenon but rather, its "linguistic" dimension. Weeds, as Karl Heinrich Hülbusch has noted, stem from vegetable gardening; it was only when Gründerzeit gardeners began to display flowers as they did vegetables that the notion of weeds took hold, also in the mind of the urban dweller. In aesthetic terms, this led to the sanction of certain wild plants, in particular of the dandelion, whose blooms are no less splendid than those of treasured species such as white and yellow narcissus or the daisy. That the dandelion is absent from meadow bouquets may be attributed also to its unpleasant sap. Yet the fanaticism with which we tear it up by its roots derives surely from its reputation as "the vegetable pest in the flower bed."

Given, on the one hand, its ornamental plant monocultures and, on the other, its production of short-lived weed communities, the art of gardening makes it impossible to read plots of land in terms of their use and capacities. The most we can discern from an area planted with ornamental plants and weeds is, firstly, that the soil has been freshly tilled and fertilized, which may possibly hamper its use;

and, secondly, that the potential interest of an owner or gardener, or perhaps only his temporary lack of interest, affords weed seeds a chance to put down roots. Constant weeding constantly reproduces the same weed community and hence uniformity, in addition to signaling rejection.

In contrast, all older plant communities—on roadsides, quarries, wasteland, countryside meadows, on the unaccounted for areas between the private and public spheres, on parking lots or on lots awaiting speculative development, on abandoned construction sites and urban industrial sites—signalize longer-term developments. They render past and present use visible and they assure, moreover, that such use is tolerated, for they render legible the fact that many people, perhaps many children, have access to an area. The diversity of plant communities and plant species fosters a discriminating gaze, provides entertaining information also for mere passers-by or non-users, and is insofar a greater source of vitality than the total care lavished on all urban green zones, care which leads to an endless, monotonous succession of ornamental plants, ornamental lawns and weeds.

The second point in our critique of the modern art of gardening is its professionalization. In the eyes of anyone who has both the necessary means and a misapprehension of professional expertise, everything is possible—technically. This fact has served to seriously devalue the longstanding experience of gardeners however amateur, regarding what grows well where and without major intervention. Local conditions need no longer be taken into account. If necessary, one simply imports new topsoil. And if rhododendrons fail to flourish alongside dry grasses, one builds drainage and irrigation. This attitude among gardeners who consider themselves landscape designers has a dual impact on our perceptions: for one, it gives rise to misinformation by disturbing the character of the landscape and, secondly, it discourages the amateur gardener.

To create a garden in defiance of the landscape and its natural conditions is an approach learned during a form of professional training premised on technical viability. The set pieces or notions grasped summarily in the design class—the ponds, canals, fountains, mounds and sculptured terrains—are ruthlessly deployed, everywhere. That water flows downhill, that geological tectonics underpin the landscape, that hillcrests sprout different vegetation than valleys, all this seems to amount to little more than the sum of the obstacles that must be eliminated by technological means.

In the park that was built in 1981 on the lower terrace of the water meadows by the River Fulda in Kassel, there are artificial mounds just high enough to obstruct the view of the ring of hills at the boundary of the Kassel Basin, those of the Kaufunger, Reinhard and Habicht forests—and these mounds were created at the very points designated panoramic sites of interest by the provision of bench seats! The art of gardening thus annihilates the magnificent geographical integrity of the Kassel Basin, of which one had a perfect view from the River Fulda's wetlands, prior to these interventions.

Gardeners faced with a large body of water seem to have nothing better to do than set a smaller body of water alongside it. One design we saw recently proposed to use a small ornamental pond to embellish a spot from which one has a panoramic vista of a hairpin bend in the River Fulda. Ponds on hillsides seem to be nothing less than the norm in the art of gardening; yet this fact is brought home nowhere so forcefully as when hilltops are redesigned as natural springs, as was the case at the Federal Garden Show in Stuttgart.

Intentionally or not, the professionals' unswerving belief in their unlimited powers serves to intimidate the layman and to foster his dependency. I buy a catalogue of the latest flowering plants. It promises me gigantic blooms. In my little garden, however, they may wither or flourish but never attain the proportions depicted on the catalogue's cover. Yet only next door, in the city's public garden, the same flowers look exactly as prescribed. Evidently the gardener knew exactly how to enrich the soil, and what poisons to use to keep away pests; the plastic sheet and the skull and cross-bones warning above each flower bed last fall were not installed in vain. Such incidents foster self-doubt in the layman. Rather than reflect on the knowledge passed down to him—on how his parents and grandparents did whatever was possible in their gardens, and let well alone whatever was not—he comes to believe he lacks the talent for gardening and should therefore relinquish his garden to professional care. And we all know where that leads: laying out the garden once and for all is not the end of it, for the professional is much more likely to claim that plants nowadays must be renewed annually, by the professional in person, and also that they will all die a sorry death, if ever the client dares presume he may manage the matter himself. The garden is thrown thus so completely off balance that it must either be manicured permanently to perfection or—much to the chagrin of onlookers—be abandoned to lie fallow for several years.

We consider the third point pertaining to the destruction of information to be academicism, which is to say, the depletion of horticultural codes through their eclectic application. The language of the art of gardening is based a priori on distinguishing and individually interpreting the two viable loci of expression such as have been manifest in our climes for centuries, namely in the distinction between the "French" and the "English" styles, which is to say, between gardens that attest to human intervention, public policy and the extension of urban aesthetics into rural areas, and those that symbolize nature, original conditions of use, pastoral landscapes and the like. Undoubtedly, the motifs found within these two contrary loci of expression have long since intermingled and great gardeners have drawn simultaneously on both style repertoires. But nowadays, the expressive potential of each is used so interchangeably, is so completely merged, as to render their respective contextual significance illegible. Moreover, a growing trend to deploy elements regardless of their origin and semantic context can be observed, even when it comes to smaller details. Japanese bonsai trees, for example, are a means of expression (albeit in miniature) that belongs, semantically speaking, in the "English garden" context, which is to say, in natural or primitively used landscapes. Such trees should therefore be deployed carefully and sparingly, wherever naturalness is to be demonstrated in a small area by recourse to a change in scale.

But what on earth are these bonsai thuja hedges, bonsai conifers and bonsai junipers supposed to signify when planted in rank and file formation? What if tulips are sprouting up between them; tulips that, were the bonsai tree a real tree, would have to be regarded as towering structures? At the Federal Garden Show in Kassel, Japanese bonsai trees had been set around a small pond and river pebbles used to decorate its banks. If one were to enlarge this landscape on a scale with real trees and real ponds, the significance of the river pebbles would be absurd. A reduction in scale therefore ought to have been considered also in their case. (We will not go into detail here, about the fact that the river pebbles bordered the forest on the one hand and granite slabs on the other; or that the bonsai trees were interspersed with rhododendron bushes of equal size, whose flowers and leaves accordingly looked inappropriately large, etc.).

Knowledge of the significance of trees seems to have dissipated entirely. In any case, the one question discussed is whether trees are "native" or alien—a minor factor, it seems to me, in the context of an artificially designed park or garden. More pertinently, a species of tree itself conveys, or at least used to convey, information that prompts associations in the viewer: either with certain locations that are associated, rightly or wrongly, with tree species; or with traditions in relation to which certain tree species are planted. The species horse chestnut, walnut and birch are worlds apart and the very fact that they originated in quite different climatic and cultural contexts assures the gardener a rich palette that must be used with great care. But if he plants all these trees indiscriminately, in one and the same arboretum, the inherited code dies away and the site loses its interest.

"Minimal intervention"—this is our adamant response to developments in the art of gardening over the past few decades. Minimal intervention is not only a concept underpinned by thrift and the ecological imperative; it is also a tool to be used at the semantic level, as a means to impart significance. Significance can never be premised on the destruction of information. Wherever that which exists, that by which one might orientate oneself is altered, a richer source of orientation must be proffered. The latter cannot be created through the indiscriminate use of signifiers, however, just as volume or noise do not, alone, suffice to produce language. Rather, the means of creating significance must be subtly introduced into the existing context and must clarify it. To thereby opt for minimal intervention is to guarantee that the significance of whatever already exists will be apprehended in full and accepted.

Views from Mount Furka (1988)

A number of events and certain institutions have recently aroused public interest in the topic of "art in the landscape." Documenta 6 got the ball rolling, so to speak, in 1977. Then followed the exhibitions at Wenkenhof, Riehen, in 1980, Merian Park, Brüglingen/Basel, in 1984, and Lullin Park, Geneva, in 1985, as well as at the permanent venues Kerguehennec Castle in Brittany and Gori Park near Pistoia. "FurkArt," which can currently be viewed at the Hotel Furkablick courtesy of the Neuchâtel-based art dealer Marc Hostettler, is the most extreme example of such ventures—extreme, owing to the show's location in an extraordinary landscape on the margins of inhabitable terrain. No, this is not about that old chestnut, "charming place" versus "the sublime," although the old hotel Furkablick certainly does prompt that historic association.

Perception of the landscape is closely bound up with the act of taking a walk. This "discovery" is attributed to the landscape architect Lancelot Brown, who organized a viewing of a landscaped park comprised of the images seen when walking along a bridle path there. Perception of the landscape has thus always tended to the integrative and abstract. The sum of the images viewed by the end of the walk amounts to an "impression of the landscape." And an impression of the landscape is what one has always had after completing any trip by stagecoach, on horseback or on foot.

Hotel Furkablick is a witness to another era, namely the railroad age. The railroad and the Alps Post stagecoach used to transport tourists to their destination. One single view at this destination had to represent the regional landscape. When the hotel guest threw back his bedroom curtains in the morning while still rubbing the sleep from his eyes, he found himself looking upon the image he was already familiar with from travel brochures and postcards and which epitomized for him the entire region: the Alps.

Nowadays, the hotels at such destinations stand vacant: the Rigi-gipfel has been demolished but the Giessbach, the Belvedere on the Rhone glacier, and of course the Furkablick are awaiting their revival. Tourism is on the rise yet they all have too few guests. Tourists on a sightseeing tour today no longer spend the night at top destinations but in-between them; and they visit them as part of a round trip by car, which is the modern-day variation on the bridle path.

The "Five Glaciers Tour," the "Three Countries Tour" and similar offerings from local tour companies highlight this new-old role of the destination. The extreme landscape visible at a destination no longer represents the entire region—"the Alps"—but is integrated instead in a more abstract and universalized image of landscape, thanks to the sightseeing tour. Marc Hostettler and the circle of artists he has gathered around him are endeavoring to give the old place a new lease of life. Art in this extreme landscape, art on Mount Furka, can serve this purpose: to combine the view of the landscape with cultural meanings. The indistinct "Aha!" moment experienced when the tourist steps out of his car on Mount Furka and reaches with a shiver for his windcheater is brought into focus by artistic interventions that open up perspectives on another dimension. The hotel itself, run as Hostettler runs it, thereby generates meaning and serves as a think tank. Even while the hotel with its wash jug and bowl sets and crocheted tablecloths pulls us by one foot back into the nineteenth century, we are stepping with the other into the futurist irreality of Panamarenko's "backpack flying machine."

FurkArt

Hostettler does not curate exhibitions. His concept, rather, is to invite a string of individual artists to create work on Mount Furka, one after another. The result is a controlled experiment that prompts reflection on the potential scope of art in the landscape. When considering the works on show there today or the remains of earlier ephemeral artworks, one tends, albeit prematurely and subjectively, to divide them up as follows. On the one hand, there are works one might equally well find elsewhere, perhaps even in a museum. In these cases, the Furka landscape serves as a backdrop. It underscores, reinforces or explains the importance of a work, or changes it. Kirkeby's stele falls into this category, for example, as does Katase's blue, anodized aluminum pool, which, mounted as it is below a natural spring between two fields of snow, naturally raises other questions than if it were installed in a green courtyard garden in the lowlands. Alone the visitor's unspoken question, as to how the artwork will survive the forthcoming eight months under snow and ice, has an impact on the statement the object makes. Into the other category fall those artworks that are not influenced by the landscape but just the reverse: these artworks send out a signal that allows the viewer a dual perspective on the landscape. A "clef" of this sort was set up last year in very explicit form. I am referring to the block of stone that Ian Hamilton Finlay had engraved with Ferdinand Hodler's signature for use in his installation. He thereby transformed the actual view from Mount Furka, that fork-shaped incision made by shale in the wraparound granite of the Central Alps, into a painting by Hodler and likewise interpreted those puffy white clouds [in Hodler's paintings] in which earlier travelers took such joy—in stark contrast to today's tourists, who demand that the cloudless blue sky in the travel brochure be permanently present for real. Without the Furka as a backdrop, Finlay's stone would be meaningless. Artworks such as this, which interpret the landscape, operate on the principle of "minimal intervention." The shift in meaning is triggered not so much by the artist's intervention in reality as by the sign we are given to perceive. Such a "shift," i.e. a shift in layers of meaning, led also to the artwork that marked the start of Marc Hostettler's ventures, namely James Lee Byars's "A Drop of Black Perfume" (1983). One stormy day on Mount Furka—and every bad to middling day up there is stormy—James Lee Byars asked some friends to come by. Then, dressed in a golden robe, he made his way to a stone on a steep slope, one of the thousand stones on the dozens of steep slopes there. Next, he asked his companions to keep their distance then, in one brief gesture, dribbled a drop of synthetic black scent onto the block of stone. Meaningless palaver in the midst of a storm, amid the scents of lobelia and stone diamond! But for those who were present, the landscape of Mount Furka was changed forever.

How the very existence of Hostettler's enterprise affects our way of seeing is illustrated by a phenomenon that no visitor can fail to note. Marco Schibig has photographed a detail of the fortifications left over there from the Second World War, in a way such as to make it seem strangely pregnant with meaning. And the contagion has spread, so hikers now regard all of the military's bunkers, hideouts, barriers and equipment as potential art objects. However, if one looks through one's photos once safely at home and beyond the reach of that spell, one wonders why one ever bothered shooting them. — And the institution FurkArt itself is also now becoming a "minimal intervention" of sorts: one that changes the location by changing how it is perceived.

A seminar

At Marc Hostettler's invitation, we attempted to hold a seminar on Mount Furka for students from the faculties of architecture, urban planning and landscape design at the University of Kassel. The aim of the seminar was not to produce an artwork or artistic photographs but, rather, photographic experimentation on the topic of landscape. Of course, the results were greatly constrained by that which had hitherto been seen as Mount Furka's greatest asset, namely its extreme beauty. The next seminar of this sort had therefore better take place in Egerkingen or Regensdorf. Three points deserve a mention nevertheless. The presence of the artist Paul-Armand Gette and the biologist Markus Ritter inspired one direction the experimentation took. The seminar dealt with the question of whether those elements of biodiversity (among plants, insects, and even stones) perceived nowadays solely in "natural scientific" terms still contribute in any way to the landscape. Everyone loves alpine flowers, but this love is no longer communicable, artistically. Was Kreidolf therefore the last integral artist of the Alps or can we get a handle in some other way on this aspect of landscape enjoyment?

Another experiment dealt with patches of snow. Almost all summer long the Alpine landscape is a patchwork of snow-covered and snow-free areas. Yet in order to clearly perceive the topography we must endeavor to render abstract this dominant element, the snow-patch. Patches of snow simultaneously underpin and mislead our perception of depth of field and distance. By gradually increasing the contrasts when taking black and white photographs, we tried to determine at which point the perspective collapses, and why.

Finally, there is one type of natural phenomena—clouds—that offers little sense of perspective because its extent cannot be measured. Painting nevertheless relies on the sky as an important marker of depth of field. In pioneering images created by advocates of perspectivism—in Masaccio/Masolino's "Miracle of the Snow," for example—clouds grow smaller the greater their distance from the foreground; and nor are Hodler's puffy white clouds entirely free of this effect. The lofty, column-free dining room at Hotel Furkablick—made famous by the artist couple Ulay and Marina Abramovic—proved to be a spaceship from which the perception of clouds could be studied as a counterpoint to the travel agencies' sky-blue propaganda.

Natura Maestra (1999)

"Nature is my teacher"—artists have been saying this repeatedly since antiquity, and still say it today. But what do they mean by it? On the popular level, the statement is always taken to mean that artists strive for a perfect imitation [of nature], which is to say for a trompe l'oeil painting or sculpture, and certainly many artists mean exactly that. Until well into the eighteenth century, the art form that best succeeded in deceiving the human eye was sculpture executed in colored wax. Nowadays, although the use of this technique for anatomical models and in Madame Tussaud's Waxworks is much admired, we no longer regard it as art.

And what about painting? To successfully conjure three-dimensional reality in the two-dimensional plane is still considered a major feat. At documenta 7 and elsewhere, the Italian artist Carl Maria Mariani was much admired for his trompe l'oeil paintings of groups of people in architectural settings, executed in the style of the Old Masters.

Zeuxis vs. Parrhasius

The tale of Zeuxis and Parrhasius is always used to illustrate that antiquity pursued this same ideal: the tale namely of their public wager as to who was the better painter. Zeuxis turned up on the marketplace with a painting of a girl holding a bunch of grapes. The grapes looked so true to life that birds swept down from on high and pecked at the painting.

"Zeuxis has already won!" cried the people, when Parrhasius arrived with his painting still wrapped up in a curtain. "Let us see," said Zeuxis, reaching to draw back the curtain. But he was badly mistaken, for the curtain was painted. Parrhasius's painting depicted a curtain. "Parrhasius is the winner," public opinion now decreed, "because Zeuxis deceived only birds whereas Parrhasius deceived Zeuxis himself." The anecdote is insofar proof of the fact that trompe l'oeil painting represents the height of artistry.

The English art historian and connoisseur Stephen Bann has traced this tale's literary fortunes through the ages. He found that a second version has been handed down, which I will briefly recount. After Zeuxis had revealed his painting and deceived even the birds with his grapes, the people "prematurely" declared him the winner. But after a while one onlooker asked: "How come the birds are not afraid of the girl? Birds have never before dared pick at grapes that a girl has in her hand!"

Art: an imitation of nature?

At this, the onlookers grew thoughtful and said, "You're right. The birds did not recognize the girl. The painting is bad." And Zeuxis replied, "Yes, the picture is bad. I will go and improve it. I'll be back in an hour." An hour later Zeuxis returned to the marketplace with his picture. And what had he changed? Everyone imagined, of course, (as we do too) that he must have painted over the girl and left only the grapes. But, on the contrary, he had painted over the grapes and left only the girl. The people urged Zeuxis to explain. He said: "The grapes were poorly painted, because they deceived the birds. But the girl is real art, because the birds did not recognize her."

So the old story is suddenly turned on its head. Art then, is not the mere imitation of visible nature, but rather a cipher that communicates something only to those who understand it. The grapes were so vivid that even the birds were deceived. But the girl was so stylized, as we would say today, that art connoisseurs alone were able to recognize her.

And this brings to mind a similar anecdote that the painter Monet related after a client had commissioned him to paint his two small children in the garden. After some time Monet delivered the painting and asked whether the client liked it. "I like the garden very much," replied the client, "but it is a pity that you didn't paint the children." And so Monet had to point out to him where in the painting the children were playing. If the story is true, then the classically oriented art lover was evidently hard put to read reality rendered in the plein air style.

Species vs. Genera

The statement "nature is my teacher" must therefore be read in the light of history, with regard both to what imitation is and to what nature is. Let us now investigate this history in several leaps and bounds—in each case in respect of the recent renaissance of interest in nature in art.

The first Christian thinker to concern himself with nature was Johannes Scotus Erigena, who resided at the court of Charles the Bald in the ninth century and wrote the book *De divisione naturae* [The Division of Nature]. He launched the debate that was to lead in the early Middle Ages to the so-called nominalist dispute, the question namely of whether nature consists primarily of species and secondarily of genera; or, to put it in more concrete terms, whether it is the existence of lions, tigers and panthers that gives rise to the term "feline predators," or vice versa. He came to realize that God created both at the same time: the species and the genera.

This view paved the way to classical natural science up to the time of Bauhin, who introduced into botany the two-part Latin name, that is, the name of the genus followed by an adjective for the species, as in *gentiana acaulis,* the stemless gentian. Linnaeus based his classification of rocks, plants and animals on this approach and thereby assumed he already knew all the genera and that future researchers would have only to discover further species.

Sugar is sweet—a substance and its accidents belong together

Even before Linnaeus, art had largely lost interest in zoology. The cabinet of curiosities—the Wunderkammer—ceded place either to the art collection or the scientists' showcase. Albrecht Dürer and Jan van Kessel painted the last rhinos. When the Dutch colonial painter Post painted Brazilian landscape idylls with an armadillo, not a sheep, in the foreground, it seemed pretty funny. Only domestic pets and the nobler of the hunted animals and heraldic symbols such as eagles and lions were still considered worth painting. And now there's this new interest, in science initially and then in naming. Paul-Armand Gette has made the latter the subject of his art. We are thinking here of his idea of hanging name tags on the spiky ribwort growing in a meadow alongside Basel's botanical garden; or of Henrik Håkansson's performances, such as his butterfly biotope at the Venice Biennale in 1997, of which more later.

At the end of the thirteenth century, William of Ockham published an important thesis that had unexpected repercussions for science as well as for the cultural realm. He discovered that substances and their accidents are inseparable. Or, put in today's terms: that a substance and its properties are indissolubly merged. Sugar is sweet. Pepper is sharp. Lemon juice is sour. Salt, in the words of the Bible, cannot lose its flavor. Nor can blood taste like wine, although this was a difficult one for religion to deal with. And the repercussions of this theory now impinge on art. Never can one thing be another. It can at best only represent it.

The image: a projective diagram of reality

In 1416, Brunelleschi invented the [linear] perspective that enables us to realistically represent space in two dimensions. After that, "image" came to mean a view of the inside of a box in which each painted object had its own exact place. The position and the dimension of objects thereby became legible. The image became a projective diagram of reality.

This too had tremendous repercussions for mathematics and the arts as well as for religion. If on the one hand, space is infinite and yet, on the other, able to be represented, then where are the supernatural things? How will we manage, in the future, to represent the fact that the Good Lord in heaven handed down tablets to Moses and prevented Abraham from sacrificing Isaac?

Durer's painting "The Adoration of the Trinity" worked with two vanishing points, a heavenly and an earthly one. But this was soon declared malpractice and the visual artist had no choice but to comply with the rules of projective geometry. It was only with the sad and ironic image "Ci gît l'espace" that Yves Klein, like a number of artists of his generation, reintroduced reflection on the mathematical character of space. Today, we labor above all under the problem of natural scale, 1:1.

Dinosaur bones, frogs' legs and Beuys's "Erdtelefon"[1]

Until then, nature had always been regarded as static, as in: everything in existence has been around since creation day. Charles Darwin was the first to invest fauna and flora with a temporal dimension:

1 ["Erdtelefon" (Earth Telephone): an art piece by Joseph Beuys from 1967.]

evolution. In the same era, discoveries of fossils gave us the pet that is now part and parcel of children's rooms everywhere: the dinosaur. Such finds had piled up during the first third of the nineteenth century, but could not yet be shown to the public for religious reasons. The English geologist Mantell invited people to view a dinosaur bone in his apartment. Among the visitors was John Martin, a renowned painter. "I was counting on you," Mantell said to him, in welcome. "Only you can breathe life into this find."

Martin retired to his studio. A little later he exhibited his painting "The Great Sea Dragons As They Lived." And he charged admission. This marked the advent of the dinosaur, neither the color nor the skin structure of which are actually known to us to this day, only variations on John Martin's image of them.

Several contemporary artists address the problematic fact that modern science presents its claims as certainties. At the Venice Biennale in 1995, Gerhard Lang showed photo constructs of imaginary beings, such as science might have invented or will invent in the future.

Electricity has haunted scientific and other minds since the eighteenth century. Galvani examined it in relation to an organic object. The frogs' legs that he had reserved for dinner twitched, since they were suspended on a copper wire and in contact with a zinc plate. The effect of this observation was both mind-blowing and restrictive. Modern physics and technology have succeeded in reducing this mysterious force to the banal level of our light switches and electric razors.

However, the German physicist Johann Wilhelm Ritter at the time considered electricity to be an actual life-giving force. Even Goethe and, above all, the Romantics shared this opinion. Beuys, following in the footsteps of Johann Wilhelm Ritter, tried to rescue electricity from banality and reinstate it as a life-giving force. I am thinking of his batteries and insulators, his wiring, his "Erdtelefon" and life-giving medical instruments.

Water

If art turns away from science and seeks to address only the incommensurable, only those events that lie beyond mundane reality, which objects remain at its disposal? I take water and clouds as my examples.

Water: Once sailors had sailed around the world and thereby swept it bare of mysterious notions, all that remained was the hope for another dimension: depth. Leonardo da Vinci had already considered this. His sketches of whirlpools, which can be found mainly in the Windsor Codex and the Leicester Codex, have hitherto always been interpreted as preliminary studies for a painting of a flood.

Alexander Perrig and, after him, Stephen Jay Gould offered a new interpretation. Rivers and streams continuously transport water from mountains to the sea. But how does water arrive back in the mountains? Not even Leonardo believed rain alone was responsible for this. In fact, no one believed it until well into the eighteenth century. The waters of the Rhine, the Danube, the Rhone and the Tiber seemed too mighty. Leonardo's drawings depict the underground rivers that lead from the sea to the mountains.

I believe this problem is addressed also by the most refined of all the Italian Baroque gardens, namely that of the Villa Lante. The garden is divided from top to bottom into sections: the spring, the mountain brook, the stream (or so I interpret the long sarcophagus-like water channel between the two buildings), and, finally, the sea, which is square so as to represent the cardinal points and upon which sail stone ships. Can this installation last forever? Somehow, the water has to return. Otherwise this miniaturized global circulation system would be missing a limb.

At documenta 8, Fabrizio Plessi showed his Roman fountain, an installation combining a Baroque cascade with a hint of the likewise

Baroque St. Peter's Square in Rome. Notes on the work claimed it represented a "Sisyphean task." I think what was meant by this was the very circuit problem I have been speaking of, namely how to return the water to the top of the cascade.

Clouds

Once painting— for example, Masolino's endeavors in his "Miracle of the Snow"—had failed to embed clouds in a linear perspective, these featured as an incommensurable phenomenon in the visible world. Goethe occupied himself greatly with clouds and used them in Faust to symbolize manifestations of the gods. His attention was drawn one day to Luke Howard's innovation: the first ever division of clouds into the three fixed categories, cumulus, stratus and cirrus. Goethe was thrilled and wrote an entire cycle of poems in honor of Luke Howard. It begins with a deliberately clumsy verse put in the mouth of the naive interlocutor and placed therefore in quotation marks:

"The world, it is so large and broad,
The sky as well so nobly high and wide,
All of this I have to take in with my eyes,
But it will not let itself be grasped by thought."

Thus he portrays that which mathematicians refer to as bad infinity, which is just big and broad, not mysterious and incommensurable. The poem therefore continues, now in Goethe's voice:

"To find yourself in the Infinite,
You must distinguish and then combine;

Therefore my winged song thanks
The man who distinguished cloud from cloud."[2]

Back to painting. Four hundred years after Masolino, Constable produced his cloud paintings: landscape paintings depicting nothing but
an overcast sky. The artist dated this series of pictures to the hour
exactly, and likewise noted the place where he had set up his easel.
One could almost suppose his series to be a meteorological report.

The German artist Gerhard Lang also works with clouds and one
of his artworks refers specifically to Constable. In 1996, Lang photographed the sky regularly, always on the same day of the month
and from the same place. Constable worked on his paintings mostly
at midday—none of them are of colorful sunsets. The difference
between them and Lang's photographs is interesting nonetheless:
in a painting even midday clouds are tinted with color whereas in a
photograph they look white.

The color tint reveals itself to be an academic convention that
must be applied even to those images seemingly made for docu-
mentary purposes. Let me explain the reason for this. The sky, even
if overcast, evinces much more striking contrasts between light and
dark than could ever possibly be reproduced on canvas. What the
canvas reflects even at its brightest points is little more than what
it reflects, or fails to absorb, at its darker points. That is the reason
brightness must be accentuated by a yellow tint, for instance, and
darkness by a touch of violet. Lang's experiment hence attests his reflection not only on meteorology but also on the theory of painting.

---

2   [Johann Wolfgang von Goethe, "Atmosphären," (1821), dedicated to the
      English meteorologist Luke Howard; trans. Stanley Godman in Kurt Badt,
      John Constable's Clouds, Routledge & Kegan Paul, 1950, p. 13.]

But can we still paint clouds today? Lang has attempted to answer this question too. He uses a photo camera to document a cloud surrounding a hill or mountain. Then he climbs into the cloud and draws it by suction into a glass bottle. His clouds—carefully preserved in well-equipped, laboratory-style boxes—are invisible. However, one is sure to find therein the condensation nuclei around which mist droplets have formed. Of course, these clouds too are precisely localized and dated.

Spontaneous vegetation vs. allotment gardens

But to return to our theme: Natura Maestra. The history of nature is the history of nature's "scientification" and, simultaneously, of its disenchantment. What therefore may be the reason a whole string of artists are occupied with nature today, yet with non-reproducible nature? One reason is that all instances of mimesis are now increasingly suspect. Many contemporary artists are occupied with plants, animals, landscape and other natural phenomena on a scale of 1:1. This has lent some momentum to an artistic genre that reached its zenith in the eighteenth century and subsequently sank into a routine: garden design. We here name three artists who have pioneered the revival of the art of gardening in our own era. Louis Le Roy, who began gardening with spontaneous vegetation, shows the importance of the incommensurable by working without a plan. What the results of his work will be is never foreseeable, not even for him; rather, his interventions challenge nature to give her response.

We also name Ian Hamilton Finlay, whom I discussed earlier. What makes his garden mysterious is not only that it is full of things growing but also that it is steeped in history. Every inhabited place on earth is a potential paradise yet simultaneously a place of past suffering and past wars.

Bernhard Lassus began his garden design work by trying to decipher the hermetic language of allotment gardeners, their windmills, ships and airplanes. He then tried to introduce this language forged by outsiders into the world of professional gardening and to make it comprehensible there. Notable in this regard is the garden he created around the former royal rope manufacture at Rochefort, a French seaport. Along with masts and rigging, he installed baskets on the site as a reminder of the fact that this was where the first begonias ever imported from Africa landed.

Nature art vs. land art

Often land art is presumed to mark the beginning of a new relationship to garden design yet it of all things is still a "classic" art form insofar as it leaves it to the viewer to deal with questions of scale. It works probably on a 1:1 scale but still calls on the viewer to see a nearby hill as a distant mountain or a dug trench as a valley.

New York artist Meg Webster highlights this problem in her works of land art, which must be seen in a certain sense as parodies. She mixes grain seeds into the earth with which she creates "hills" in her studio and in galleries. Initially, as long as the seed has not yet germinated, every visitor understands that the hill is meant to represent a distant mountain. Yet the minute cereal starts to sprout, the 1:1 scale rears its head and the distant mountain becomes a modest heap of earth in a gallery.

Beuys' forest project in Kassel is also on a 1:1 scale: the reference to the incommensurable forest, to the "7,000 Oaks," must be conjured in the mind. However, the viewer can only ever see a few trees at one time, which are identifiable as part of the forest project owing only to the large basalt rock installed beside them. The forest as a whole remains invisible—but as the proverb says, even in reality one cannot ever see the forest for the trees …

Henrik Håkansson's butterfly biotope at the Venice Biennale in 1997 won great acclaim. Here, if one comes at the right time, one can witness on a 1:1 scale the miracle of caterpillars transforming first into pupae then into butterflies. We understand Håkansson's work as a reference to one of the possible ways in which our minds perceive nature as a system. Håkansson's project "The Wall of Voo-Doo" makes this clearer. His wall consists of wet peat on which tropical plants are growing. The plants serve as food for the stick insects that inhabit the wall. The humidity of the wall—and hence also its stability as well as the life of the plants and insects—is electronically monitored and automatically maintained at a constant level by hydrostats. Finally, Håkansson turns off the automatic system and challenges the audience to use a water tap to adjust the humidity. Thereupon the wall falls apart.

Håkansson's "Wall of Voo-Doo," in this interpretation, is a little too didactic yet instructive nonetheless. Nature in our present-day perception is a self-regulating system but one that mankind—although fully blind, or blind in one eye only—continues to tinker with. Whether this image of nature as a system is at all viable and whether we will be able to fill it one day with increasing knowledge is a question crucial to the future of mankind. The image of the system has now replaced the old image of the exploitable quarry. We do not know what new notion will replace our image of nature as a self-regulating mechanism. Nor do we know of any artists currently working on this issue.

Current Trends in Garden Design (1999)

There is—unfortunately or fortunately?—no Charles Jencks of garden art able to spot and list existing trends or predict upcoming trends. The only thing we know for sure is this: that professional routine unfolds on the sidelines of future art forms. The profession made manifest in garden shows, national events, public facilities or private commissions has long since been occupied with indiscriminately pooling all the traditional elements of garden design and combining them in ways such that their contrary meanings cancel each other out. Here we have ponds with natural banks and a fountain, trees beneath which groups of flowers grow, or dwarf shrubs amid giant tulips, and the like. — And why is no one complaining about this? Why are there no vocal critics? — Because flowers are popular, green is always pleasant and trees are always great, regardless of whether irises are obliged to bloom among river pebbles and azaleas between granite slabs.

Since the 1960s, outsiders, artists mostly, have contributed to the renewal of garden art. Let's name those pioneers: Louis Le Roy, Ian Hamilton Finlay and Bernard Lassus. Their approaches have also found their way into professional studios and hence there is great potential, now, for developments to go all which ways. It therefore makes no sense at the moment to speak of the "current state" of garden design—yet it is possible to identify a number of trends and I shall try to do so here:

1. Disciplined professionalism: the traditional means of garden design are once again deployed skillfully and purposefully, such that their meanings can be demonstrated in full without thereby cancelling each other out. Here too, the code can be used critically and reflectively.

2. The artistic trend: garden design is understood here as performance art, because it not only creates works of visual art but also deliberately stages the paradox inherent to this art form: landscape is represented by landscape. This duplication creates literary double meanings: Finlay's garden is "really" a battlefield.

3. The architectural trend: here, the garden and the built environment are not set up as polar opposites. Rather, architectural elements, the further their distance from the main building, are either gradually absorbed or entirely replaced by natural elements: via stairs, terraces, parapets, canals and bridges, one reaches hedges and paths and, finally, the conclusive green of the actual garden.

4. The poetic trend: The private and hermetic poetry of windmills and garden-dwarf gardens is made intelligible by a highly articulate language. Allusions and arrangements evoke images, ideas and dreams that far surpass the garden itself.

5. The natural trend: ecology is now the subject of our relationship to nature. Ecology is not visible, however, but can be detected only by laboratory tests. Nevertheless, there is a need for "natural" outdoor spaces. A scattering of woody plants, a broad mix of flora and indiscernible maintenance measures together contrive a sense of "unspoiled nature."

6. The social trend: gardens are there to participate in, are for games and for children. They should not be perfectly planned and realized all in one go. Visitors too must be allowed to make practical contributions, to bring along ideas and plants and make their own visions reality—as long as they take other potential participants into consideration.

Yes, that's right. Work yourself into a tizzy about this list. I'm not too happy with it either. Any such classification is simultaneously unjust and instructive.

And now, let me put the list to the test! In the summer of 1997, heartwarming activity could be observed in Lausanne. There were thirty-two temporary gardens in the city center, here detailed below.[1] The city administration had made available some funding (very little!) plus thirty-two lots ranging in size from quite big to really tiny—the "lot" was often simply a part of a stairway, a street or a roof—and then invited young landscape architects and other teams to design them. A walk to these gardens—many of which I saw, although I never did find all of them—initially appears to buck the trends listed above. As different as these gardens were, one could still sense a "new spirit" common to all of them, but admittedly, one not easily defined. — Let me describe to you some of those gardens, namely those that have remained most vivid in my memory.

– To the left and right of the steps leading to the hilltop cathedral, tall poles were erected then interlinked by string. Hops sprouted

[1]   The thirty-two gardens are documented in the book Lausanne jardins, Une envie de ville heureuse, Ed. du Peribole, 1998, ISBN 2-97000191-0-8. The garden designers are:

Hops Garden, Promenade Curtat: Olivier Lasserre, Olivier Donzé, Laurent Salin, Jean-Blaise Gardiol, Jean-Claude Deschamps, Jean-Claude Maret.

East Hillsides of the Cité: Françoise Crémel, Thierry Le Goff, Isabelle Schmit, Paris.

Plant tubs in rue de la Tour: Setsuko Nagasawa, Atelier 89, architectes associés, Philippe Bonhôte, Franck Neau, Geneva/Paris.

Cuboid grid, Promenade Schnetzler: Marie and Bernard Zurbuchen-Henz, Sarah Nedir, Ursula Schmocker-Willi, Oberrieden.

Quai d'Osches in the Port of Ouchy: Jean-Jacques Borgeaud, Cécile Presset, Jacques Droz, Christian Junker, Lausanne.

Esplanade de Montbenon: Kathryn Gustafson, Vashon Island, François Paris, Ivry-sur-Seine.

Promenade Derrière-Bourg supérieur: City Lausanne Department of Parks and Gardens.

La Ficelle (Lausanne-Ouchy métro): Gilles Clément, Christophe Ponceau, Paris.

on this structure. Right there, in the city center, this climbing plant was able to show not only how high it could grow but also how its vertical strivings and vegetal structure had, perhaps, inspired architects of the Gothic era.

- Beyond the cathedral, behind a row of medieval houses on the western slope of City Hill, a strip of land shored up by a perimeter wall offers a fine view of all kinds of courtyards, boutiques and garages. This strip was recently redesigned in its entirety yet thereby also subdivided by slight trellises in order to suggest that each section of the strip belongs to the narrow house it fronts. The strip therefore intimates a private garden—yet clearly remains a public right of way for passers-by.

- In the port of Ouchy, what was obviously once a garden still occupies a section of a narrow embankment. However, it is impossible to see either how this space was previously used or how it looks now, since—as is generally the case with gardens—it has been completely enclosed by a slatted wall and thus rendered inaccessible. So passers-by now peer between the slats in order to catch a glimpse of its doubtless paradisiacal yet barely identifiable interior.

- "Lawns" were created on the lookout platform of the Esplanade de Mont Benon, except these were not lawns one might walk on but, rather, plots densely planted with low-growing plants whose respective shades of green strongly contrasted each other. So one area was blue-green, the next perhaps the color of fresh green grass and another gray-green: a treat for the eyes of a closet watercolor painter like myself!

- Cuboid plant tubs were set in a row down the middle of a narrow pedestrian zone. Gardeners had secreted tubers in them, from which erupted in springtime great stems of white lily. Once passers-by had stolen all the lilies, only those airborne seeds already present in the tubs or newly arrived there sprouted: nettles, mainly. Despite the decline of the noble lily and the rise of the weed, the tubs remained an uplifting sight.

– And now what else comes to mind? Oh, yes: a group of young landscape architects tried to display plants as well as stones and wood in large cubes made of grating, laid out such as to create a grid-like system of walkways. On the day of my visit, the interior of the most beautiful cube was covered with nasturtium creepers. — And then there's the Derrière-Bourg nursery, a boardwalk on which the city nursery annually lays out a number of ornamental flowerbeds full of pansies, begonias or asters, depending on the season; except in the year I'm thinking of they planted vegetables there instead, arranged in a way such as to weirdly exaggerate the contrasts between their shapes and leaf shades. — And another thing: Gilles Clément, who designed the Citroen Park in Paris, planted lots of wild flowers along what was hitherto a bare strip of grass beneath the "Ficelle," Lausanne's cable car: and the result was the kind of flower-filled meadow I used to see as a child around Alpine farms. And what remains now of my initial classification, after this colorful parade? — Gilles Clément, whom I had hitherto classified under Architectural (#3), appears now under #5. Natural trend. I now class the young garden architects' cuboid grid under #2. Artistic trend and the trellises and hint of medieval ambiance in the port under #4. Poetic. Professionalism is gently mocking itself with its ornamentally arranged vegetables (note that the city nursery itself came up with this design) and thus represents #1: Disciplined professionalism. The experiment with lilies in the middle of the pedestrian zone belongs under #6: Social trend, even though the result was negative. Nettles are the social penalty for those egoists who privatized the lilies. So, our list is perhaps not too bad at all, given that we have found a representative of each trend.

In 1987, "The Voyage to Tahiti" led to a former military training zone in Kassel. At various points on this "voyage," an actor read aloud texts by George Forster, who went with Captain Cook to Tahiti in 1772. This served as a soundtrack while people gazed upon the Dönche Nature Reserve, a place for which Forster's descriptions of a paradise isle seemed equally apt. Photo: Klaus Hoppe (above)

5DM

Fahrkarte
nach Tahiti
an Bord der
Landscape

Gruss aus Tahiti

In 1988, "The Voyage to Tahiti" was presented in Bosiva, a neighborhood in the north of Milan characterized by abandoned industrial plant, disused railway tracks and ruins, colorful southern flora, and the remains of farmsteads and noble villas. A souvenir bearing the name "Bovisola" was used to view the ten points covered on the walk. Photos: Martin Schmitz

Breadfruit trees and exotic potted plants from a city nursery numbered among the props used when staging "The Voyage to Tahiti," both in the Bovisa neighborhood of Milan and on the Dönche Nature Reserve in Kassel. Photos: Martin Schmitz (above), Monika Nikolić (below)

Actions staged as part of the undergraduate course "Perception & Traffic" taught by Lucius Burckhardt and Helmut Holzapfel in 1992/93 included inter alia the "Motorists' Walk" and the occupation of public space normally reserved for parked cars. A seminar took place in an outdoor space on which two cars might otherwise have been parked. Photos: Bertram Weisshaar

"ZEBRA crossing"—participants in a stroll through Kassel in 1993 ignored all the existing zebra crossings and intersection lights. They had brought along a zebra-striped carpet (Gerhard Lang), with the intention of rolling it out at any spot they chose on a six-lane highway, so as to be able to cross in safety. The action drew attention to the misappropriation of city dwellers' right to walk. Photo: Angela Siever

"The Villa Medici Travel Agency," 1998. Repair workshops, wrecked cars and industrial wasteland are the side of Rome one never sees on a postcard or in travel guides. In order to illustrate his strollology theory, Lucius Burckhardt developed ten guided walks of the city of Rome, in cooperation with a group of local students. And anyone who took part in one or two walks was able to say: "Now, that's the real Rome!" Photo: Annemarie Burckhart

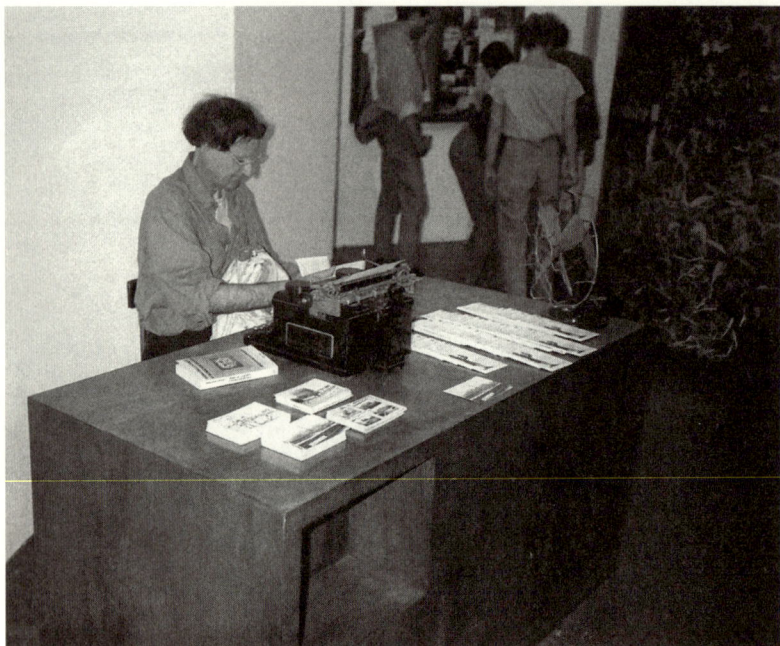

In 1988, Lucius Burckhardt accepted an invitation to the 17th Triennale in Milan. A mock travel agency offering "The Voyage to Tahiti" was set up in the "Landscape" section of the show. When Armstrong landed on the moon, he radioed to earth, to share his first impressions. What did he see on the moon? — A landscape, of course. Actually, one he could have seen without ever flying to the moon. The Steingletscher [glacier], the Furka Pass or the canyons of Colorado would have done the trick just as well. Photos: Martin Schmitz

STROLLOLOGY

Strollological Observations on Perception of the Environment and the Tasks Facing Our Generation (1996)

Aesthetic aspects of the environment have never before concerned people to the extent they do today. Never before were so many committees caught up in permit procedures; never before were such powerful organizations at work to protect the environment, the landscape, monuments, and a sense of local identity; never has it been so difficult to erect a new building in a historical location, or on a landscape that still bears traces of earlier gardens or agriculture. Yet despite all these safeguards, procedures and rejected construction proposals, complaints about the "ugly-fication" of the environment and the destruction of the landscape are growing louder by the day.

My science, which is called strollology, attempts to analyze this phenomenon. Strollology examines the sequences in which a person perceives his surroundings. For it is not as if we find ourselves "beamed" all of a sudden to Piccadilly Circus or the Cancelleria; instead we find our way there, one way or another. We leave our hotel on the Via Nomentana or the Pincio, catch a bus or flag a cab—younger people go on foot. We check out the streets, cross squares, stroll along the Corso, perhaps take in the Palazzo Vidone, the Linottte and St. Andrea della Valle, and are thus sufficiently prepared also for the Cancelleria to fall into place. A parachutist who happened to land among the endless cars parked in the narrow alley in front of the Cancelleria would gain a quite different impression of the architecture than we do.

In the old world, the intact world, any context explored strollologically served as an explanatory complement to the actual object of a visit. For example, the Cancelleria is not situated just anywhere, such as in a park, on a hillside, or on a large square flanked by two fountains. And if the nineteenth century had ever erected an imitation Cancelleria, then the context selected, its driveways, flowerbeds and fountains, would have explained the building as a Gründerzeit[1] replica.

A building supported thus by its context has a relatively easy time of expressing itself. And much has been clarified already: we are in Rome, in the Cardinals' Palace district; or we are on a nineteenth-century boulevard in a commercial and administrative district; or we are in a park whose genesis we are able to date, and are arriving now at the palace. The architectural statement, the architects' message, can be limited under such circumstances to the narrow field of stylistic contrivance; the architect can fulfill the stylistic ideal or, much to the Classicists' horror and Robert Venturi's delight, deviate from it. Either message is certain to be clear to the visitor, for his stroll has equipped him to read facades.

Let us speak as strollologists also of the landscape for a moment. In the nineteenth century, the age of railroads and terminals, the landscape shrank to a postcard cliché: this is Ostend, and this Scheveningen, Interlaken or the isle of Mont Saint-Michel. The stroll was reduced thus to the choice of a holiday destination, the purchase of a ticket and the rental of a hotel room with a view to match the postcard. The railroad journey was in a sense also a strollological context. Yet experience of the landscape prior to the Golden Age of railroads was a very different matter: the way was as important as the goal. Perhaps a person would have left town on foot or on horseback via a brick city gateway, seen strangers at their work, forded a river,

---

1 ["The Founder Epoch" refers to the early phase of industrialization and economic growth in Germany and Austria, before the great stock market crash of 1873.]

entered a forest or climbed a hill. He may have chosen another route back to his home town and then, in the evening, tired and weary, have described the landscape to his dear ones: that is how things are in Saint Germain or in the Jura near Besancon, and the forest of Fontainebleau is like this. Much of that which the stroller related at home he had never really seen, and much of that which he had seen was omitted from his account. The image he conjured was a collage of previous knowledge and fragments garnered along his way. The outcome was nevertheless certain knowledge—he now knew the forest of Fontainebleau.

Did he find it beautiful? Of course: for everything he saw of agriculture and natural growth on his travels was beautiful. Poetry since the days of Theocritus and Horace and the paintings of Neapolitan and Dutch Masters had prepared him for this beauty, had schooled his eye. And, moreover, he regarded this landscape with disinterest, in Immanuel Kant's sense of the term, meaning he did not seek to derive any personal benefit from it. He was in search neither of mushrooms nor of a suitable place to till the soil. The urban dweller's lack of familiarity with the rural landscape was precisely what enabled him to appreciate its aesthetic qualities.

And now I wish to describe why and to what extent our generation is the first to find itself in a novel situation vis-à-vis the object observed, be it a building or a landscape. And the explanation is once again strollological. It is not objects themselves that have changed, but the context. I'll name here some of the changes.

One actually does arrive in front of many an interesting building in much the same way as our parachutist, but from below now, from the subway. I have traveled from the Gare de l'Est to the Louvre metro station and find myself now in the Rue de Rivoli. Where am I? What is that? And how rapidly the picture changes: now I am in the courtyard of the Louvre or in the Tuileries Gardens. Without my prior knowledge, my city map or my travel guide, I am at a loss.

I park my car and head for the city forest. Gas stations, factories (abandoned ones mostly), a second-hand rubber dealer with a stock of old tires, a farmer on a tractor who is spraying his field with a white powder or vapor and, finally, trees. Are they valiant warriors, bowed by the tide of time, or is the forest here dying? And if so, whose fault may that be? Possibly mine, it is said, insofar as I drive a car and have a centrally heated home. And who drinks the water from beneath the sprayed field? Again, I do. So I am implicated in what is happening around me, after all, and by no means alien or disinterested, as Kant would have it.

Another example: let's say I go to the park, back to the Tuileries Gardens. In historic times one used to cross the built-up city, the city in which every last square meter was exploited and the king used his great wealth to plant a green oasis, the Tuileries Gardens. So I walk through the "stone city,"[2] cut through the palace and find myself gazing in delight upon this precious public park. Yet since the nineteenth century, the Tuileries Gardens have come to present a quite other aspect: we arrive now from the Champs Elysées, cut through the grounds that were laid out for the World Exhibitions, search between the Seine and the Place de la Concorde for a way to reach the entrance and ultimately find ourselves in a place not so very unlike the previous grounds. The experience of "I am now setting foot in the park" has been lost.

And now let us leave these anyhow still classical situations and take a look around those infinite zones we might best describe as "metropolises." These are the zones in which the city strives to be the countryside and where everyone, whether building a home or a factory, surrounds himself with as much greenery as possible. The same

2   [A reference to Werner Hegemann's book *Das steinerne Berlin* (Berlin of Stone), Kiepenheuer, Berlin 1930.]

is true of the zones in which the countryside aspires to be urban and every small town mayor is in search of an investor prepared to make him a gift of a tower block or, at the least, of a railroad station with an underground section, a pedestrian level and a multistory parking lot. — And now, my discovery: in those zones of our environment inhabited or visited by the majority, the strollological context that fosters understanding of what we see has completely disintegrated.

We are therefore the first generation of people for whom the aesthetic experience does not occur automatically. Instead, the place itself must explain its aesthetic intent. When we create a park, the park can no longer rely on the fact that we proceed from the town and through a gate to a green space and hence know we are visiting the park. Rather, the park must now substantiate by means of its interior design the extent to which it contrasts with its surroundings. So, without us even taking a single step, it must give us the strollological explanation: "You have come from the city to the park."

The same holds true also for architecture. Architecture can no longer rely on us grasping its greater significance thanks to its location alone and so must assert its singularity by deviating slightly from the stylistic ideal. For instance, a new bank must now introduce a slightly variant nuance to the banking district. Now, an acclimatized suburban cube that has been incorporated in a partly green, partly concrete-braced artificial plane must fall back on a conveniently ambivalent statement: I am in the suburbs but I am resolutely urban; I am a bank, but a bank like no other…

To reiterate: we are the first generation to have to construct a new aesthetic, a strollological aesthetic. Strollological, for the simple reason that the way or route to a place can no longer be taken for granted, but must be reproduced in, or represented by, the object itself. The multilayered message that a building, garden or cultivated landscape must deliver can no longer depend only on an architect's flash of genius. It is not enough for the enterprising architect to say "Where there is no place, I will create a place myself:" there are plenty such aesthetic cactuses dotted about already and, indeed, it is they which have contributed so decisively to the much lamented deterioration of the natural environment. What is required here, rather, is design intelligence, intelligence that conveys a dual message: information about the context as well as about the object in question.

The Science of Strollology (1995)

When, after a long pause, there was a renewed surge of interest in the landscape and new publications on the English landscape were able once again to fill a shelf or two, the ways in which we perceived the environment and the stroll itself caught the eye also of literary historians. If we understand their publications correctly, literary historians examine such topics as "a literary code" and they hence see the stroll as a means to represent both the external and internal realms. Even if this interpretation is correct, our investigation of the walk begins somewhat earlier. We are interested in the walk not as a means of representation, but rather as a mode of perception. However, such perception is premised on cultural baggage derived from earlier representations, for only in exceptional cases is man capable of perceiving that which has not already been mediated and made visible to him by pictorial or literary means.

Such cultural mediation is generally a guide to how to select and filter out certain impressions. The hundreds of thousands of bits of information that confront us when we take a walk cannot all be processed. If something like a landscape image is to take shape before our mind's eye, all irrelevant information must be suppressed or repressed. When a child returns from a walk she says she has found a colorful tin can that she ultimately threw into a pit, where it made a sound like thunder. When an adult returns home, he describes things he ought to have seen in the area but that are actually partly invisible to him or that he is unable to analyze. The basalt peaks with their pine-covered plateaus, the brooks wearing away the limestone or the heath with its scattering of bogs. — These are things he was aware of, even before he set out on a walk. Enjoyment of the walk lay in his greater or lesser ability to recognize those elements already underscored in literature and to filter out any distracting elements, such as a discarded Coke can or the scaffolding around the church tower in the village. If such distractions are too major to be easily overlooked then we fall back on another mechanism that comes into play: the landscape appears to have been "ruined," and the environment "damaged."

Our investigation will therefore focus at least in equal measure on what a person actually encounters during a walk and on his preconceptions. Perception here is not to be understood as a one-way street, for a system stands between the stroller and his field of view, one that steers his reflections, and his reflections have an impact on the object, and may even lead in special cases to physical intervention, namely the removal of the distracting element. Such intervention at its most structured may comprise action by associations for the protection of the local environment or landscape and the conservation of nature or cultural heritage. We will return later to restorative endeavors of this sort, which are inspired by specific forms of perception.

The investigation pursues a line similar to Gerhard Hard's critique of geography. Hard impressively characterizes the scientific and literary system that exists between the viewer and the environment. The geographer is in search of that which is "typical," and it is he who stipulates by what criteria something may be taken for a heath, moorland or an industrial landscape. The next task—subsumption—falls to the viewer. It is he who must decide what density of a hardy heather or juniper bush justifies the use of the term "heath" or whether the plain before his eyes is actually something else, a steppe or a tundra or whatever; or whether the heath, perhaps—to return now to those restorative interventions—has been neglected, or destroyed by planting tree stock or by failing to put sheep out to pasture.

We learned from our geography teacher that the billowing smokestacks, pit frames and blue flat caps of shift workers are "typical" of the Ruhr District. In consequence, a cultural heritage preservation office in the Ruhr today protects such features as a matter of course (naturally with the exception of the shift workers and the plumes of smoke) —but only there; because anywhere else, it would be strictly forbidden to suddenly erect a smokestack or a pit frame. — Critiques serve thus to highlight the fact that current perceptions are determined by insights premised on earlier perceptions. Subsumption as a perception technique is thus an obstacle to the renewal of information. A vicious circle ensues: because something is like this or that, it is called so or so; and if it has always been called so or so then it must be like this or that. — That which we call strollology must therefore strive to simultaneously identify not only our modes of perception per se but also how these are determined, for only then will it be possible to arrive at new and unusual judgments on matters long since known.

The primal walk

Our primal walk took place in 1976 in Riede, Emstal. Devised by Karl Heinrich Hülbusch, it followed the traditional loop: the walker leaves the village and passes briefly through an agricultural zone in order to reach the forest, where he traverses several clearings before finally coming upon an impressive one with a panoramic view, where, significantly, he finds a paved barbeque area. From there, he descends into the fertile plain, crosses fields, eventually passes by a characteristic group of poplars and then arrives back at the village, more precisely, in its only pub. There, our thirsty walker finds a photographic landscape: wallpaper depicting the sublimity of Alpine scenery with an Alpine lake and snow-capped mountains provides the requisite contrast to the charming agricultural landscape he has just experienced.

Our primal circuit had been marked on a map and the participants' task was to additionally pencil in the most remarkable spots, the "charming places." Later, in the pub, we compared the maps.

What we found in each case was a line broken by distinctive points, a composition somewhat akin to a string of pearls. Participants had, notably, mostly marked the same points. One could thus surmise that their perception of landscape had been shaped in a uniform fashion. It became clear in subsequent discussions, moreover, that visual or literary factors had influenced their decision as to what made a place distinctive. All of them had found passing by a castle when leaving the village a poetic experience and some even professed to believe they had seen a fountain there too, so strongly is this instance shaped by the well-known line: "At the fountain by the gate there stands a linden tree." The ascent from there had led to a spot predetermined by the presence of a stone bank and table and likely thus to draw the walker's attention to the view of village rooftops and the rolling hills beyond. Here too, set pieces had sprung to mind, mostly of the romantic sort. "On Saturday evenings, the pastor reviews his sermon here," said one participant. "Jean Paul wrote his novels here when the weather was good," claimed another. The next spot had been a bend in the road that disappeared into the forest—and there was no end to the literary connotations this time—before leading to a clearing (where an eighteenth-century obelisk stood) and to the barbeque area (where a horse chestnut tree looking totally out of place betrayed that a former lord of the manor here once aspired to something better). It then descended into the fields (which the villagers call "the pantry"), passed the group of poplars and led, of course, back to the pub; these were places associated with visual or literary cultural fragments.

The overall impression

These various literary connotations or, rather, the spots themselves give rise to that persistent impression of the landscape, which is finally taken away as a souvenir. The viewer accomplishes a remarkable feat of integration insofar as he now subsumes the path out of the village, the entrance to the forest and the barbecue area under the single term "typical North Hessian landscape." Suddenly, the castle, the village, the local economy, the basalt peaks—that very landscape familiar either from the Atlas of North Hessian Geography or a travel brochure—stand out more prominently than any individual spots experienced in person.

This feat of integration is made possible by the ingenious term "landscape," which enables us to filter from a heterogeneous environment a single entity that makes all we have seen communicable. It is this capacity of the term landscape to subsume in a single image an environment comprised of numerous bits of information that led to its use in quite different contexts. One speaks of a seascape, a cityscape or, more abstractly, of the German university landscape, whenever one wants to quickly communicate the import of a multifaceted phenomenon. "This discipline is not at all suited to the German higher education landscape" sounds just as logical—and is, logically speaking, just as unfounded—as the claim that a pit frame is not at all suited to a North German peat bog. The claim needs no justification; everything suits, because at the aesthetic level agreement is easily reached.

On the communicative capacity of language

In our seminars we investigated with students the evocative capacity of language in descriptions of landscape. Reading stories, fairy tales, novels and in particular, travelogues conjures images of landscape in our mind's eye. This poses two questions for us. One is: How much (or how little) does the author predetermine and how much is the work of our own imagination? The second is: Can words describe landscapes to us in a way such as to convey a clear image of them?

How few words historical storytellers use to tell their tales, how few qualities they convey of the environments they see, and how rich the image we profess to see when we read the stories of Sinbad the Sailor or the forest fairy tales about Red Riding Hood, Sleeping Beauty, or Hansel and Gretel!

Ernst Robert Curtius explored the literary launch of set pieces, of literary landscapes with their requisite furnishings: shady places, cool springs and hedgerows. The perceptive capacities honed by such medieval traditions are so great that we today need recall only a few words of a text in order to conjure meticulously prepared landscapes in our mind's eye. But what if the author wants to portray highly specific, geographically characteristic or extraordinary landscapes? — The language of literary narrative is still too underdeveloped for such feats. In the case of one eighteenth-century text (Hirschfeld's *Herschenberg*), most readers see mountains or hills of stately height arise before them, unless they happen to know that the region being described is a part of present-day Denmark. It is also interesting to note how authors fall back on preliminary verbal padding when called upon to describe scenic highlights, because they already sense that words alone will not suffice to describe the "most charming place"—as in the case of Isola Bella in *Wilhelm Meister's Apprenticeship* or Jean Paul's *Titan;* or in the description of the sunrise on the Brocken in Heine's work; or on the Rigi in Mark Twain's. But let's not further pursue that topic here.

Metaphorical aspects of the landscape

We accept Gerhard Hard's critique of geography and broaden it to include the various tasks of today's engineer. The natural sciences now work largely with the system concept: organisms—and likewise apparent entities arbitrarily isolated by researchers, such as environments or landscapes—are hence read as systems, i.e., as entities that to a certain degree automatically counteract their own dissolution. The causal chains at work within such entities are so interlinked that the entities' "reaction" to external influences is internal consolidation. Wounds heal. Societies and groups become established. Ecosystems "function" and landscapes "bear" interventions to a certain extent. This system character attributed by science to the aforementioned organisms and entities is a metaphor that explains to us the existence of such real or apparently self-sustaining entities. Engineering as an applied science now adopts this metaphor as reality and hopes also to apply it. Engineers have wrought the greatest destruction when attempting to intervene in a systematic manner in supposedly fully understood ecosystems: in irrigation systems in the Indus Valley, in dams in Pakistan, in the Aswan Dam or the Tennessee Valley Administration.

Strollology now fears that the same thing is happening in so-called landscape protection, namely that the system as metaphor is mistaken for a real system. For one, the geographically described landscape is a scientific construct. Components of an environment impossible to describe, on account of its sheer complexity, were arbitrarily selected in order to compose a—in aesthetic terms—logical image. The logic here is premised on the alleged operability of the landscape insofar as self-sustaining capacities are attributed to it. And now comes the apparent savior, the landscape engineer, and makes use of this giant toy as he likes. He believes that the reductive view taken by science for the sake of description constitutes a reality; and he therefore operates at the level of this reduced metaphor, as if it were possible to intervene at that level. Alone the attentive stroller senses the great damage being done here, damage that the next generation will have to undo—just as today, in the Indus estuary, 2,400 World Bank-funded pump stations have to pump off the water that earlier generations brought to the area through irrigation and which has meanwhile led to oversalinated soil.

Strollology's task, therefore, is to gather impressions and string them together, to create impressive image sequences without renouncing traditional metaphors, for the latter alone make the images thus obtained communicable; and likewise without creating the impression that the portrayal of an entity suffices to exhaustively describe that entity and render it comprehensible. Strollology is hence a tool with which previously unseen parts of the environment can be made visible as well as an effective means of criticizing conventional perception itself. We want now to show how we have applied strollology in both respects in urban and in rural environments and thereby obtained tangible results.

The destination and the way

The trip and the walk can have two different meanings: they can either be the means to reach a destination, whereby the destination is of paramount importance; or they may be an end in themselves, undertaken for pleasure's sake or to gain knowledge through travel or, if undertaken on foot, for the simple enjoyment of stretching one's legs. Every trip has a little of both: a pilgrimage may initially appear to be focused exclusively on a destination yet the journey itself is a powerful experience, not least owing to the devotional highlights found at different points along the route. Modern modes of transport tend to make the journey itself seem insignificant and abstract, for they focus only on the destination. The subway offers an abstract form of travel oriented purely to the target destination and likewise the now popular "non-stop quick hop" routes. Flight, which early pioneers imagined primarily as a trip, not simply as a means to reach a destination, is also now an extremely abstract means to arrive quickly at one's goal. This can be explained in strollological terms by the fact that the view of earth from an airplane cabin window is much less interesting than it was once imagined to be.

In this chapter we examine the extent to which our perception of landscape depends on the mode of transport used for a trip or a walk. The trip on foot, on horseback, or by horse and cart were the first modes available, as we know from historical memoirs. A whole world has been lost since those modes disappeared: the world of coachmen and inns, a world of encounters between nations, classes and ranks, for every traveler, from the prince to the journeyman, had to rely on roadside inns. Contact with the localities traveled was indispensable, for food supplies and hay and oats for the horses had to be purchased en route from farmers, traders or innkeepers.

When it comes to the landscape experience, traditional travel may be said to follow the "string of pearls" model. Our perception registers the typical places and qualities, filters out incidental aspects and accomplishes that feat of integration we attributed earlier to the walker. From the wealth of information that impacts the eye and all other senses we select those bits we believe we have seen before or that can be subsumed in our previous knowledge; this and this alone makes them apt for re-cognition; and we store them in our memories, or record them in narratives and transcripts. Here, the feat of integration consists in our capacity to process fleeting sequences of heterogeneous impressions—the walker or traveler leaves a city, crosses an agricultural zone and comes upon a forest, where the trail leads him up hill and down valley, past a body of water and over a bridge—and to integrate these in a single image that we then hold to be "typical" of the area traveled.

This perception of landscape accomplished by the integration of heterogeneous impressions stands in stark contrast to the perception of landscape fostered in the nineteenth century by a new mode of transport: the railroad. From the very start, rail travel was oriented to the destination. Its administration made this very clear, for anyone boarding a train requires a ticket to his chosen destination. The traveler must therefore know before starting a journey where he wants to get off and spend some time. Only very few rail offers deviate from this model, for example, the "Mystery Tour" on special trains for short trips. The conventional rail vacation is extremely oriented to a fixed destination. The traveler spends a great deal of time choosing a resort, consults brochures, travel agencies, colleagues and neighbors, and ends up with great expectations of the landscape experience the resort is likely to provide.

Construction of railroads made certain resorts popular in the course of the nineteenth century and they provide clues to the railroad-related landscape experience, i.e. the experience rail travelers had of their destinations. Not all typical nineteenth-century railroad destinations can actually be reached by rail; often a short crossing by boat is necessary, or an ascent by mule or with a porter. All the more evident is it thus, that the destinations in question had extraordinary qualities. The destination had to guarantee at a single point that "typical" something accomplished during a walk by a feat of integration. The nineteenth-century guest takes up residence in his hotel room, throws back the curtains, looks though the window and—as long as he has booked an expensive room—sees before him the ideal image of the typical Alps or the typical North Sea or the typical Mediterranean landscape. Ideally, the image framed by his window will be exactly the one he has already seen in the travel brochures.

These nineteenth-century destinations have now often lost their clientele; or they have won a quite different clientele. The large hotel blocks stand vacant at panoramic spots in the Alps or in the similarly extreme landscapes of northern Germany or Italy—on Helgoland, in Naples (where the size of the city and its views of Mount Vesuvius and Capri ensures hotels a steady stream of visitors), or on Capri itself (where the joys of bathing have replaced delights for the eye); and likewise in France, at Mont Saint-Michel and

Saint-Malo; the large panoramic hotels in Austria and Switzerland are literally vacant too, on the Semmering, the Rigigipfel (demolished) and Mount Furka (Hotel Furka has been demolished, the Furkablick turned into an art gallery). The Belvedere Rhone Glacier stood empty for many years while thousands of motorists whizzed by daily or even made a stop there. Alone the Hotel Giessbach has been revived, thanks to a group of nostalgic tourists. What does this mean? The construction of railroads and the cable cars that went with them meant the landscapes judged suitable for tourism were not explored on foot but merely perceived as an image. The tourist spent his fourteen days or three weeks in a hotel—on a terrace or in a winter garden, often without ever leaving the building—and saw through the window a typical image already integrated by nature. This image had to be striking enough to constantly impart information. It must be mentioned too that perfectly beautiful weather was not yet so much in demand as it is today. In winter gardens with panoramic outlooks we actually used to enjoy changes in the weather; and exposed places, such as the Furka or Helgoland, provided welcome shifts: dark clouds before the window soon ceding to a broad blue sky, or vice versa.

The aforementioned former destinations are not deserted nowadays, at least not if located on a roadside; but the hotel rooms are deserted. The motorcar has brought us a new mode of transport that, since it is steered individually and not bound to follow tracks, initially appears to herald the revival of the walk. Someone who goes for a drive need not have a fixed destination in mind. He can set off, gaze through the window, integrate the things he sees in a single landscape, as a walker does, and then change direction if dissatisfied by the impressions garnered, or park and while away some time, if a certain spot on the string of pearls strikes him as especially remarkable. In many respects, however, a drive does not recreate the same conditions as the walk of yore.

First, the scope of travel has much increased. While a walk on foot or a ride on horseback allows one to cross a village, river, valley, hills, etc. and integrate in one's mind eye and hence perceive the characteristics of a limited landscape, travel by car facilitates access to much larger vistas. While the walker reports on the peculiarities of the nearby Habicht Forest, the motorist talks of Tuscany, Burgundy and the Provence, which he has just visited by car over Pentecost. We are accordingly now required to accomplish a more complex feat of integration: more heterogeneous impressions must be integrated in much more abstract ideal landscapes. Anyone traveling through Burgundy sees big cities, highways, factories, ugly settlements and yes, also the vineyards, wine-growing villages, and Romanesque or Gothic churches he had reckoned with. But what constitutes "typical Burgundy" today? The feat of integration is too demanding and the subsumption of all one sees in the single image learned of in school impossible. So our motorized tourist returns home downhearted and tells his friends that Burgundy, too, is no longer what it used to be.

Evidently, the improved accessibility of more remote areas and the difficulty of successfully integrating all one's impressions of them have fostered the need for a new type of landscape perception, one that we see as a kind of abstraction. The tourist travels namely to several similar points. This is also a reason why he drives past the old "panoramic hotels." Today, the Rhone Glacier alone is never touted; only the "Five Glaciers Trip."The Swiss mail truck company now offers a "Passes Trip" as well as the "Three Countries Trip." The latter starts in Grison Canton and covers a bit of the South Tyrol and a slice of Austria. What information does such a trip convey, above and beyond the day-tripper's sense of pride at having visited five glaciers, three mountain passes or three countries?

Obviously, the tourist is in search of the ideal image of the glacier, in search of the ultimate, essential *glacial-ness* of glaciers, which can apparently be identified only after viewing several samples. Similarly, the "Three Countries Trip:" it tends to abstraction insofar as one pays for cigarettes here in francs and there in lira or shillings; but Alps are Alps from wherever you look at them.

The increase in motorists and the construction of freeways have challenged the notion that a drive is a kind of motorized walk. The idea that one is free to choose one's route is now largely rhetorical; in practice, a trip by car requires some planning and relatively long stretches of it cannot be easily modified or interrupted. The crisscross local road system is now overlaid by the linear system of freeways. To drive from one hotel to the next is now history, rendered redundant by new offers: the tourist location is touted only as the "base camp" from where one embarks on brief excursions. The thousands of tourists who drive by the Hotel Furkablick or the Rhone Glacier each summer spend the night at one of the "starting blocks" on a major road through the Alps, in Interlaken or Montreux, Merano or Innsbruck. The destination and the stretch of road beyond it are touted as a single package deal: a tourist location no longer advertises its own qualities but explains rather, how convenient a springboard it is for further travel. However, given the severe congestion prevalent on road networks in tourist areas, this form of vacation too will soon be history.

The city and the countryside

We read the walk as a sequence, as a string of pearls that demands a feat of integration, namely to produce an image of the typical landscape. But this feat of integration in its original form was based initially on yet another sequence, namely the transition from the city to the countryside. The landscape was invented by urban dwellers. Urban societies that necessarily still source foodstuffs in the countryside but whose only connection with it is their power and money—and whose foodstuffs hence arrive in the city in the form of tributes, taxes, interest, ground rents or commodities—tend to develop an aesthetics of landscape, because the urban dweller so disconnected from agricultural production leaves the city to go for a walk and sees the countryside only in aesthetic terms or, as Kant puts it, without interest. He has namely no vested interest, no direct stake in the production process, and so potato or sunflower fields do not bring investments and yields to mind, and nor are poppies and cornflowers harmful weeds, in his eyes, but seem to him like everything else to be a natural part of the landscape. Even the country folk so alien to him yet so likeable—those "happy People of the Fields"—are part of the landscape, are what painters call staffage or props. To transform phenomena into an aesthetic image a border must be crossed, in this case the city limits marked by a gate. In analogy, although sociologically more problematic, one could imagine the farmer entering the city and regarding buildings there likewise "without interest."

The contrast, both aesthetic and economic, between the city and the countryside thus underpins the basic pattern of classic perception as shaped by the walk. The economic prerequisite is the lack of vested interest, the purely indirect relationship to income or profit generated by agricultural activity. Even if the occasional walker happens to own or lease a plot of land, or make purchases, in his role of walker he joins the ranks of the "disinterested urban dwellers." The impact of the look of the landscape, for its part, is determined by the existence (or not) of distinctive city limits. There has to be a point, a border, at which aesthetic perception is switched on or switched off. This is the reason classic perception as shaped by the walk is now in crisis and must be redefined.

Today's walker, who is simultaneously a consumer of TV, radio and newspapers, participates or, more precisely, is implicated in agricultural production and in the current condition of fallow land. Everyone has heard that the forests are dying and so the sight of a scrawny or perhaps withered tree is a rude reminder for the urban consumer of heating oil: it fuels his personal share in the guilt. On the other hand, the walker can observe today that the "happy People of the Fields" are up to something other than merrily binding ears of corn. The urban dweller eyes with suspicion the mysterious sacks and containers stacked up by the stables and likewise the strange vehicles spreading powders or liquids on the fields. Are these fertilizers or poisons? Will our bodies absorb them along with our food and drinking water? Here, the culprit becomes the victim, the injured party the aggressor; we urban dwellers feel guilty about our part in killing off the forest yet are simultaneously outraged to see our essential raw materials being ruined by chemicals—and feel powerless to stop it happening. And what about the cattle, now that it no longer stands around picturesquely in a clearing? True, we cannot see it, but we rightly presume it to be on the far side of those extremely long walls from behind which trucks appear, laden with dung and headed for the fields, fields where vegetation is sparse, not because of a lack of dung but because of its sheer abundance. The walker who sees all this and necessarily gives it some thought since he's confronted with it time after time daily is no longer quite the disinterested observer. But then, what is he?

The second component of the crisis of our perception of the landscape relates to the suburbs. We move nowadays in a continuum that we call the metropolis. By that we mean this mixture of buildings and green spaces that now sprawls across what used to be the city or used to be the countryside. We know the following statement provokes protest, but we make it anyhow: "Never before have our cities been as green as they are today." Not a single administrative building, not a single pedestrian zone has failed to render its limited space unusable by planting rampant vegetation purchased from nurseries. We will return later to the fact that the very ubiquity of urban greenery can render actual gardens invisible. Changes in the former countryside are easier to see. No rural town is at peace until it too, like the city, has a few too low high-rise buildings. And even in villages, at the least the local council offices are expanded such that one could easily take them for Deutsche Bank. And none of this happens, let us emphasize, without the requisite dwarf shrubs and steppe grasses being planted in former farmland, where they struggle unsuccessfully to assert themselves in the face of adventive sunflowers and giant hogweed. — And so we must ask ourselves once again: Is our image of landscape in crisis simply because a distinct border between the countryside and the city no longer exists?

Here we must touch upon a third point that we will not discuss conclusively, however: the confusion of the landscape and nature. Such confusion is a latent companion every time we look at or try to represent the landscape. The urban dweller walking in the countryside takes pleasure in signs of different types of agricultural processing or non-processing. The classic landscape paintings of the Italian and Dutch painters show both: the interventions made by the farmer-landowner as well as unspoiled nature, here symbolized perhaps by the portrayal of old, half-dead veteran trees that are surely not destined to land in a carpentry workshop or on a fire. Both options are obviously well worth considering: using a thing—or letting it lie fallow.

In this respect too, we are currently experiencing momentous change: use is intensifying and more land is being left fallow. The economic reasons for this need hardly be explained here. Also understandable is the aesthetic phenomenon that ensues from this development, namely, that the denser and more homogeneous agricultural use becomes, the more the walker loses his aesthetic interest in it. We don't pull on our hiking boots in order to see endless fields of grain and poultry factories. In the future, we'll more likely head for fallow land; but pitfalls are in store, there too. Any land neglected by its users, be they farmers, the Bundeswehr [German Federal Armed Forces] or whoever, becomes unstable. That which we witness, glad or incredulous—adventive weeds, the prickly jungle of thistles, then the emergence of the first alder thickets and, finally, after a few years, the inaccessibility of these areas—has still to be discussed. For now, at least, the matter is on the agenda.

Making things visible

Faced with this crisis of the perception of landscape, we take two divergent approaches, both of which are an attempt to use something visible to satisfy our longing for the natural.

The one tendency is to seek naturalness in the extreme landscape. Only a location in which we are not implicated can be aesthetically perceived. Just as a search began in the eighteenth century for the last blank spots on the map, so today, the search is on for the last unspoiled edges of the world. It is clear, however, that the latter are not only *not* uninhabited but also doubtless given over in part to tourism.

Perhaps such unspoiled-unexploited areas actually do still exist, or even tribes of people who have never yet seen a tourist. Yet they are not within our reach. It is unnecessary however for such unspoiled-unexploited places to exist in the here and now, if they happen to exist within a specially adopted system of signs. And the extreme landscape provides such signs. While, historically, initially, the landscape experience was satisfied by elements of the charming landscape and then eventually, in the eighteenth century, took on elements of the, in Burke's sense, "sublime" landscape, today we seek the very opposite, or at least the opposite of "charming." Some travel agencies specialize in trips of this sort: Ireland, Iceland, hikes in the northern tundra and steppes, cruises between cliffs and icebergs with a view of Spartan fishing villages, or treks by camel or mule through the desert, the Atlas or the Himalayas, whereby the ideal of diversity still alive and kicking in the minds of certain landscape designers cedes dramatically to the lure of solitary expanses.

Travel agencies cannot convey the adventurous landscape of a jungle trek but cigarette advertising can at least give it a good try: a Jeep hauled onto a raft, the faithful dog, boots, a slouch hat, a bottle of whiskey and, of course, a cigarette. This so trammeled system of signs beyond the conventionally sublime—trans-sublimity, we might call it— now serves to communicate to today's traveler (the one with a guilty conscience thanks to environmental propaganda) what was previously the situation of the disinterested observer, namely of he who is not implicated in what is happening around him and can therefore perceive it in aesthetic terms.

The other, likewise commercial (although in a different line of business) mediated system of signs is that of ecology. Ecology is invisible. It is a scientific construct that first requires an operable definition of goals and thereafter must be proven by scientific means. But this is of little concern to the urban dweller stricken by a guilty conscience. He wants to see ecology in simple, legible terms—and immediately. This is why landscape nurseries now offer organic vegetation alongside their dwarf shrubs and large-petal tulips. Of course, the organic flower meadows that the urban gardener plants are not really organic. You can tell that alone from the fact they need full-time care. For they are nothing less than interrupted successions, transition states artificially brought to a halt between care and the absence of care, between the urban lawn mowed weekly and the wasteland full of scrub. After all, even the "real" alpine flower meadow, on which commercial mixed-seed bags are modeled, used to be exploited pretty intensively as part of a rigid scheme of farming and its urban counterpart must likewise be coddled with fertilizers and novel means of loosening or even ventilating the soil. But the image thus produced brings relief to the troubled conscience of any urban dweller no longer able to take much pleasure in the disposable flora on offer in conventional city nurseries.

The "Voyage to Tahiti"

The "Voyage to Tahiti" referenced the paradoxes inherent to unspoiled nature and ecology. It took the form of a walk staged with students through the Dönche area of Kassel, after we had read Georg Forster's "A Voyage Around The World," in particular his descriptions of the island of Tahiti. Bougainville had declared Tahiti the picture of paradise before Cook and Forster arrived, so Forster already knew what to expect or, rather, how he should respond to what he found there: the clef indicated charming, natural and pure. The landscape and the lives of the people had to convey appropriate information. Some landscape formations with their clean streams, picturesque trees and tame birds did in fact correspond to painters' images of paradise. Then there was the breadfruit tree, whose very name conjures a particular fairy-tale form of paradise: a tree whose fruit is bread! That is a true Utopia! And finally, the good-natured and trusting population one was so ready to forgive, at least until a silver spoon vanished from Captain Cook's table. The people led a simple, sensible life, formed natural hierarchies and lived by mutual assistance. The discovery that all the breadfruit trees belonged to one rich man who was too fat to move and thus always had his concubines feed him was evil however.

The "voyage" through Tahiti in the Dönche consisted in the fact that excerpts from Georg Forster's diary entries were read aloud at certain spots on our walk, wherever they seemed apt to describe similarities or associations with the present Kassel landscape. The punch line of the story, so to speak, and one that underscored the paradox of the unspoiled area, was the fact that the Dönche had served until only a few years earlier as a military training ground for tank drivers. The terrain already riddled with Second World War shell craters had thus been trampled and churned up for years yet had meanwhile sufficed for some sparse and fleeting vegetation to dare raise its head between the caterpillar tracks. Once the tanks had pulled out, the terrain prepared to welcome rare pioneer plants and launch its impending natural successions. Unlike fallow agricultural land, the unfertilized, humus-poor soil here gradually transformed itself into that stopgap final state, the alder swamp. The intermediate stages are absolutely lovely so the situations on Tahiti described by Georg Forster could be easily identified or helped along by the play-acting of some humorous students. A Turkish bakery supplied the breadfruit we carefully suspended in the scrawny trees and the tropical vegetation was loaned from a nursery. The indigenous dwellings that Georg Forster claimed resembled birdcages had been erected by the leading lights in German architecture on the edge of the Dönche, under the name "documenta urbana." A critical reading of the carefully planned walk proved under those circumstances superfluous: the meaning of the artwork struck the participants instantly. And many of them must have smiled years later, when committed conservationists demanded that the humus layer forming in the Dönche be removed again in order that rare pioneer plants might hold their own and not be swamped by ordinary grass or even alder. They estimated the cost of the job would be 300,000 Deutschmarks. That the Bundeswehr could do it more cheaply was kept scrupulously under wraps.

Urban garden design

As we have seen, the traditional landscape experience was rooted essentially in that moment of transition from an urban to a rural setting, the moment namely when a walker steps out through the city gate. Similarly, the aesthetic impact of any urban garden lies in the fact that one comes upon it unexpectedly. It thrives on the contrast between the stone city and the sudden glimpse of a lush monastery courtyard, a cloister or a courtyard garden in the densely populated city. After the long walk through Venice, the stoniest city of all, Princess Papadopoli's garden must once have seemed paradisiacal. Yet when we arrive there from the open-plan bus station today, it doesn't look convincing at all. Something unchanged looks different under different circumstances.

The same can be said of the Tuileries Gardens in Paris. They were previously flanked on one side by royal palaces and the built city and later by the city ramparts and, strollologically speaking, how they were approached determined their impact. Strolling through the city, opening the gates, catching sight of the green oasis—all of that constitutes a sequence. And we must consider this fact now, when we commission the Gardens' restoration in the historic style of Palissy and Le Nôtre: here too, something unchanged looks different under different circumstances. Now, if one regards Paris in the light of nineteenth-century urban expansion, say, from a standpoint on the Champs-Elysées, that transition from the city to the park is sought in vain. The latter with its rows of trees ends in the World Exhibition zone, i.e., in front of the Grand Palais and the Petit Palais with their park-like grounds. Then one crosses the vast expanse of the Place de la Concorde and enters the Tuileries Gardens, which feature quasi as a continuation of the urban axis beginning at the Arc de Triomphe on the Étoile. If one considers the relationship between perception and movement, one might call this the nineteenth-century carriage-ride city par excellence: Les Invalides, the Champs de Mars, the World Exhibition zone, the Tuileries Gardens and the Champs-Elysées were specifically adapted to carriage traffic.

The Tuileries were hence not experienced as a garden at all, but as a single stage of a carriageway.

As for today's traffic, it is probably safe to assume that most visitors now enter the Tuileries Gardens from the subway station. Which is to say, they experience absolutely no transition at all, but rather, reach their decision to visit the Tuileries while still at home. They take no stroll to speak of, but instead experience the Métro, a non-place, before finding themselves suddenly at their destination, where they hope to enjoy a pleasant hour or two in the park.

This poses entirely new challenges for the park. The experience of transition has ceased to exist, owing either to the greening of the "carriage city" or to the "non-approach" style of an arrival by Métro. The excitement the garden must create thus no longer ensues from a shift, from the transition from a city to a park, but must be completely engendered by the garden itself. This confronts garden architecture with a wholly new task. We are the first generation for which the park must in and of itself create a certain tension, a sense of excitement as its aesthetic justification and experiential raison d'être. Whenever the superordinate category "green oasis in the city of stone" disappears, not even the previously elaborated semiotics denoting the more formal or the more scenic garden is of any help.

The experience of Markus Gnüchtel (then a student, now a graduate engineer) helped clarify our thoughts on this subject. The mayor of Wülfrath wrote a letter asking us to send him a talented undergraduate who might re-design Wülfrath's city park as his or her thesis project. The Wülfrath student who eagerly answered this request found a considerable stock of old trees on land adjacent to the City Hall, namely the park bequeathed to the city earlier, by a wealthy manufacturer. The student noted that the park required some maintenance but he saw no reason to re-design it. He then went to the mayor and asked why he wanted the park altered. The answer was that he, the mayor, had long since considered the park pretty enough, but that individual citizens or civic initiatives were actually increasingly wont to ask why Wülfrath did not have a city park.

This paradoxical situation can be explained only in strollological terms. If nothing about the park itself had changed then the problem had to lie in the way it was approached. The question, therefore, was: What had changed lately in the city of Wülfrath and thereby rendered the large and centrally located beautiful city park invisible? Two factors, long-term and short-term, were found to have had an impact. Wülfrath owes its original wealth to stone quarried on the outskirts of the city; quarries still surrounded the city in the inter-war period. Once the quarries were depleted it was decided to plant trees in them—an action apparently launched by Alwin Seifert in person. These trees have since grown tall and therefore possibly rival the hitherto predominant tree stock in the park. A recent development seems even more important—and will surely come as no surprise. The shopping street leading to the City Hall has been converted into a pedestrian zone. And pedestrian zones being what they are, every square foot not devoted to generating revenue has been planted. This pseudo park extends as far as City Hall then opens onto what one must necessarily now call the "former" city park. — Of the various solutions proposed, we mention here just one ironic one: to reduce the park's surface area by ten meters all along its border and thus increase its distance from its green surroundings and also to enclose it by a picket fence with very few entrances.

One example of a park that endeavors to generate this tension under its own steam, so to speak, is the public park on the so-called island in Saarbrücken (Architect: Peter Latz). The island port facility was once Saarbrücken's economic center, a major trading hub surrounded by storage buildings and port facilities. Here, Minette of Lorraine met Saarland coal and Baron Röchling transported his steel. The park created at this spot was supposed to preserve the remnants of the industrial past for future generations of citizens. The basic elements of the new park were to be the foundation walls, original cobbled streets and spontaneous vegetation on the ruins.

Well, in Saarbrücken, abandoned and derelict factories and the rampant vegetation that subsequently squats them are nothing out of the ordinary. The average on-looker's comment on a park created from these elements is therefore likely to be: "What's new?" The designer must therefore devise a means to raise the ruins and their spontaneous vegetation from the banal to the consciously visible realm. Anyone arriving from the city at the park today notices first and foremost the—patently fake—ruins of a bizarre building. Was this once an aqueduct? The masses of downward flowing water almost suggest it. Or was it an arena, some kind of Colosseum, as its circular form suggests? Or was it an old factory? The bricks and the shape of the windows seem to say it was. But, above all, it is a fake ruin: the bricks are new and excessively glazed and the ironwork is painted a poisonous blue-green. The site culminates in a pond from whose bed masonry rises like some sunken city, a water-drenched Pompeii: but patently, this too is fake. And the counterfeiter has spared no pains to highlight that his archaeological ground plan is fake. What are all these historical fakes supposed to mean? — They serve namely to make the now completely redundant ruins in the former port facility appear suddenly "real."

The same aesthetic scam is used for the spontaneous vegetation. Southern dry vegetation with its colorful blossoms on crumbling walls, mosses on former traffic routes and alder sprouting forth from cracks—all of this is ubiquitous in the Saar's formerly industrial regions, in its disused glass factories and ceramic factories, its collieries and mines, and the gigantic casting and rolling mills at Völklingen. So, how may the viewer's gaze be directed to the beauty and significance of this spontaneous vegetation? — The answer is: by interspersing it namely with well-tended "gardened" sections. In the center of the park, the walker passes through a designed area, essentially comprising the usual brick rotunda and iron profiles in blue-green, laid out as a formal garden with low trimmed box-hedges, colorful flowerbeds and flowering shrubs. However, it suddenly seems as if the horticultural care has ceased, for spontaneous vegetation now begins. It too is cared for, of course, for it represents an interrupted transition state; yet its juxtaposition with the formal garden lends it greater authenticity, makes it worth looking at, enjoyable. We are now no longer someplace on the outer edges of the industrial zone, where no one but young people (who feel unobserved there) wants to hang out. We are actually in a suspenseful urban park.

Art on the cityscape

Once one is clear about why the urban park is in crisis and where the solution may lie—namely in the creative production of meaning and suspense in the garden context—then the much discussed issues loosely grouped under the heading "art on the cityscape" may perhaps be easier to understand. Our cities are filled with works of art more numerous than ever. Most of them have fallen completely below the public's radar. From time to time, art critics make well-intentioned or ironic proposals, such as to gather together these works of art and exhibit them elsewhere or in new combinations, or perhaps to put them temporarily in storage. Nevertheless, numerous artists continue to be commissioned annually to beautify various venues and sites.

Artworks in public space do not always fall into oblivion. On the contrary, some even cause a sensation. One spectacular example was the trial regarding a massive curved steel plate sculpture installed by Serra in New York on a public square the users of which, banking and insurance clerks in the main, sued for its removal—and won. One nostalgically compares such events with the social consensus and general applause that allegedly accounted for and accompanied the erection of the Bismarck monument in Hamburg, the Goethe/Schiller monument in Weimar and the Tell monument in Altdorf. It remains to be seen whether those supportive majorities really did exist or whether, in fact, potent minorities simply so successfully articulated and archived their own applause that we now believe it to have been universal. What is clear is that today's society is different; the cultural hierarchy is no longer pyramid-shaped with an elite at the top and, beneath that, a broad middle class seeking eagerly to ape it and, eventually, much further down but basically pursuing the same line, the "masses." Our cultural elites today are minorities themselves; they are subcultures within their own culture. They see themselves as avant-garde and no one stops them doing so, unless, that is, their statements and trend-setting manifestations clash with signs and symbols of importance to other social groups and classes. This is precisely why the museum—in its broadest sense of a public collection and exhibition of modern and contemporary art—plays such an important role today, because it is only in such contexts, i.e. in a public show of experimental art, that the code is fixed. Anyone who has paid admission to an art venue is no longer in any doubt about the fact that the objects on display there are art; and nor will he complain that it is demanded of him there to decipher the layers of meaning investing such objects. Even the usual jokes, for example, about whether a thing is art or simply the sprinkler system, are not funny in this venue; and neither are the reverse jokes that read fire extinguishers and scrap heaps as art—such jokes are fun only on the cityscape.

The nostalgic dream of a nineteenth-century consensus on art in public space, on Goethe/Schiller, Tell & Co. leads us to erroneously assume that even today's art in public space would find acceptance if only it were created in harmony with its surroundings. That is why the cry regularly goes up, for the artist or artists in question to be involved "in good time" in the re-design of this or that square. Yet it is precisely, those artworks in harmony with their environment that fall most quickly into oblivion, owing to the banality we described above. If, in consequence, we demand that an artwork should not be in harmony, but in a state of tension with its environment, we are not talking about the kind of tension that drove the local residents or those named as plaintiffs in the Serra trial up the wall. We believe, rather, that a public square and the artwork in it must relate to each other in a way such as to engender a certain tension that might equally be called suspense: the same tension or suspense we demanded earlier of the urban park. This tension or suspense can be generated, however, only when the artist is able to see and get to know the location in advance. Only then can his work, above and beyond its inherent meaning, prompt an additional interpretation or, possibly, a critical misinterpretation of the square and thus generate meaning without necessarily causing offense. One artist who works in this way is Norbert Radermacher and we can name as one example of his work his use of a bicycle stand to adorn a public square, a stand to which are attached not only the bicycles left there temporarily by the public but also a horse, the statue of a horse. A more critical work of his was to install at a vacant lot—a lot long since vacant—a sign showing the outline of the Hagia Sofia. Or, finally, the two lifebuoys that Radermacher hung in Ludwigshafen on a highway ramp leading to the bridge over the Rhine, although one could see nothing there initially but concrete walls.

The city outskirts

Our strollological critique of the cityscape is premised among other things on the fact that an earlier prerequisite of perception—the moment of transition from the city to the countryside, or its symbol, the city rampart—no longer exists. This transition has ceded now to our current state, which is the endless metropolis. — This is true on a large scale but not in the narrower sense. Something like a border does still exist around a city but it conveys in its present form a different experience than it used to. We discussed this too, during our strollological seminars. One walk led to the Riedwiese [meadow] on the western outskirts of Kassel, where we symbolically marked the border of the city by spanning a red band along the edge of the built-up area. Of course, our endeavor failed; and its educational impact lay in its very infeasibility. And of course our band was much too short to mark the jagged line traced by the last protruding row of large bungalows and their gardens, then across the (for good reason not built upon) Riedwiese itself and, finally, to the vacant—and now rare—lots still hopefully awaiting a buyer. The four-fold image of the "countryside" beyond this property development was likewise dramatic: the spontaneous vegetation on those investment lots awaiting a client; the vegetation on the Riedwiese, a protected nature reserve; the "thistle-phase" succession on arable land left to lie fallow; and, finally, the artificial, ennobled fallow land of the historic Wilhelmshöhe Park in Kassel. Somewhere there are horses grazing; a tennis club is provocatively situated at a most unsuitable spot; and most areas have been given over to the dog owners who stroll daily through this new wasteland.

The walk to the city outskirts is also a means to critique the sudden revival of Great Green Concepts. Whenever little can be done in the field of urban development, people begin talking again about green corridors and a green belt around the city. The desired objective is the walker who strides purposefully from his apartment to the next green corridor, wanders then along a radial axis to the city outskirts and finally—although this is so ridiculous one is ashamed to write it down—walks or cycles to the green belt around the city. — The practice of strollology makes clear, however, that such plans should stay on the drawing board and never be realized. For one, because to pass gradually through increasingly dense stretches of greenery to reach the outskirts and then to walk in circles in a green belt does not correlate the sequence that a walk conceived for suspense must necessarily include. It is precisely this careful dosage that renders greenery invisible to the stroller. It does not do the walk any harm, mind you, but the walk certainly becomes more impressive when it leads through contrasting neighborhoods: through narrow streets, between public buildings, residential districts and then, finally, through the countryside.

If ever the green of the outskirts were reconfigured as a landscaped green belt—which is highly unlikely—it would cease to be impressive. We recommend, by way of contrast, "Greenery Born of Poor Planning." Any area earmarked for integration in a development (i.e. construction) zone, from which agriculture has been driven out yet where buyers have not yet arrived, attains its diversity owing to poor planning and misguided speculation. It is to these phenomena that we owe areas overgrown with goldenrod and blackberry bushes. If they were in the care of the city gardeners, there would be only grass, paving stones and barbeques. Hence, poor planning is ecological insofar as it contributes to the conservation of species diversity. Just as little green plants in the jungle wander from place to place and are able to spread wherever a storm or lightning has felled a few trees and created a clearing, so too the plants on our city outskirts spread across land awaiting development, from one vacant lot to another. The higher rival speculators drive land prices, the longer it takes an owner to begin to build. So on various lots we find evidence of different conditions of ownership: we can read these off from the flat rosettes of newly sown thistles that will grow tall and bloom within a year and under whose protective shield blackberries will eventually prosper and, finally, shrubs and even trees. What could be nicer and more interesting to see than such constantly evolving vegetation?

The aim of the walks, therefore, is to counter urban planners' and landscape architects' stereotypical images with urban dwellers' real images. These images, let us repeat, are impressive only when they are elements of a sequence. Green planning must therefore seek not to maintain the continuity of green corridors and belts, but to consciously break it up. Every residential area should be only a short walk from the city outskirts or from a green space in the city and the latter space (location permitting) should preferably lie close to a river and be not only formally landscaped but also subject to the shifts common to vacant lots and property speculation which ensure variation.

We would like to offer another example of a city that has trouble with its outskirts. That city is Basel. Many spots on its outskirts are border crossings yet it is lucky enough to have within its limits large green open spaces on the banks of the Rhine. In Basel, too, pedants worked on a greenbelt plan and finally proposed to insert green zones as buffers between individual districts. These green zones were meant to assure access to the outskirts. The task allocated these green zones is paradoxical: they are simultaneously intended to separate districts from each other and yet also to be green meeting places for the adjacent neighborhoods, where people can hang out or, alternately, make their way to the green outskirts. Fortunately, land for new development is so scarce in Basel and the city already so densely built-up that these pedantic planning proposals never left the drawing board.

A strollologically-based concept for leading the residents of each district to a central spot that simultaneously offers a typical image of the city's position on the Rhine puts such heady planning back on its feet. A glance at the map of Basel shows that almost all districts, with the exception of the already most advantaged ones, are so situated as to be able to secure and build upon such a view of the Rhine. This would result in a sequence of six images on the left bank and four on the right bank, comprised of "each district's respective view of the Rhine." Depending on their location, these could be landscaped in a more urban or more garden-like style and would ultimately be ideal spots to head to for short walks, trips to the playground or encounters with one's fellow citizens.

Urban criticism

Our seminars, insofar as they address the city, seek to render visible that which is actually and generally available and visible but which urban dwellers apparently now fail to perceive. The urban environment has slowly but steadily deteriorated. Each measure takes something away from the city's residents. Yet such loss is always spoken of proudly as a gift to the people, namely the gift of greater security. The slow but steady incidence of loss on the one hand and the smiling promise of security on the other dulls people's sense of urban deterioration. At the point where I have long since felt a little insecure about crossing the road, a crosswalk suddenly pops up. I am glad about that, of course, for it makes me feel safe. But now I am no longer free to cross a 60-meter stretch of road—that is my loss. Soon, the crosswalk is no longer seen as safe since a motorist turned right there and ran over a pedestrian. I feel insecure again and so the City Council installs intersection lights for my benefit. Once again I feel safer of course, but I now have to wait up to three minutes to cross the road and when I finally reach the tram stop, the tram is long gone—my loss.

All these little deteriorations, which amount in total to a serious loss of quality, seem mundane and uninteresting. In consequence, they cannot be addressed in seminar-style classes for the participants assure each other constantly that they are of the same opinion and thereby bore themselves silly. Our approach—the "action teaching" focus on taking a scientific stroll together—put some life back into the issue. It is to be hoped that the participants will remember their view of such strolls in the future, when installed at some municipal desk or drawing board. Several such actions are described below—but it is only by imitating them that one could ever hope to recapture their spirit of light-hearted fun.

A considerable loss of public space can be put down to parked vehicles. A parked car is permitted to occupy public space that is valued at hundreds or even thousands of Deutschmarks—but why only a car? I could just as well install my closet, kitchen stove or desk in the street. Our seminar group once realized this idea of setting up one's desk in the street on Neue Fahrt, an access road for Kassel's downtown pedestrian zone. The night before the action, we parked tables and chairs for thirty people in a nearby car park. At 8 a.m. we put them out on the street in such a way as to occupy the space the larger sort of delivery truck needs to park and turn around. Then there we sat for two hours, discussing urban transport. As the action was intended to provoke the public, not the authorities, we had sought permission for our action beforehand. As a result, the professor was obliged to wave a red and white-checkered flag for the entire duration of the event. Question: Why are the owners of parked cars not also obliged to do so? There was nothing to see except the public's reaction. This was limited to the motorist's usual spectrum of expressive gestures: a beep of a horn, a shake of the head, a finger pointed at the forehead or a dangerously close drive by. They all had the right to react as they did—and none of them showed an ounce of curiosity.

Probably all my students are also motorists. The view through a windshield is therefore nothing new for them. Another action of ours served to reproduce the view through a windshield but in an alienated form, without the usual protective surrounding of a car. We made portable windscreens from transparent plastic sheets then marched two-by-two along a stretch of slip road (the Frankfurter Strasse on the Weinberg), spread out so as to block the road. There is no sidewalk beside this stretch of road, only a brick wall, and hence no safe place to dodge the traffic. The experience is difficult to describe. The motorist's usual sense of safety evaporated. The danger felt immediate. Not that we had exposed ourselves to any real danger here, since a police car followed our parade. Our acute sense of danger therefore appears all the more remarkable.

Another walk addressed the issue of urban yards. What does one find between two inner-city shopping streets, between Königsstrasse and Neue Fahrt in Kassel, for example, or between Königsstrasse and Karlsstrasse or Obere Gasse? The distance between these streets equals at least the combined depths of two standard buildings plus a yard. — In cities in Southern Europe and even in some older towns in Germany, such yards are lively places used for commercial or business purposes and are also often open to the public. They provide consumers not only with goods and services, but also with passages and shortcuts through the city streets. While preparing this walk, we quickly discovered that such yards are generally full of parked cars and that only one exit is kept open. Valuable urban land thus serves businesspeople as a place to park their car from 8 a.m. until they drive off again at 7 p.m. Some obviously very important service providers have a customized driveway leading from the yard to the first or second floor of the building, so that they can park their cars in front of their dental or legal practice. A system of security grilles separates them on the ramps. What really annoyed us was, firstly, that these parking spaces with their attendant grille-and-ramp constructions occupy the very sorts of space that small and less profitable service providers and manufacturers are sadly lacking in downtown Kassel. Moreover, if smaller businesses and service providers ever occupied such yards and the through traffic accordingly increased, both tenants and the public would keep an eye on the place: locking all the grilles would therefore become superfluous. At certain locations, a single door blocks a crucial right of way. If anyone wants to see a prime example of this, there is one next to a shop on Friedrichsplatz that leads—or would, if it were open—to the yard between Königsstrasse and Karlsstrasse. On that door and others like it, we stuck our preprinted stickers announcing that, "The mouse demands a right of way."

Other walks addressed issues of noise and nighttime lighting. We used decibel meters at the noisiest spots in town to register the noise of motor vehicles, trams, industrial noise and irregular, socially generated noise or music. The type of noise is at least as critical as the volume. Noise may convey varying degrees of information and we were able to establish that it is not least the content of such information that people experience as a disturbance. Evidently, noise that is relatively loud but conveys little information (constant traffic on a nearby highway, for example) is easy to bear while other types (such as the music student practicing next door) "get on people's nerves." The extent to which high decibel levels produce real damage naturally cannot be established on a walk.

Saving light is no priority in cities nowadays. Yet the walker's experience is that large amounts of light are deployed often to useless ends. His sense of insecurity at night is not diminished by making ugly facades as bright as day. It would be more effective to turn the spotlight on the actual street itself. Moreover, street lighting is relative. If it and other private sources of urban light have to compete and their race to outshine each other reaches absurd proportions, the effect of all the lighting is lost. Our nocturnal walk and conversations showed that the discussion of pedestrian safety by night should not be handled reductively as a problem of lighting alone.

Significant places

Talk on our walks always turned to whether Kassel lost its "significant places" during the bombardments of 1943. By significant places, we didn't mean only important buildings but simply any place held in collective memory as the site of a major historical event or one at which matters of great public interest unfold. We discussed the significant places that Hoffmann-Axthelm proposed to the city, which would in essence replace vanished historical buildings and hence have a direct impact on the viewer, without further mediation or possible readings, owing alone to the fact that they stand in his way. A controversial point was always whether reference to an actual site serves to convey a sense of history or, in other words, whether it matters at all that Kassel's City Hall is located below the tram tracks on Old Market Square or that a corner tower of the former fortress stood right in the middle of Steinweg.

The other extreme of meaningful urban planning is still Sir Patrick Geddes' "Dunfermline" model. Geddes' model is closer to our approach, for one, because it is concerned not with history but with stories, not with places but with transitions. Sir Patrick made Dunfermline important by investing certain paths, especially those taken by schoolchildren, with sequences of meanings: they passed, for example, from a place of craft to one of industry then to a trading point and then to the City Hall. Another led from the residential area to gardens and from there to the market and to the women's places of employment at the time. The model Dunfermline definitely deserves much closer examination.

Bearing in mind the formula "meaningful places are stories," we dreamt up with the students various scenarios that could have taken place on the streets of Kassel. We then reenacted them near their likely locations. Such scenes were: the Landgrave of Kassel invites the astronomer Jobst Bürgi to calculate the necessary depth of the city's new fortifications from a ballistic point of view. However, the population is more interested in the astrologer Bürgi and asks him to draw up horoscopes. Our group therefore meets at the central square, Am Stern, where we begin to predict each other's futures.

As everyone knows, the Brothers Grimm once sent to Niederzwehren for Ms. Viehmann so she could tell them old tales. However, once in the Brothers' study, Ms. Viehmann was as dumb as a fish and she later explained that she had no wish to tell children's tales to such distinguished gentlemen.

We acted out this scene at the Gatekeeper's House on Grimmplatz, whereby the joke, this time around, was supposed to be that Ms. Viehmann would not be able to make it there owing to delays in public transport. But when we (the seminar group) arrived at the Square and saw there was no traffic at all on Wilhelmshöher Allee and also that Ms. Viehmann was peacefully ambling down the street with the heavy tread of an aging farmer's wife and far away from the pedestrian zone, we really had a good laugh. On Theatre Square above the Karlsaue we played a scene from recent German history: the residents of Kassel watching Willy Brandt and Willi Stoph arriving each in a separate helicopter for a meeting on the Karlswiese. We had to add our own soundtrack, however, to our staging of the helicopters. The purpose of these actions was to remind ourselves, that even a bombed out and hence somewhat ahistorical reconstructed city is full of history in the form of stories. Undoubtedly, the site of a scene plays a role, but much more important is to revive stories and bring them back into public consciousness. In doing so, solutions must be sought that bring the past back to life by narrative means, not by pursuing Hoffmann-Axthelm's formula for the reconstruction of mere cubes, nor by installing the now so popular plaques. But there is no recipe for how this might be done in general, since each individual case has its own peculiarities.

What Do Explorers Discover? (1987)

What do explorers discover? — This question came up in a seminar after students and I had been reading texts about landscape in which poets and travel writers describe places they have visited—but what did they see there? And do their texts convey to the reader what was special about a place or only those things that are already part and parcel of the literary genre "landscape description:" charming wetlands, rugged gorges and distant mountain ranges?

And if indeed landscape is shaped in advance this way by images from literature, then what do explorers see? What does Linné report on from Greenland, Bougainville and La Perouse, or Humboldt from America and the South Seas? Some such sea voyagers must have sensed their own failings and had painters and writers join them on board. And yet neither the little paintings by Hodges nor the texts of Adalbert von Chamisso convey anything really new about the New World, or not in such a way as to inspire us to sail away to those islands. — But something new may be found perhaps also at home, the Kassel students said to themselves, and they decided to investigate some texts about Tahiti—those written by Georg Forster, who once accompanied Captain Cook on a voyage there—at a site in Kassel. Could it be that Forster's descriptions of a paradisiacal island apply equally to a former Federal Army tank-drivers' training ground?

One sees that which one has learned to see

The perception of landscape has to be learned. This is as true in any historical epoch as it is for any individual. Our cultural circles have become skilled in the perception of landscape because Roman poets, late-Renaissance painters and English landscape gardeners knew how to depict the landscape. The landscape is therefore a component of our collective consciousness, our cultural legacy.

When Armstrong landed on the moon, he radioed to earth, to share his first impressions. What did he see on the moon? — A landscape, of course! And indeed, one he needn't have flown to the moon to see, for he could have seen similar sights on the Steingletscher [glacier], on Mount Furka or in the canyons of Colorado. What did Georg Forster see on Tahiti? — He saw that which he expected to see: a charming landscape. And one so charming indeed that any reader of his since the eighteenth century has always known exactly how things look on Tahiti. When Jean Paul wants to describe the Isola Bella in the Lago Maggiore, to what does he compare it? — To Tahiti, of course!

Are there any new paradises in existence?

Captain Cook and Georg Forster did not sail around the world to see landscapes. Rather, they hoped to discover nature. Their first triumph was scientific, namely the discovery of new species of bird, fish and plant. All these were given a Latin name in the traditional manner. Natural science is one possible alienated means of appropriating nature. The other is art, which in its eighteenth-century manifestation meant the art of gardening. The true, unintentional yet much greater triumph of the explorers' research trip was, therefore, the fact that they brought new landscapes to Europe. Except that these new landscapes were the old ones … For no one ever sees anything he has not already learned to perceive and to describe as landscape.

Which is beautiful—the natural or the cultivated landscape? The question remains unanswered to this day. Which is the more attractive—a deserted alpine valley with whistling marmots and, in the distance, a herd of chamois; or a bench beneath the lime tree on a farm, from where one commands a fine view of the yard, stables, fields and orchards? The most beautiful thing of all would be if human beings were a part of nature. On Tahiti the "good savage" awaits us.

The sensible society

The "good savage" must still exist today. We haven't ever met one ourselves but friends of ours spent their vacation at his place: for a small sum, he rented them a little house, sold them some jugs and woven stuff that had long since been in his family, and even had Coca Cola on offer at almost cost price. Georg Forster would loved to have told his landgrave how sensibly and harmoniously a folk might live, with a hierarchy between rich and poor, for sure, yet no sign of pomp, war, crime or punishment. Yet there, among all the good savages, he ran into the fat savage: a nobleman who moved no body part except for his jaw, and this only when beautiful girls put yet another tidbit into his mouth. Well, what a spanner in the works of the so urgently needed enlightenment in Hessen he was.

Death was in Arcadia

Tahiti is paradise, for sure. Yet some work must be done there too. Even if the name "breadfruit tree" sounds like something from Dreamland, we learn that it must nonetheless be planted and cared for like any tree. Some cultivate it; others eat the fruits of their labor. Nor is paradise totally perfect. There is a remarkable lack of certain things: of nails, for example. Ultimately this proves fortunate for visitors: for if paradise were perfect, one could do no trade there. Only the need for nails can satisfy our hunger for breadfruit. Wherever there is labor, there is the division of labor; wherever there is the division of labor, there is domination; wherever there is domination, there is war. As peaceful as Tahiti claims to be, it too has a political past. The former king is alive no longer. In the wake of war, conquest and rebellion, a new king is on the throne. "I too was in Arcadia:" the goatherds come upon a sarcophagus or is it, as Ian Hamilton Finlay claims, actually a German tank? Are there former battlefields in paradise? Is Arcadia a deserted military training ground?

Tahiti is a deserted military training ground. Only in those places where human beings have destroyed nature does a really beautiful landscape come into being. Only in those places where a forest has been felled do flowers grow. Only in those places where tanks have left their furrowed tracks does a biotope develop. Paradise was not peaceful because the lion slept with the lamb—which is in any case an improbable scenario—but because it was in reality a battlefield.

Disruptions and end states.

Nature today is no longer in the countryside, for farmers there have long since destroyed it. Nature today is in the city or at least on the city margins: on gravel pits, construction sites, abandoned industrial plants, disused quarries and slag heaps, between railway sidings, along walls, or in the hands of the Federal Army. Conservationists today can no longer cordon off certain areas and wait for the right type of flora to establish itself. Rather, they must ensure that the traditional types of disruption continue to occur: that peat is cut from time to time, and stone quarried, and gravel extracted; and that a tank thunders occasionally through the Dönche. Otherwise, all of a sudden, there will be no landscape at all.

Mountaineering on Sylt.
In Conversation with Nikolaus Wyss (1989)

Nikolaus Wyss: Which issues are of concern to a strollologist, a scientist of walking?
Lucius Burckhardt: The discipline strollology could just as well go under the name "aesthetics of landscape." For no strollologist is concerned with the ideal form of a hiking boot or the optimal composition of a hiker's packed lunch. We inquire, rather, why landscape is beautiful and in what its beauty consists.

And how do you come up with answers to such questions?
We reconstruct an ideal walk for example—a model walk, so to speak. The classic walk would go something like this: the urban dweller senses that spring is on the way and steps through the gates of the city to go and roam about the countryside. The aesthetic problem here is that he sees a variety of things on his walk. He crosses a valley, fords a stream, sees a farm, climbs a hill to enjoy the view and then wanders through a forest before finally making his way back into town. Namely, he makes a round trip and notices a highly diverse range of objects. Once home he manages to sum up the impressions garnered on his walk. He explains how very lovely it is on the outskirts of Zurich or Bern or wherever; or that the walk from Baden to Mount Lägern is beautiful. And if you persist in asking this walker what he has seen you realize he's roamed through six or seven very different places, all of which exist in their own right, independently of each other. And yet the walker nonetheless feels he may characterize all of them as a single environment. In his imagination, all his individual perceptions merge into one. He manages to integrate them in a single image in his mind's eye. And this is the essential

issue in strollology: How is it possible to characterize a landscape when the landscape thus characterized is nowhere to be found? That which the walker talks about once home—the Basel area or Mount Lägern—is ultimately a chimera, something conjured in the course of a stroll that then takes concrete shape in his mind's eye.

You speak of an ideal type of urban dweller who throws open the city gates and delves into the countryside—a romantic image!
The landscape we are discussing here could not exist without the city. For no one but an urban dweller ever sees the city outskirts as a landscape.

So how do things look to country folk out for a stroll?
A farmer goes to see whether his neighbor will harvest more cabbage than he will or whether his cherries are ripe or whether so-and-so has already spread dung. His perception of the landscape is another thing altogether. He speaks primarily about its use, exploitation and yield—in marked contrast to the urban dweller, for he regards the landscape neither with a vested interest nor with a quick eye for soil quality or the most suitable site for seed potatoes. The urban dweller perceives the landscape quasi in aesthetic terms. He likes the way the trail winds around the hill and it never strikes him that this same trail might be a hindrance to rationalized agriculture.

The concept of landscape can be seen thus to be rooted historically in the city. Odes to the landscape, whether Greek or Roman, are always of urban origin. Vergil, for example, discovered landscape as a subject at the very moment when urban dwellers were able to cease grubbing around in the soil and leave grain production for the city of Rome to armies of slaves in Sicily. The Romans went so far as to not even look at the landscape—and hence all the more intense and wistful their experience of it in poems or paintings. Indeed, Roman villas were always built at the most beautiful vantage points yet without windows in their exterior walls. Murals on such villas' interior walls delighted residents, however, with their depictions of landscapes and flute-playing goatherds by a pond. The sight of slaves beyond the door, toiling at their labor and drenched in sweat, would have detracted from cultivated Romans' pleasure in the landscape. The man who works the land is part and parcel of the urban dweller's image of the landscape, certainly, but exists nonetheless at a remove from him, in a different world completely. The goatherd and the peasant in this image are staffage, mere props. The most intelligent thing ever to have been written about the stroll can be found in Schiller's poem on the subject. The city dweller sees a peasant and says: "O happy People of the Fields, not yet Waken'd to freedom." Schiller's urban dweller implies that peasants are a part of these climes, a part of this rural fabric, and may count themselves lucky, to be able to work there, because theirs is a natural condition; whereas we urban dwellers are not so lucky, because we have woken to freedom, which is a great burden. We must entertain complex thoughts and can no longer participate actively in the landscape, because we have gained consciousness, an awareness of freedom, and are therefore able to enjoy landscape only in aesthetic terms.

A dangerous poem.
This poem is the most revolutionary one of all for the science of strollology, because it shows the wholly paradoxical nature of a society divided into urban and rural realms. In Schiller's day, an urban minority ruled a rural majority and so could dictate the aesthetic canon, dictate what beauty supposedly was. And, at the same time, it felt guilty and responsible for what was happening out there in the fields. Today, however, urban dwellers comprise the majority and can therefore rest assured that their opinions on the landscape are majority opinion. This is very evident in ecological debates. Today, it is we urban dwellers who accuse farmers of not farming in a good and

ecological manner yet we ourselves put them in this predicament, since we want nice fresh fruit from the countryside at reasonable prices. We urban dwellers lay down terms and conditions that make rationalized agriculture necessary yet when we take a walk in the countryside we complain that farmers are ruining the landscape. And it was we urban dwellers' conflicting interests that Schiller acknowledged in his poem.

Things are a little different today, given that even farmers take a walk in the urban sense of the term.

We are faced with a new situation now, for the city and the countryside are no longer polar opposites. Today we find endless nuances of one thing only: the metropolis. We have to cope with a city that never ends, a city without limits. Everything belongs to the city, everything takes place in the city and the city is gobbling up the countryside. Likewise in sociological terms: a distinction between the city and the countryside is no longer feasible. The forester lives in the city and drives each morning to the forest and each afternoon to his office in the city. Farmers in Holland often live in the city and drive each morning to a field, to plant tulip bulbs there, whereas bank employees these days, as we know, naturally live in the countryside.

Earlier, you said the beauty of the landscape was simply an image in the mind's eye of the urban dweller. What will happen to our perceptions of landscape now that there are neither irrefutably urban types nor purely natural folk in our metropolis?

As a strollologist I am deeply concerned with this question, and it is one we have already addressed by making a practical experiment, namely the aforementioned model walk.

We were invited to organize a walk as part of the Milan Triennale last fall, the theme of which was "Oltre la città la Metropoli." The location we chose was a typical metropolitan district, where eighteenth-century aristocrats built their summer residences in what was then a rural setting dotted with agricultural laborers' settlements. All of this still exists alongside the more recently built chemical factories, gas works and industrial settlements which have likewise become outdated and been abandoned in turn. Some factories are at risk of collapse; others have already been demolished for safety's sake. Land speculation is rife and it is hoped things there will take a more urban turn but it is still too early to say. For now, it's a biologists' and ecologists' paradise, with spontaneous vegetation rampant along the railroad tracks and freeway embankments. Plants flourish there likewise on waste dumps rich in compost and in the many illegal allotment gardens around which makeshift fences have been built from all kinds of material. In certain neighborhoods the city administration is enhancing the environment by creating parks. Gypsies have settled there with their mounts. Bovisa is the name of this area, where tens of thousands live. "Better" Milanese frown at the mention of the neighborhood's name and no one would ever think of taking a walk there of their own volition.

Our walk relied in essence on a distancing effect. We assumed that the benefits of discovering and observing the neighborhood could be seen only through a stranger's eyes, so to speak, and therefore chose for our purposes an eighteenth-century explorer, Captain Cook, and his diarist, Georg Forster. We—that is, myself and a group of students from Milan and Kassel—selected twelve stations, such as the railroad station, an industrial site, a nice little garden, the gypsy settlement and a small castle, at each of which an actor read aloud a page from George Forster's diary of the exploration of Tahiti. We chose diary excerpts that matched at least in part the spots where they were read. And the fact that they were halfway appropriate and halfway inappropriate served both to create distance and to generate new knowledge.

How far do you really do justice to such surroundings when you treat them with irony? Do you not somehow project something at the expense of this landscape?

It is quite patently a projection. However, the distanced perspective allows us to gain a better understanding of how illogically we look at cities. Take spontaneous vegetation, for example: on railroad embankments and waste dumps one finds the same African plants that florists sell for lots of money in city stores, plants that are regarded as weeds in Bovisa. The city nursery receives orders to get rid of them and sow grass instead. And if we walkers now visit such a place and hear how Captain Cook and Georg Forster discovered tropical plants that are now on sale in our local florist's store then it opens our eyes and certain things fall into place; and in that respect we add something to the neighborhood and render visible that which, although present, had hitherto been overlooked.

It's a long road, historically speaking, from the desire to take a walk beyond the city gates to the desire to take a walk in the metropolis.

The history of the walk also provides an answer to the question of what people experience as beautiful in their respective epoch. Goatherds playing their flute by water seem conventional to us—no poet would sing an ode to landscape that way now. It was obvious by the late eighteenth century that the "charming place" would cede to the sublime. Formidable and awe-inspiring things such as steep cliffs and waterfalls then gained in appeal. Artists had crossed the Gotthard for centuries and yet the mountains left them cold; their eyes were set instead on marvelous Italy. But all of a sudden, the lofty mountain range and its peculiar aesthetic qualities held great appeal for them. The history of the walk clearly shows that people have not always been looking for the same thing. Transportation plays a role too. Changes in modes of transport wrought changes in people's perceptions of landscape.

The first major shift was the railroad introduced in 1840. It allowed one to travel a certain distance at speed. Because a train stops only at stations, the path to a place became increasingly unimportant and destinations increasingly important for the walker, who had meanwhile been reduced to a tourist. Famous and legendary hotels awaited him at the target destination: the Rigi-Gipfel, the Giessbach, the Furka and the Belvedere Rhone Glacier were all hotels sought out by the tourist who, if at all possible, booked a room with a view of the local "must-see" sight. His vacation experience rested on the fact that the view and the postcard of it were identical. He was able to throw back the curtains each morning in the most expensive room in the hotel and enjoy the very same view he was already familiar with from a postcard or the hotel brochure. Almost all such destination hotels are now run down. Some have already been demolished, others bailed out by nostalgic fans. The sublime is no longer "in" when it comes to vacations; and this, despite the shortage of tourist accommodation and despite the fact that hordes of people still pass by those panoramic spots. The motorists overnight down in the valley, however, and spend only a few minutes in any sublime spot—after all, they manage to pack in two or three of them in a single day.

The advent of the motorcar and popular propaganda for the Topolino and Volkswagen in the 1930s put the route traveled back at the heart of the landscape experience—even before freeways were built. The motorized walk quasi revived the phenomenon of taking a walk. The motorist passes through many places that vary in appearance and, once home, must describe the area he has traveled in a few pithy phrases, as if it were a single entity. But the motorist who takes a walk by car, so to speak, no longer talks about how things look on Mount Lägern or in the Basel area, for he can now report on the far-flung regions of Tuscany, Spain or Burgundy. He can say exactly how Burgundy looks. His capacity to integrate all he has seen in his mind's eye is remarkable yet also overstretched; so he is tempted to relate instead whatever he has read in travel guides, such as the Baedeker or Guide Bleu. But, as we all know, neither Burgundy nor Tuscany are quite like the brochures would have us believe and nowhere will one find the point the motorized walker loosely describes, the one point where it is possible to say: Now, that is Tuscany in a nutshell. Or: That's Burgundy for you. Often, too, the feeling that Burgundy is no longer what it used to be, that the locals who live there have ruined it, overwhelms the home-comer.

And the motorized walker is even more dependent on his personal interpretations than any traveller on foot is, since all his many impressions must be greatly reduced to some "typical" essence, even though this doesn't actually exist.

Tour operators' brochures exploit this to the hilt. I recently read an advertisement for holidays on Cyprus: "Cyprus is like mountaineering on Sylt." Now, what on earth is that supposed to mean? Presumably that there are beaches on Cyprus like those on Sylt as well as mountains either as flat as those on Sylt or that don't exist on Sylt at all, but only on Cyprus. People try to cover everything in one go, to make a package deal of it: a single all-in offer on which all one's dreams and desires can be projected. Someone sees a long sandy beach and runs the headline: "Voilà la France."

Switzerland has no sandy beaches to offer...
Swiss marketing nowadays rarely promotes typical destinations. Walks are being touted again but they no longer revolve around one particular panoramic spot or a typical landscape but appeal instead to people's interest in collecting: the mail truck in the Engadine, for example, carries advertisements for the "Three Countries Trip." Evidently, for people who come from large countries such as the United States, visiting three countries in one day is a sensation. The feat of integrating myriad impressions in this case is very impressive for a

blanket term must be found for all three countries. In Interlaken one can take the "Five Glaciers Trip" or the "Mountain Passes Trip." So one no longer makes a pilgrimage to the Rhone Glacier, which in itself would be interesting enough. Instead, one collects or "does" three or five glaciers all in one go.

But what becomes of a person once he has collected all the glaciers, all the mountain passes and all the hills? Does he not get terribly bored?
I'm pessimistic on the whole both about these excessive demands made on the walker and about the development of the landscape per se. Conservation has picked up speed recently and that also brings change. Unfortunately, protection of the environment follows ill-considered principles that have only a short-term impact.

What is the most common concern of landscape conservationists?
Diversity. A landscape should be diverse, a trip through a landscape should be diverse, a walk should be diverse. Everything should be diverse. Diversity is by far the most common criterion, the reason most often cited for protecting a landscape. That worries me, because implicit in this much acclaimed diversity is the risk of making everything the same. If everything is diverse then everything is the same. Cyprus on Sylt is the diverse landscape, is an example of how diversity irons out difference. Wherever one actively alters landscape, one creates diversity and promotes uniformity.

For example?
In the Federal Republic [of Germany], there are places people feel should be artificially landscaped because brown coal was mined there previously, in open cast mines. People want to reclaim this lunar landscape and, in fact, every new application for permission to mine a site must now include plans for its future re-cultivation, so the licensing authority can be sure how a site will look once the

mining is over. The plans are generally for a "diverse" landscape: a small lake, a holiday village or a hill. And nothing is more boring or uniform than the countless diverse landscapes being produced in this way. What a relief it would be if someone came along and said: "Oh, throw that hill into the lake, level the entire landscape and then let's see whether we shouldn't create a heath for a change!" Best of all, would be to keep this wild lunar landscape as it is. But there are precise regulations specifying how sheer the embankment slopes can be and so, alone for security reasons, the moonscape is being robbed of its sublimity.

To meet the growing demand for diversity, ever more ambitious efforts are put into "staging" a landscape, Disneyland-style. This is the case with the "Alpamare, South Seas Bathers' Paradise" on Lake Zurich.
I see that as the logical conclusion to landscape development. Everything is everywhere, so one need no longer take a trip. The trip comes to you. The landscape event, for example, or the Finnish-Japanese-style spa experience including views of a mural painting of an Alpine landscape fringed with palms. That is how one reduces the walk to point zero.

There are fitness centers there too, so the walker still gets some exercise ... What would you, as a strollologist, do to counter this trend?
I limit my advice to suggesting that we take a break and reflect on the point we are at. Perhaps after that we'd be able to renounce with a smile a great many things we currently believe to be vital. After all, our notions of what makes a beautiful landscape are historically determined and subject to change. In ten years time we'll see beauty in things we now wouldn't give a passing glance to; and the stuff we rave about now will be out of fashion. Bearing that in mind helps relativize our certainty that whatever we are doing is the right thing to do. We have to realize that we're really doing our descendants no

favor when we alter a landscape. For if we alter it, then only because we don't find its present state beautiful; and we thereby create something that is beautiful, in our eyes, but may well register as uncool, kitsch or disgraceful on our descendants' aesthetic scale. They would perhaps really love the lunar landscapes that we are about to fill in.

The logical conclusion would be to do nothing more at all?
One logical conclusion would be to talk things over more, to discuss where the beauty lies in a landscape that we have not yet even recognized as one. Talking about landscapes sure beats using bulldozers to change them. Certain landscapes have blossomed simply because they were painted or because odes to them were sung. Heathland was initially a by-product of peat production and the artists' colony Worpswede was not a destination. There was nothing at all sublime about it until a few artists landed there more or less by chance some eighty or ninety years ago, which in turn prompted a few curious urban dwellers from nearby Bremen to seek it out. Because those artists painted pictures of the peat landscape and Rilke wrote about it, simply because it was talked about and its praises sung, this supposedly ugly by-product of agriculture became a thing of beauty.

Does value accrue to one landscape always at the expense of another?
A society may well increase its overall wealth. We all know from our physics class the zero-sum model. People say the world is neither beautiful nor ugly, that there are beautiful places and ugly places, and that the average is zero. I refute that. I believe that putting work into a place, writing about it or interpreting poetry and painting can enhance its beauty. Even though people now take vacations in Florida, Worpswede remains a part of our rural wealth, just as a view of the Alps from Munich or Lucerne is. Worpswede is in this sense immortal and remains an important chapter both of our art history and of the science of strollology. Taking a walk creates beauty.

A Matter of Looking and Recognizing.
In Conversation with Thomas Fuchs (1993)

Thomas Fuchs: Briefly put, the aim of all science is to acquire knowledge of things as yet unknown. Researchers seek answers to questions. Which questions does strollology raise and which insights may we expect to gain from it?

Lucius Burckhardt: The research topic in strollology, the science of walking, is the aesthetics of space. Here, the basic question is: What is landscape? What is a cityscape? Landscape can be perceived, actually, only in the course of a walk. Let's take as our example an inhabitant of Kassel who sets out on a stroll. He sees the city outskirts, goes across a field or through a village, passes by a stream or a quarry then, at mid point on his walk, he climbs a hill, enjoys the view then finally finds his way back to Kassel by taking a path through a forest. Once home, he says he has been in Habicht Forest or Kaufunger Forest, where things look this way or that. In essence, he describes an image of landscape. However, an image of landscape was nowhere to be seen on his walk. Our man in Kassel saw a stream, a quarry, etc., and combined these details in his mind's eye so as to create an overall picture. Our stroller described the landscape of Habicht Forest yet none of it looks anything like he said it does. That is why the term "landscape" is of such great interest to we strollologists, we scientists of walking: for us, it denotes the integrative power of perception. Our work also consists in correcting certain approaches to preservation of the landscape, those namely which seek at times to preserve the so-called typical landscape. Yet, in our opinion, this typical landscape does not exist. What these well intentioned but overly hasty conservationists present as being worthy of preservation is a construct.

You mean that certain images of landscapes have come to predominate in our mind's eye and accordingly determine how we relate to the landscape as well as how we deal with it?

Yes, and landscape painters of the nineteenth century are a good case in point, for what they conjured on their canvases still influences our notions of landscape today. Only recently I heard a story about Barbizon Forest, which was home to an artists' colony one hundred and fifty years ago. Barbizon Forest is now protected by the type of conservationist who runs around with reproductions of the Barbizon painters' work under his arm and tell visitors: "Here, this is what we need to protect, just as it looks in this painting." And yet, however faithfully such landscape paintings reproduce an original scene, they are unfailingly a product of certain preconceptions. And when landscape conservationists seek to protect landscapes that they personally have preconceived, they run risk of chasing their own tails.

Images of landscape are constructed, however, not only by visual means but also by images we draw on in language, by metaphors.

All perception is tied up with language. We cannot think without drawing on words. One question pursued in my strollology seminars is therefore: What can language convey? Whether we read a description of a landscape in a novel, a magazine, a travel brochure or a textbook, the same questions always arise: To what extent does language convey images? How much can it convey of what we really see? Let's imagine someone reading a travel brochure about a seaside resort in Schleswig-Holstein. The resort's image appeals to the reader so he books a hotel and sets off for a two-week stay there. Has the language of the text conveyed the situation or might it have been equally applicable to a bay in central Italy? In our seminars we experimented with landscapes conjured by language and landscapes that exist in reality. We undertook our "Voyage to Tahiti." The location we chose for this was the Dönche in Kassel, which used to be a military training ground but is now a designated conservation area on the outskirts of which new developments sprang up in the early 1980s, "documenta urbana" among them. We sought out several points on the Dönche then read aloud there texts written by Captain Cook's diarist Georg Forster during an exploration of Tahiti in the eighteenth century. While listening to his descriptions of the lovely scenery in Tahiti, we looked around and found that they were applicable also to the Dönche landscape. Thus the "Voyage to Tahiti" was, on the one hand, a means to experience the interplay of language and walking and, on the other, it allowed us to see that which is otherwise self-evident and familiar to us on the Dönche landscape with an outsider's eyes, thanks to the alienating impact of stepping for the duration of the walk into the role of an historical explorer of exotic climes.

Then one could say the academic walk is a teaching tool for the science of strollology?
It is a matter of looking and recognizing. Any academic walk such as the Tahiti one serves the didactic processing of knowledge. The content doesn't fall out of the blue, of course, but is discussed at great length during seminars. Ideas are often very hazy at the start.

What underpins strollology in an urban context, for example, in the case of a project like your latest one, "ZEBRA crossing"?
The premise for the city walks is that we no longer really see our everyday surroundings. Urban dwellers' quality of life has been whittled away in a process so gradual it was barely perceptible. When the number of cars increased, the street ceased to be an area one might play in. Then zebra crossings[1] were installed and people were happy

---

1 [British term for pedestrian crosswalks marked with white stripes]

to be able at least to cross the street in safety. This [loss of the street as public space] basically constitutes a permanent expropriation but we fail to perceive it as such and may even regard it as beneficial, since we appear to gain something in return. The zebra crossing is safe and secure, they say, but in fact we should be able to cross any road safely, anywhere. And over time, the zebra crossing itself comes to be regarded as too unsafe and is replaced by a set of traffic lights at which one must wait for a signal before crossing. This expropriation always takes place bit by bit, so we cannot easily see and experience the total loss. City walks—such as "ZEBRA crossing," the one we staged in Kassel city center—are intended to convey this specific insight, insight into what we have lost. The subject in this case is the road network. The shopping street network is lost to us now. It has ceded to the pedestrian strip of Obere Königsstrasse, with all the economic repercussions this entails for property values, store rents and the range of available goods.

You often present your actions in fun and witty ways.
Any walk we undertake as part of our seminar is designed to leave a strong impression and to communicate an experience. One example is an action with students co-hosted last year by my colleague Helmut Holzapfel and I. We were annoyed about the way parked cars clutter public space downtown. We therefore placed desks along the roadside, at points where parking is permitted. Two or three desks took up the same amount of space as one car. We sat down at our desks and held our seminar. Of course, we were able to observe lots of honking and cursing about this pointless obstacle blocking the road. People were very upset about the parked desks but made no complaints about the cars alongside them. This shows how perceptions of unremarked social conditions are schooled.

The use of artistic means, the play with associations, means participants in the scientific walks need some experience of seeing the artistic angle, for the viewpoints you deal with are not exactly routine or commonplace. Are not the limits of what you do quickly reached and its beneficial effects therefore limited to the small circle of those very few, who understand the actions? What do you make of the reproach that your walks are an elitist activity comprehensible only to intellectuals?

The walks are indeed experimental in form. The scientific walks are an outcome of the seminars and are oriented to students' interests. Of course we also try to catch the public eye and we inform the press. But that is precisely what leads to occasional misunderstandings. The desk action I just mentioned went over pretty well. In another case, however, we were met with incomprehension. We played at being cars, marched down the road holding windshields in front of our faces. That didn't go down well at all. On the contrary; one journalist told us we were plain crazy. And people didn't see the humor of it. But it was a lesson for us, too, in that respect, to note that our symbolism had not sufficed to put our message across.

So the science of strollology leads us from looking to recognition. It also points out what might be imaginable. The difficult question is always, how do we go from knowledge to action? How can we assess an action's social and political impact?

I do believe that our work is acknowledged to be a valid critical approach—for example, in the landscape conservation context I mentioned earlier. Landscape conservationists seek to protect the typical landscape. This turns everything into something typical. When everything becomes typical, the landscape's diversity and originality are lost. With our critical approach, we were able to point out the risk inherent to this trend towards "typification" in landscape conservation. Our concerns were voiced increasingly in public and professional discussions. Or, let's take perceptions of the city! Our generation lives in part under novel circumstances. We are witnessing the dissolution of borders between the city and the countryside, and this entails a loss of perception. The countryside is now full of modern buildings and the city is comprehensively landscaped. Our scientific walks were an attempt to re-experience the contrast between the city and the countryside and to highlight the fact that this contrast has now largely been lost. The consequence for design, for urban planning is that we must now look for new contrasts, new sources of suspense. And we designers and planners must consciously create such suspense. Anyone who designs a park today must incorporate the user's experience of the shift in context, the shift from the city to the park. In the past, people really did leave the city to visit a park. In eighteenth-century Paris, one still walked through narrow stone streets to reach the Tuileries Gardens. Today, one arrives there from the spacious tree-lined sidewalks of the Champs-Elysées. Moreover, on entering the Tuileries Gardens one finds just as much asphalt and just as much green as on the Champs-Elysées. So, if we were to build the Tuileries Gardens today, we would have to create this suspense, this shift symbolically, would have to draw on the art of gardening and landscape planning to conjure an impression of this shift "from the city to the park." This is a wholly new challenge and one to which few landscape gardeners have yet risen.

Strollology—A New Science (1998)

No generation of urban dwellers has ever had as much green space at its disposal as ours does: and no generation of urban dwellers has ever complained as much as ours does about the lack of green space in our cities — How to explain this apparent contrariness? — Well, firstly, by making a clear distinction between the gardens of yore and the urban greenery we have today. And, secondly, by drawing on the tools of a new science I have founded, namely the science of walking, also known as strollology. In conclusion we will ask ourselves, where a revival of the art of gardening and garden design is most likely to start.

Today's urban green spaces originated in what civil engineers call "roadside garnish." From freeway entrance and exit ramps to access roads and major city squares (though the latter are now not so much squares as traffic intersections) through to smaller branch roads and the apologies for vegetation set before, after and in the middle of every traffic circle, there is no end to this "roadside garnish." Its characteristics are: it consists of bushes, preferably thorny ones that make areas unusable, as well as of plants that can withstand large doses of canine feces and be maintained with minimum care after being purchased at great expense from nurseries and growers. The same aesthetic, but with different characteristics, continues also beyond the threshold of numerous buildings: no city hall, no bank, no insurance company, no hospital, no courthouse, no canteen and no police station gets by today without greenery in the form of the small-leaved rubber plant.

In newer neighborhoods we are confronted with a second type of vegetation that is equally monotonous. This is not a part of roadside garnish but of "public parks" or "public recreational zones." From there, it spreads to the green "keep your distance" markers found around or between public buildings or those belonging to private construction companies, collective housing associations or private individuals. They all employ gardeners and the gardeners all went to the same school, all read the same magazines, all receive notice of the same special offers from the same nurseries and growers and all face the same pressures, namely stuff is expensive to buy and must be easy to maintain. The rich flora formerly found in private gardens has been reduced here to a half dozen species.

The lawn predominates, of course, and is dotted with irises, dog roses and peonies. Tree stock is limited to the two species resistant to gas fumes: the black locust and the maple, accompanied, at times, by two "specials"—the gingko and catalpa—which have already become the norm. And, wait, there's one more thing I've noticed lately: the frequent, mostly senseless use of the white cypress.

What makes these plants or green distance markers between buildings so boring is, that they say nothing at all—they are unintelligible. A stroll among private gardens or even past the front gardens of modest terraced houses provides a great deal of information about the residents. This guy allows his plant population to age, that one is obviously a botanical connoisseur who knows what he's buying, this one simply grabbed a few things off the shelves of his local garden center… And here, I observe year after year a botanical rarity evidently cared for meticulously by its owner. I'm thinking now of a rare clematis in a front garden in my neighborhood.

The green distance markers between buildings never betray this kind of fact or conclusion about residents of course. They don't even make it possible for me to tell, whether the City Parks Department or companies hired by the buildings' owners supplied the greenery. Consequently, it is equally impossible—given that architecture lets me down here too—to say whether these buildings are residential accommodation or private offices, medical clinics or perhaps public offices with little visitor traffic. Consequently, such a walk bores me and—here it comes—I end up complaining about the lack of green space. If the same or similar greenery surrounds me wherever I go, wherever I walk, then I am bound to no longer notice it—or even to claim it doesn't exist. Today's urban dwellers should therefore lament not the lack of green space but the lack of effort put into designing green space distinctively.

Let us now turn to the science of walking. A brief introduction: the walk does not lead to a single, spectacular destination and then back again; and what we say from memory about the walk does not describe an individual image but synthesizes a string of impressions. The classic walker leaves the city, passes through the suburbs and an agricultural zone, traverses a forest, crosses a bridge, climbs a hill and then returns to the city after a detour through a deep valley. Once there, he says (depending on where he has been): the Jura is like this, the Vosges, the Vienna Woods, the Wetterau are like that. And what he describes is not a single place that actually exists, a place he has seen, but rather a synthesis of sequences of hill, valley, forest and agriculture. The walk is thus a chain, a string of pearls made up of more expressive and then less expressive passages that are ultimately synthesized in the mind's eye. Similarly, the walk in a city: one's memory—"Paris was like this"—does not describe the Eiffel Tower but rather a synthesis of the boulevards, squares, side streets and parks one has rushed through. The effectiveness of parks and gardens rests however, not on the fact that we make our way to them expressly, by taxi for example, but on the fact that they suddenly open up before us, beyond the streets and alleyways. In Paris, I walk from the Madeleine across the Place Vendôme, through the Rue Royale, arrive thus at the gate of the Tuileries Gardens—and I breathe out! And now the strollological counterpart: I arrive from the Champs Elysées, walk past the Grand Palais and the Petit Palais, cross the Place de la Concorde and—am not at all impressed by the Tuileries Gardens. The eighteenth-century walk still takes effect; the nineteenth-century one is merely tiring. I know a small German town that, strollologically speaking, had a well-designed shopping area: the shopping street led to Town Hall Square and the Town Hall and behind the Town Hall began the Town Park. In the 1980s, this town, like all small and medium-sized towns, fell for a seductive role model: it created a pedestrianized shopping zone. As a result, residents complained to the mayor that their town did not have a park. It does have one and a rather lovely one at that; but one barely notices it after making one's way through the tree-lined shopping street and the Town Hall's rubber plant collection. What is one to advise the mayor? — The emergency measure we proposed was to fence off the park and put a sentry on the gate.

One place where one can still experience the strollological efficacy of tiny green spaces is Venice. Wherever greenery is scarce, it continues to exert its magic. Arriving from the Rialto Bridge we cut across the historic city center to reach the railroad station, thereby pass the Frari church and the Scuola di San Rocco, remain the whole time within stone streets with severe facades and then arrive, finally, with a sigh of relief, in the Papadopoli Garden. What a sense one has there of the pride of Princess Papadopoli, who used her great wealth to create this gem in Venice! If we arrive from the other direction, however, from the bus station, this garden appears pretty shabby to us: two or three old trees surrounded by bits of ivy trampled underfoot and littered with Coke cans. Without the right approach, the magic evaporates. One of the perversions of urban planning is its insistence on continuous green corridors. For this type of modern planner, the ideal city looks like this: only a few steps away from home, I find myself in a street that belongs to the green corridor system; from there I can walk to the outskirts then all around the city while remaining always beneath fume-proof maple or black locust trees. I therefore will never see the green of the city because I will never even notice its opposite, the stone city. The green corridor system will multiply complaints about the lack of green space.

If I then keep a lookout for where public garden art, which is to say the art of creating beautiful and effective public parks, might find positive role models and inspiration, I manage to identify three approaches: private amateur gardening through to naive gardens of the sort often derided as kitsch; the attempts of artists to use the medium of garden art; and, finally, pseudo-wild gardens that strive to look natural.

In our suburbs we see many gardens distinguished either by formal knowledge or by meaningful, expressive designs incorporating trees, hedges and bodies of water as well as those which evince skill in dealing with the world of plants, namely the use of bloom sequences or leaf combinations that prompt legible associations with "landscapes."

The seemingly primitive allotment gardens "discovered" or rehabilitated by Bernard Lassus mark a first step to revival. "Educated" onlookers when faced with garden gnomes and windmills in small front gardens generally laugh. And it's true, that not all such gnome gardens are masterpieces. And yet at least some of them attest to artistic endeavor that expresses various meanings in a private language, perhaps unintelligible for outsiders. Or, in other words, if the designers of such gardens were to express themselves in a universal language of art instead of in their private language, their gardens would be works of art. As Lassus discovered, many of the encrypted symbols they use are attempts to create space or distance. The windmill in the small front garden should not be regarded as an isolated object for, in combination with the house facade painted in yellow or light blue, it produces—if the viewer tries to see the yellow as a sandy beach and the blue as the blue of the sea—the impression of an endless Nordic plain. And, lo and behold, suddenly one discovers a model ship on the roof ridge—on the "horizon," so to speak.

From there it is only a small leap to my assertion that it is artists who pave the way to a revival of garden art. I say a revival of art, not new art, since the novelty of such art lies in the fact that it draws on the traditions of garden design and fills them once again with meaning. In Switzerland, the Garden Summer staged in Lausanne in 1997—which led to the production of thirty-two small city gardens—was proof that artistic ideas can inspire developments in professional horticultural art.

A long-standing concern of the art of gardening is to represent nature. The recent attempts to depict nature by means of gardening must therefore be considered as art, not as ecology. Ecology is not visible. If the feeling that agriculture is conducted ecologically is a part of our sense of wellbeing then gardens too must appear to be natural. It is a common belief that a flower-filled meadow is more ecological than a green lawn. Yet the flower-filled meadow in the countryside is not natural at all, but a by-product of a specific, perhaps now extinct form of dairy farming. A flower-filled meadow in the city demands just as much care, fertilizer and labor as a green lawn does. However, if we have reached the point today where the green lawn makes us think only of gasoline-powered lawnmowers and fertilizing equipment whereas the flower-filled meadow banishes such associations from our minds then it is indeed most welcome!

The representation of landscape by landscape in the landscape garden is an old artistic technique that began in England in the mid eighteenth century. It comes up against its artistic limits given that nature—if one's medium is nature—can be imitated only on the scale of 1:1. So, ultimately, only princes and kings were in a position to create truly natural gardens. The issue, today, however, is definitely something else again: namely, to represent naturalness on a reduced scale that can fit into our urban systems. And that is the problem: for this can be done only by recourse to representative, i.e. artistic means. Remember the city gardeners' "roadside garnish" mentioned earlier. Their sweepingly destructive hedges are copied from nature, no doubt, yet they are conceivably unnatural or at least appear to be so. It is a mistake to plant the bushes so extensively and thereby fail to consider the strollological aspect. A correctly deployed dog-rose bush may well evoke a sensation of naturalness. On the other hand, we should recall the aforementioned garden gnomes and windmill gardens. They really are a case of artistic means being used to create landscape, even if only for the owner who has opted for a private encryption and decrypted it for himself alone. The chance passer-by smiles and shakes his head: "Garden gnomes." Here, in my opinion, more work on the development of the future city park is required. This park has to begin somewhere, not to sink into the endless road-side garnish and leafy tree stock. The entrance zone is where the code changes: previously we were truly in the city and now we are in the artificial yet also artistically portrayed nature. Previously, we saw things on a scale of 1:1 and now they extend incommensurably. Outside, the arrangements are rational and in here they are arbitrary, but meaningful. — These are very general rules, but I do think that disregarding them has led to the miserable garden design we have witnessed in the recent past and that is likely soon to cede to a new awakening.

On Movement And Vantage Points—The Strollologist's Experience (1999)

Those who addressed you prior to me have spoiled you, no doubt, with their polished lectures. My lecture is a patchwork of loose thoughts, partly on the current state of affairs, partly about how things were back then, in Ulm.[1] For our objective here, after all, is to revive the spirit of Ulm. I can see now, in my mind's eye, the remarkable ruins of the library in Ulm, which was stocked to two thirds with volumes on mechanisms and gear trains and to one third with aesthetic books of the kind we actually longed for.

Well, Ulm is in fact a history of insights into what happens when one seeks to use rational methods—by which one does not progress from one certainty to another but, rather, from a certainty to a growing sense of doubt. In my opinion, Ulm epitomizes this approach. Ulm has various tendencies and orientations, of course, and also much to its credit. I'll tell you straight off, where I stand. I follow somehow in the steps of Horst Rittel, a mathematician who came to Ulm then spent some time at the University of Stuttgart then disappeared off to Berkeley before finally, regrettably, dying of cancer in Germany.

A position which attempted namely to make a science of decision-making in design, and actually always progressed, not from one certainty to another but, rather, from doubt to doubt—design here in the sense of an attempt to remedy a problem by recourse to inventiveness or organization. And then, there are those difficulties inherent to human thought—and in particular to human thought in

---

1   [LB is referring to the Hochschule für Gestaltung, Ulm (Ulm University of Applied Arts)]

a collective context, which is to say, in a team. And design teams are the issue here, for the designer works with other people. The point, therefore, is to reflect as a team on the methodological approach and so-called solutions.

The first thing is: it is very difficult to define problems. One never knows exactly, what problems are. Parameters must be set before one can remedy them. Yet they are essentially without limits and merge with further problems. Problems have blurred contours. And the design process gives them hard, i.e. non-blurred edges.

I have cited an example. The fact that elderly people can no longer live with their offspring is a problem. A parameter is therefore set, namely to place old homeless folk in an old folks' home. This serves in some way to limit the problem. Problems cannot be remedied. They are wicked—to cite a mathematical term Rittel very frequently used. One cannot remedy them. One can only limit them. And the more one seeks to limit them, the more fatal the solution. There are small solutions and small improvements and then one tries out the total solution, which is like cracking a nut with a sledgehammer.

I have cited an example. To avoid mosquito bites, one can span a net in front of the window or one can drain all the lakes in the vicinity: the major or the minor solution. The remedy for a problem depends on constraints, on certain conditions—and mostly on the cost factor: a thing may only cost this or that much. Therein lies the discrepancy between the objective and the problem.

An example: a route to a school involves crossing a major road. Various solutions are possible: an underpass, an overpass, intersection lights or whatever. And there is a constraint, since the remedy for the problem may not cost more than one hundred thousand Deutschmarks. So the discrepancy here is: a child could be run over—and: the budget may not exceed one hundred thousand Deutschmarks.

Then the interventions: the allocation of pros and cons. Interventions do not solve the problem; they simply allocate pros and cons differently. So, the driver must step on the brake and the school-kids can cross. Someone benefits and someone loses out. Most design solutions are a matter of assuring certain population groups either advantages or disadvantages. I am not talking here about a design for porcelain cups but about the sum of decisions taken to remedy a problem.

One piece of wisdom that can be traced back to the pre-war national economist, Gunnar Myrdal is: it is never a case of objectives and means. Objectives and means are one and the same thing. Or vice versa. And to say, "That is my objective and this is simply my means" is to spout ideology.

Take the prohibition of cannabis, for example, and its enforcement by the police. One can say, "All young people are kept under control in order to stamp out cannabis." Or one can say, "Cannabis is stamped out in order to keep young people under control." So the means and the objective are interchangeable. The police say the one thing, of course, and young people think the opposite.

Decisions—precisely because they are so complex—tend towards simplification the minute they are reached in collective contexts (for example, when a planner has to present his proposals to policymakers). And such simplification leads namely to so-called simple solutions. At the local government level—so my theory—everything culminates in construction. Therefore, the problem of old people leads to an old folks' home; the problem of blind people leads to a home for the blind. Thus, attempts are made to remedy problems by erecting a building. This amounts to a reductive phase in the decision-making process, which is inherent not to the matter in hand but to the collective context.

And here, the role of naming the problem comes into play again. Who is empowered to give the problem a name? Problems are so general and they have blurred contours. One never really knows exactly, which one should remedy and which not. One problem, for instance, is that it always rains on Sundays. In this case, however, nobody can prompt a decision-making process—not because that would be impossible, but because no political party or group would ever take it up as a cause. There are problems one can name. In the summertime, young people hang out and sweat. Therefore, we need a swimming pool. That is an identifiable solution. So, now we are back where we began. There are many problems; their contours are blurred; they are intermingled, and to name them isolates them from one another; and then so-called solutions are applied to them.

Applying solutions was also one of the tasks in Ulm. And in the first phase—I'll structure this somewhat here—it was endeavored to introduce a clear conceptual approach in order to deal with problems, all the way through to design solutions. This step-by-step approach was named ZASPAK, which is an acronym of the following German words: Z for objective *(Ziel)*: name the objective; A for analysis *(Analyse)*: analyze the problem; S *(Synthese)*: synthesize one's analysis; P *(Plan)*: formulate a plan; A *(Ausführung)*: move towards implementation; and K *(Kontrolle)*: monitor the result. Sounds totally rational, does it not? So, ZASPAK means, name the objective, analyze the problem, synthesize the analysis, formulate a plan, implement it and then monitor the result.

Then, as we discussed yesterday for example, there are the doubts to which ZASPAK gives rise. We spoke about how a problem might be solved. As a first step I proposed, "Name the objective." Thereupon someone pointed out, quite rightly, "One doesn't know at the start, what the objective is. One knows at the end, why one has done a thing, but to name the objective at the start is possible only when dealing with very simple tasks. In the case of more complex tasks one can only really identify the objective at the end."

This has an impact on analysis. Which is to say: analysis was the latest fad at the time, back when databanks and data compilation first came on the scene. So: to analyze a problem gives rise to far too much data, more than might be used effectively afterwards.

Then comes synthesis. That is a wonderful, mysterious word. How one proceeds from analysis to synthesis was never really explained; one simply set out to synthesize. This means: the wastepaper basket soon fills up.

Synthesis culminates in a plan. The plan is implemented then monitored in the light of the objective. The monitoring phase occurs very late however. By that time, one has pretty much done everything. Even if the monitoring process reveals that this or that was pointless, it is actually too late to be of any use.

I would now like—and this is actually the unstructured part of my lecture—to name several tasks. You will say, "Those are not design tasks, strictly speaking." They are simply the tasks involved in the human decision-making process yet in my opinion, they underpin a theory of design. For they remedy—or "solve"—problems.

I wish to name some of them here; the simple tasks first, then the more complex ones. A simple example is a family, asking, "What shall we do tomorrow afternoon? — It's Sunday." The two suggestions are, firstly, "Let's go to an art museum" and secondly, "Let's visit our sick aunt." One is aesthetic, the other ethical.

Yesterday we were told this is one and the same thing. We are faced with a problem. And this problem—whether to visit our sick aunt or go to an art museum—is not one we will be able to solve, because these activities, these decisions do not co-exist on the same level: for one of them tends towards aesthetics whereas the other is most definitely an ethical decision—so, here, we already have a problem that cannot be solved.

I once carried out an exercise with my students. We wanted to see how much thought the population really gives to alternative solutions. And we made our preparations. We said: our way of measuring time is actually pretty strange. These twelve hours—why not have twenty-four of them and be done with it? And then, when do they change? At midnight: a strange time, when most people are in bed already while others are not. The time could change in the gray light of dawn, for instance, and then once again, in the evening. And instead of twelve hours, it might just as well be ten. That would make more sense. That was the case in fact during the French Revolution but it was later revoked. Some very rare clocks that measure ten hours of a hundred minutes each do exist. In short, we thought this was a simple solution. But we had this problem: if the first ten hours of the day begin in the gray light of dawn, and the ten hours of night begin in the evening, then summer and winter would not be the same, of course. So we said, the hours are not always the same length. By daytime, there are ten hours. One divides the time between dawn and the evening into ten hours. And it will always be announced, how long the hours are. And they are accordingly shorter by night in the summertime, and longer in the wintertime.

We hit the streets, armed with this plan, and we spoke to passers-by. Students went around in pairs, asking, "Do you have a moment? We have a problem. People are up in arms, and no longer satisfied with time. We have come up with a proposal, and we would like to hear your opinion on the matter." Well, we had actually expected to be given a good clip around the ear, or for irate people to respond with "What nonsense!" That was not the case at all however. Instead, very many people took a great deal of time to give the matter some thought. Inevitably we heard the questions, "Well, what do Norwegians do? They suddenly have an incredibly short day and a very long night. So, when they work a six-hour day, do they actually need work only a few minutes? How does that work?" Then someone says, "Yes, they can. But they can also work the night shift and be paid the night rate. Then the hours are terribly long." The strange thing was that many people also offered another solution: our students had to listen to incredible theories on how to improve time-keeping. We see, things are given thought, and the only thing lacking is decision-making. We have an outdated, centuries-old system of time. All our watches and everything else run to its rhythm, and so on. We cannot change it now, but we are not really happy with it.

The next planning problem is a very common and trite one: we are planning an intersection. Every city council has to deal with this. Engineers identify the objectives. The objectives are: to reduce the risk of accidents, to increase the speed of traffic, and to keep costs low. The reduction in accident risk is relative. We know every city keeps statistics on accidents and documents them on city maps. This means one can say: this type of intersection has many small accidents while this type of intersection has fewer yet more severe accidents; that type of intersection has actually proved its worth but it was very complicated and expensive to build, and so on. What is not discussed—either by the expert committees or parliament—is the question: How many accidents are we prepared to tolerate? Which could so easily be answered, thanks to the available statistics. Do you want five accidents per year, or eight or ten? And then one might say: Would you prefer lots of little accidents, or…? All that is implicit in these questions. But of course, this is not discussed. The strange thing is that no one says, "We want no more accidents"—but merely acts as if that is what is meant.

The reason this interests me brings me to the next problem now concerning our communities, namely mad cow disease—for the maxim here is: We want to be absolutely free of disease. While, in the case of accidents, one says there are one hundred thousand accidents to eighty million people, one says fifty million cows equals zero mad cow disease, i.e. no mad cow disease. This is obviously a total solution, and leads to correspondingly high costs. Then the European Union proposed that Britain should kill and burn all its cows. Then it was figured out, how many billions that would cost—and no one wanted to pay for it. But the amazing thing in this case is, that people wanted nothing less than a total solution. The distribution was very strange indeed: in England, tens of thousands of cases; in Switzerland, seven hundred such cases, I believe; and no cases at all in France, or so one says—so France says. And the less said about Germany, the better.

Everyone knows that the English have smuggled cows. This means: Ireland was not under sanction, so cattle could be shipped there from England, and likewise from Ireland to Europe. So it was not very difficult to bring English cows to Europe and it is therefore highly unlikely that any country had zero cases.

Well. Then came the news: mad cow disease is the same as Creuzfeldt-Jakob disease and can therefore be passed on to humans. A totally unclear hypothesis led people to hazard a positive claim, namely that Creuzfeldt-Jakob disease had affected only very old people—and later, in two or three cases in England, also young people. People said, "Aha, now that is the result of mad cow disease."

While people tolerate hundreds of thousands of road accidents, in this case they tolerate only a zero solution, which is to say total freedom from disease. Of course, I wouldn't want to catch it either. But it amazes me, how much more protected one is. Already, to catch Creuzfeldt-Jakob disease from a cow is extremely unlikely in Europe, on the continent. One is more likely to be bitten by a crocodile in Rotis!

But it has consequences nonetheless: in the United States now, no one with a UK stamp in his passport may donate blood. One must show one's passport before donating blood and, if one has visited the UK in the previous decade, one cannot donate blood—which amounts to a massive intervention in the face of a monstrous improbability. I'm simply contrasting that and traffic problems.

Yes, now we are doing something really big. We are planning the just war. Two just wars are currently underway. So, we are planning the just war. We have objectives too. The objectives are parallel: to liberate Kuwait, and to liberate Kosovo; and then to bring Saddam Hussein before an international tribunal and to bring Milosević before an international tribunal. Then: do not lose face—do not lose face here. Something must be done here—and something must be done there. And, of course, we also finally get to try out our weapons.

The entire business is subject to severe constraints, to restrictive conditions. You see, the problem has far-reaching repercussions; it cannot be isolated. The Chinese do not want to join in; the Russians do not want to join in. In the first case, it is the Kurds one may not hurt, in the second case, the Montenegrins. It is very difficult to decide what to do. We are all aware of that.

I am not speaking in favor of the war or against the war. I am saying, we are planning the just war and we face enormous difficulties in doing so. Success is not in sight. Both wars are ongoing. One can say: Kuwait has been liberated; Kosovo has not been liberated. As far as the secondary objective, Saddam Hussein / Milosević, is concerned, the result is largely contrary to the original intention. Both men's power has increased exponentially, as a result of these wars.

What lessons can we learn from this resolution, from this design? First, it was not possible to extract the problem itself, with its own inherent system, from the overall system. It was not possible to draw a sharp boundary between the problem we hoped to deal with and the rest of the world. This means: the problem is too tightly interwoven with the rest of the world. Second lesson: there is no room for experiment; there are no maneuvers in war—there is only war. And everything one has already done—one has broken pots; and broken pots cannot be glued back together. There is no turning back. We can say: we have done the right thing. Or: we have done something wrong. But we cannot say: that was just an exercise; we will do it properly next time. A problem such as this exists once only.

Now I want to set another task. And I set this task in memory of the mathematician Horst Rittel, now deceased, who once worked in Ulm, as I said. This is the example he used to set his students as a planning task. He'd say, "We have a city. The city needs a systematic fire department. And, although the city council has decided to build four firehouses, it is up to you to position them throughout the city. Let us now discuss where the firehouses should be located."

The four firehouses are likely to be located within a circle—if the city is a conventional city and more or less describes a circle on a map. They are thus all equidistant from the city center and the city margins. Four firehouses form a square in the city, a regular one. There is a lobby that says: The square must be as close to the center as possible. That is where the major assets are—the Deutsche Bank, the Dresdner Bank. If they burn down, we'll all be broke. Then there is the justice lobby. It says: But the forest ranger still lives ten kilometers beyond the city limits. He too belongs to our city. If his house catches fire, the fire department must reach it as quickly as possible. In other words, the circle of firehouses must be equidistant from the city center and the city margins.

Everyone has an equal right to be extinguished; the fire department arrives in a half-hour or in three-quarters of an hour. Everyone has an equal right—the ranger beyond the city limits and the Deutsche Bank in the city center. Then along come the insurance companies. Of course they wreck this fair solution. They say we are actually better off when a house that has burned for twenty minutes burns down completely. That costs us less than having to repair a ruin. So either put out a fire in ten minutes or forget it—it's pointless. That puts the firehouses pretty close to the center again.

One can therefore propose a few solutions. All of them have something to offer. The argument is always fair on some level or other—the forester hopes the fire is put out, even if it takes three quarters of an hour—and the money argument amounts to saying, we need one district in which a fire can be put out in ten minutes; and, as to the rest, we will drive over simply to sweep up the ashes or spray down the neighboring houses. We have to take decisions, therefore, based on arguments made on different levels. That is the problem.

Now we are doing something major again: we want to save the environment. Everyone surely wants to save the environment. The environment—that is difficult to define. The environment is plants, animals, and everything around us; and all of it is dying. There is the Endangered List and all that. So we want to save it all. There are also people who say, the environment has a history; everything has evolved. So we imagine climbing into a time machine to take a look at environmental history. And now, let us run by Germany in 1648. It is rather swampy—in this area here, for example, we hear toads croaking everywhere, and so on. We meet a farmer and say, "How wonderful for you. There are still real swamps here, and very rare toads, and storks everywhere. You have a wonderful environment." And he replies: "We have a terrible time of it. There are marauding soldiers everywhere; the Thirty Years' War has just ended, and all the soldiers are sitting around in the woods. When a farmer shows up, he is killed. And these marshes—we cannot till them. We can only till the hills, because our plows are suited only to this dry soil. We lead a dog's life." So the intact environment eludes us, here too.

So, we learned something there. And then we get back into our time machine, and step out in the Ruhr District in 1880. We meet a worker, and say, "These are disgusting conditions in which you live here—the soot, the smoke, the metal oxides in the air. You will not live beyond forty. Your lungs will be ruined by then." He says, "What do you have against smoke? I'm looking for work. I always go wherever the chimney is belching the most smoke and ask whether they can use me."

The environment is obviously very subjective—or: it needs a subject. We say we are saving the environment—and it is our environment. For some reason we have now set our minds on the fact that species diversity comprises our environment. Yet when we look into the time machine, we see other people had very different environments. Environment in the sixteenth century meant marshland, persistent marauders, deserters and epidemics. Environment in the nineteenth century meant a population explosion and the search for work. And the sole source of happiness was a smoking chimney. And now we suddenly want, yes, to save the midwife toad and the kingfisher.

I am not disputing our plan to save the environment. I am all for the Greens myself. I simply would like us to be clear about the decision-making system that we use here. Our environment has obvious objectives. And these objectives need a subject. The word environment indeed means something that surrounds man, which is to say, it has a subject. I think it is nonsense or an oddity of science, to imagine one can write environmental history simply by pointing out that it rained a great deal in 1600, and so on and so forth. That is not environmental history; it is climatic history. Environmental history is whether people at that time were afraid of something, and of what they were afraid—for one needs a subject. When we say "Let's save the environment," we are saving something that has a variable subject, and a change of subject implies a change in the material with which we must work.

From our vantage point today, we see competing objectives. Some are in favor of "biodiversity." They want to save certain species. And others say they actually want to save the potentially natural vegetation and biology, fauna and flora. The latter is contradictory, because the potentially natural flora and fauna of a region comprises a fairly limited range of species. Back when primeval Germanic forests stood here, there were relatively few species. You ask, "So how come all the little flowers have survived? There are thousands of species of flowers and insects that feed on the forest." They have survived thanks to disasters. Which is to say, one part of the forest burned after lightning had struck; and another just disappeared, for example after the Danube had sought to follow another route. Huge disasters of a kind we in our Europe can no longer tolerate have occurred in the past. And the flora followed the disasters. This means: little flowers exist only because large trees fell down at some point, and created a gap.

Kingfishers exist only because shifting currents created new river-banks and new clearings suitable for nesting. And so on.

The question is therefore: How can we preserve biodiversity? Probably we are the ones preserving it already, thanks to the disruptions we cause. It is said already, there are more animal and plant species in the cities now, than on agricultural land. And man, the disrupter, is a preserver of species. Yet he plays this role unconsciously, and it is a role we could organize much more effectively. But we need to bear in mind that we are engaged here in an activity that has a variable subject and a variable object—hence, in a difficult task.

Where does all this lead? Yes, our planning methods will be more complex than Ulm's "ZASPAK": name the objective, analyze the problem, synthesize—I think I must have put you off that approach by now.

The ways in which we can do all this must take a more collective form and leave more room for discussion. And they must also include mechanisms that allow decisions to be reached on arguments that engage with a problem on different levels. That means: whether we visit an aunt or an art museum—the ethical and aesthetic solutions must be discussed. And given that some things simply cannot be discussed, our last resort is the vote: Who wants to visit his aunt, who wants to go to the art museum? We as a society cannot solve such problems as these, for arguments about them unfold on different levels and therefore do not intersect, except in the ballot box. And which mechanisms ensue from voting. Aunt museums?

It is fantastic what solutions are offered nowadays. The public hospital, with art inside: its corridors an art museum and its rooms for patients. What is the impact now, of us having suddenly found a solution? Evidently, certain constraints have loosened. This means our previous approach to the issue was: There are hospitals and there are museums. That was a constraint—that set a limit. And now, along comes someone who loosens that constraint. I believe this is an important process: to recognize that so-called constraints are likewise design variables. Admittedly, design variables of a sort somewhat difficult to alter—but design variables nonetheless. And that is certainly something we have learned from this.

The other thing we learn is: there was the famous Zwicky Box, which played a role in Ulm also. Zwicky was also a brilliant mathematician. He always made tables: What are the possible solutions, and where is something still missing? One can write up solutions in terms of the way they are formulated, and then see whether they may be combined. That means: You write everything down and then draw a road running right through the table. What is compatible with what? What is compatible with this? One usually imagines there is only one road. And whoever does not agree, i.e. the client, simply holds another opinion. As I mentioned earlier, we know that different lines of argument do not always run on the same level—there are numerous solutions to every problem. It would be an incredible coincidence, were only one solution to exist. If there is only one solution, that is the realm of functionalism. Functionalism says: This is the one best solution. The best spectacles—so stop designing spectacles: that is the one-stop functional solution to the spectacles problem. In reality, best solutions, optima, do exist; they operate on waves. There are optima and then there are worse solutions. And then, on another level, there is another optimum. One pair of spectacles has the best glass, but it is quite heavy; the other is made of plastic, but it is very light and therefore doesn't hurt one. So, there is one thing with two optima. Most solutions have very many optima. And at the start of the design process we really need to invest in the variability range.

And, ultimately, we must find mechanisms by which we might reach a decision. If we do not come to a decision because we cannot discuss things exhaustively then political views are in play; but there are, in fact, many things that we can thrash out. So my advice is, take a broad approach to design from the start, and make more rational use of paper and printing ink. Thank you.

Bibliography

Strollology. A minor subject (Strollology als Nebenfach = Spaziergangswissenschaften—ein Gespräch zwischen Hans Ulrich Obrist, Annemarie und Lucius Burckhardt), auf www.kunstaspekte.de/diskurs). Strollology—a conversation during a taxi-ride in Bordeaux between Hans Ulrich Obrist and Annemarie and Lucius Burckhardt, on the occasion of the exhibition "Mutations." – In: *Inhabituel,* exhib. cat., Dena Foundation for Contemporary Art, Paris 2005, p. 34–37 (Eng.), 164–165 (Ital.), 178–180 (Ger.). In: Mira Cómo se Mueven, *See how They Move*, exhib. cat., Madrid 2005, Fundación Telefónica (Span./Eng.). – In: *Warum ist Landschaft schön? Die Spaziergangswissenschaft*, Markus Ritter and Martin Schmitz (eds.), Berlin 2006, p. 5–11.

Landscape

Landscape Development and the Structure of Society (Landschaftsentwicklung und Gesellschaftsstruktur). – In: *Die Ware Landschaft*, Friedrich Achleitner (ed.), Salzburg 1977. – In: *Die Kinder fressen ihre Revolution*, Bazon Brock (ed.), Cologne 1985, p. 206–213. – In: *Landschaftswahrnehmung und Landschaftserfahrung – Arbeiten zur sozialwissenschaftlich orientierten Freiraumplanung,* vol. 10, Gert Gröning and Ulfert Herlyn (eds.), Munich 1990, p. 105–116. – In: *Warum ist Landschaft schön? Die Spaziergangswissenschaft*, Markus Ritter and Martin Schmitz (eds.), Berlin 2006, p. 19–32.

Why Is Landscape Beautiful? (Warum ist Landschaft schön?) – In: *Basler Magazin* supplement to *Basler Zeitung* no. 45, 10. 11. 1979, p. 1–5. – In: *Warum ist Landschaft schön? Die Spaziergangswissenschaft*, Markus Ritter and Martin Schmitz (eds.), Berlin 2006, p. 33–41. – In: *Lucius Burckhardt Writings. Rethinking Man-made Environments. Politics, Landscape & Design*, Jesko Fezer and Martin Schmitz (eds.) Vienna/ New York 2012, p. 133–141.

Ecology—Only a Fashion? (Ökologie – nur eine Mode?) – In: *Werk und Zeit* no. 4, 1984. – In: *Die Kinder fressen ihre Revolution*, Bazon Brock (ed.), Cologne 1985, p. 220–224. – In: *Warum ist Landschaft schön? Die Spaziergangswissenschaft*, Markus Ritter and Martin Schmitz, Berlin 2006, p. 42–48.

Nature Is Invisible (Natur ist unsichtbar) – In: *Anthos* 28/3, 1989, p. 2–7 (Ger./Fr./Eng.).

Nature has neither core / Nor outer rind… (Natur hat weder Kern noch Schale). – In: *Imitationen,* Jörg Huber et al. (eds.), exhib. cat., Museum für Gestaltung Zurich 1989, Basel and Frankfurt/Main 1989, p. 67–70.

Aesthetics and Ecology (Ästhetik und Ökologie) – In: *Bauwelt* 81/39, 1990, p. 1968–1972. – In: *Werk und Zeit* no. 3, 1990, p. 22–26. – In: *Der Gartenbau*, 111/39, 1990, p. 1913–1917. – In: *Basler Magazin* supplement to *Basler Zeitung*. 44, 3. 11. 1990, p. 6–7. – In: *GHK Fachbereich Stadtplanung und Landschaftsplanung*, reprint no. 20. – In: *Le design au-delà du visible*, Les essais du Centre Pompidou, Paris 1991 – In: *Design = unsichtbar*, Hans Höger (ed.), Ostfildern 1995, p. 151–161. – In: *Warum ist Landschaft schön? Die Spaziergangswissenschaft*, Markus Ritter and Martin Schmitz (eds.), Berlin 2006, p. 67–81. – In: *Lucius Burckhardt Writings. Rethinking Man-made Environments. Politics, Landscape & Design*, Jesko Fezer and Martin Schmitz (eds.) Vienna/New York 2012, p. 212–224.

Aesthetics of the Landscape (Ästhetik der Landschaft) – In: *Passagen/Passages* no. 11, 1991, p. 3–5 (Ger./Fr./Eng.). – In: *Die Eroberung der Landschaft – Semmering–Rax–Schneeberg*, Wolfgang Kos (ed.), exhib. cat. no. 295, Niederösterreichische Landesausstellung Schloss Gloggnitz, Vienna 1992, p. 63–68. – In: *Warum ist Landschaft schön? Die Spaziergangswissenschaft*, Markus Ritter and Martin Schmitz (eds.), Berlin 2006, p. 82–90.

Landscape Is Transitory (Landschaft ist transitorisch – Umweltgeschichte können wir nur aus heutiger Sicht schreiben – Das uns bekannte verklären wir, sobald es zu verschwinden droht). – In: *Topos – European Landscape Magazine* 6, 1994, p. 38–44. – In: *Design = unsichtbar*, Hans Höger (ed.), Ostfildern 1995, p. 165–170. – In: *Warum ist Landschaft schön? Die Spaziergangswissenschaft*, Markus Ritter and Martin Schmitz (eds.), Berlin 2006, p. 90–97.

Wasteland As Context. Is There Any Such Thing as the Postmodern Landscape? (Brache als Kontext – Postmoderne Landschaften – gibt es das?) – In: *Wespennest – Zeitschrift für brauchbare Texte und Bilder* 110, 1998, p. 56–61. – In: *Ist es hier schön – Landschaft nach der ökologischen Krise*, Anton Holzer and Wieland Elfferding (eds.), Vienna 2000, p. 141–152. – In: *Warum ist Landschaft schön? Die Spaziergangswissenschaft*, Markus Ritter and Martin Schmitz (eds.), Berlin 2006, p. 97–113. – In: *Lucius Burckhardt Writings. Rethinking Man-made Environments. Politics, Landscape & Design*, Jesko Fezer and Martin Schmitz (eds.) Vienna/New York 2012, p. 249–263.

Landscape (Landschaft). – In: *Natur – Arbeit – Ästhetik: anlässlich des 5ten Todestages von Karola Bloch*, Francesca Vidal (ed.), *Bloch Jahrbuch* 1998/1999 = Talheimer Sammlung kritisches Wissen 34, Mössingen-Talheim 1998, p. 76–83. – In: *Warum ist Landschaft schön? Die Spaziergangswissenschaft*, Markus Ritter and Martin Schmitz (eds.), Berlin 2006, p. 114–123.

Gardens and the Art of Gardening

Gardening—An Art and A Necessity (Gärtnern – Kunst und Notwendigkeit). – In: *Basler Magazin* supplement to *Basler Zeitung* no. 21, 25. 6. 1977, p. 1–2. – In: *Warum ist Landschaft schön? Die Spaziergangswissenschaft*, Markus Ritter and Martin Schmitz (eds.), Berlin 2006, p.131–139. – In: *Lucius Burckhardt Writings. Rethinking Man-made Environments. Politics, Landscape & Design*, Jesko Fezer and Martin Schmitz (eds.) Vienna/New York 2012, p.123–132.

No Man's Land (Niemandsland – Wo Anne ihren ersten Kuss bekam). – In: *Werkbund – Material* no. 2, 1980. – In: *Grün in der Stadt*, Michael Andritzky and Klaus Spitzer (eds.), Reinbek 1981. – In: *Die Kinder fressen ihre Revolution*, Bazon Brock (ed.), Cologne 1985, p. 199–200. – In: *Wer plant die Planung? Architektur, Politik und Mensch,* Jesko Fezer and Martin Schmitz (eds.), Berlin 2004, p. 321–322. – In: *Warum ist Landschaft schön? Die Spaziergangswissenschaft*, Markus Ritter and Martin Schmitz (eds.), Berlin 2006, p. 140–141.

Destroyed By Tender Loving Care (Durch Pflege zerstört). – In: *Deutsche Bauzeitung* no. 6, 1981. – In: *Die Kinder fressen ihre Revolution*, Bazon Brock (ed.), Cologne 1985, p. 193–196. – In: *Warum ist Landschaft schön? Die Spaziergangswissenschaft*, Markus Ritter and Martin Schmitz (eds.), Berlin 2006, p. 142–145.

Reason Slumbers in the Garden (Die Vernunft schläft im Garten). – In: Museum Fridericianum (eds.), *Schlaf der Vernunft*. exhib. cat, Kassel 1988, p. 189–198 (Ger./Eng.) – In: *Warum ist Landschaft schön? Die Spaziergangswissenschaft*, Markus Ritter and Martin Schmitz (eds.), Berlin 2006, p. 146–156.

Gardens Are Images (Gärten sind Bilder). – In: *Natur im Griff – Bundesgartenschauen am Beispiel Frankfurt*, Michael Damian and Thomas Ormond (eds.), Frankfurt/Main 1989, p. 19–26. – In: *Warum ist Landschaft schön? Die Spaziergangswissenschaft*, Markus Ritter and Martin Schmitz (eds.), Berlin 2006, p.156–166.

In Nature's Garden (Der Garten der Arten, written for the 400th anniversary of the Botanical Institute Basel, November 1989, first published in: *Warum ist Landschaft schön? Die Spaziergangswissenschaft*, Markus Ritter and Martin Schmitz (eds.), Berlin 2006, p. 166–176.

Nature and the Garden in Classicism (Natur und Garten im Klassizismus). – In: *Der Monat* no. 177, 1963, p. 43–52. – In: *Warum ist Landschaft schön? Die Spaziergangswissenschaft*, Markus Ritter and Martin Schmitz (eds.), Berlin 2006, p. 177–197.

Garden Design—New Trends (Gartenkunst wohin?). – In: *Grün in der Stadt*, Michael Andritzky and Klaus Spitzer (eds.), Reinbek 1981. – In: *Die Kinder fressen ihre Revolution*, Bazon Brock (ed.), Cologne 1985, p. 307–314. – In: *Warum ist Landschaft schön? Die Spaziergangswissenschaft*, Markus Ritter and Martin Schmitz (eds.), Berlin 2006, p. 197–207.

A Critique of the Art of Gardening (Kritik der Gartenkunst). – In: *Docu-Bulletin* Oct. 1983, p. 939. – In: *Die Kinder fressen ihre Revolution*, Bazon Brock (ed.), Cologne 1985, p. 422–427. – In: *Le design au-delà du visible*, Les essais du Centre Pompidou, Paris 1991, p. 97–106. – In: *Warum ist Landschaft schön? Die Spaziergangswissenschaft*, Markus Ritter and Martin Schmitz (eds.), Berlin 2006, p. 207–216. – In: *Lucius Burckhardt Writings. Rethinking Man-made Environments. Politics, Landscape & Design*, Jesko Fezer and Martin Schmitz (eds.) Vienna/New York 2012, p. 195–203.

Views from Mount Furka (Furkablick). – In: *Docu-bulletin* Jul. 1988, p. 5–14 (Ger./Fr.) – In: *Warum ist Landschaft schön? Die Spaziergangswissenschaft*, Markus Ritter and Martin Schmitz (eds.), Berlin 2006, p. 216–221.

Natura Maestra (Natura Maestra – Über Pflanzen, Tiere, Landschaft und andere Phänomene in Natur und Kunst). In: *Künstler als Gärtner*, Paolo Bianchi (ed.), *Kunstforum international* vol. 145, Cologne 1999, p. 181–192. – In: *Warum ist Landschaft schön? Die Spaziergangswissenschaft*, Markus Ritter and Martin Schmitz (eds.), Berlin 2006, p. 222–235.

Current Trends in Garden Design (Tendenze attuali dell'arte dei giardini). In: *Domus* no. 817, 1999, p. 4–6. In: *Warum ist Landschaft schön? Die Spaziergangswissenschaft*, Markus Ritter and Martin Schmitz (eds.), Berlin 2006, p. 236–241.

The Science of Strollogy

Strollological Observations on Perception of the Environment and the Tasks Facing Our Generation (Promenadologische Betrachtungen über die Wahrnehmung der Umwelt und die Aufgaben unserer Generation, written for an exhibition planned by Herzog & de Meuron for Centre Pompidou, 1996) – In: *Warum ist Landschaft schön? Die Spaziergangswissenschaft*, Markus Ritter and Martin Schmitz (eds.), Berlin 2006, p. 251–256. – In: *Lucius Burckhardt Writings. Rethinking Man-made Environments. Politics, Landscape & Design*, Jesko Fezer and Martin Schmitz (eds.) Vienna/New York 2012, p. 239–248.

The Science of Strollology (Spaziergangswissenschaft, 1995) first published in: *Warum ist Landschaft schön? Die Spaziergangswissenschaft*, Markus Ritter and Martin Schmitz (eds.), Berlin 2006. p. 257–300.

What Do Explorers Discover? (Was entdecken Entdecker?) – In: *Die Fahrt nach Tahiti* (with texts by Georg Forster, Jürgen von Reuß and Stephen Bann), Fachbereich Stadtplanung und Landschaftsplanung der Gesamthochschule Kassel (eds.), *Schriftenreihe der Gesamthochschule Kassel* vol. 11, Kassel 1988. – In: *Le design au-delà du visible*, Les essais du Centre Pompidou, Paris 1991, p. 85–88 under the title "Que découvrent les explorateurs?" – In: *Warum ist Landschaft schön? Die Spaziergangswissenschaft*, Markus Ritter and Martin Schmitz (eds.), Berlin 2006, p. 301–305.

Mountaineering on Sylt. In Conversation with Nikolaus Wyss (Bergsteigen auf Sylt – Ein Promenadologe auf freien Füssen – Nikolaus Wyss sprach mit dem Spaziergangswissenschafter Lucius Burckhardt). – In: *Das Magazin – Tages-Anzeiger* and *Berner Zeitung* no. 12, 23./25. 3. 1989, p. 30–36. – In: *Bauwelt* 81/7–8, 1990, p. 311–315. – In: *Le design au-delà du visible*, Les essais du Centre Pompidou, Paris 1991, p. 71–84. – In: *Warum ist Landschaft schön? Die Spaziergangswissenschaft*, Markus Ritter and Martin Schmitz (eds.), Berlin 2006, p. 306–319.

A Matter of Looking and Recognizing. In Conversation with Thomas Fuchs (Es geht um das Sehen und Erkennen. Interview mit Thomas Fuchs). – In: *Garten und Landschaft* 103/10, 1993. – In: *Design = unsichtbar*, Hans Höger (ed.), Ostfildern 1995, p. 195–200. – In: *Warum ist Landschaft schön? Die Spaziergangswissenschaft*, Markus Ritter and Martin Schmitz (eds.), Berlin 2006, p. 320–326.

Strollology—A New Science (Promenadologie – Eine neue Wissenschaft). – In: *Passagen/Passages* no. 24, 1998, p. 3–5 (Ger./Eng./Fr.). – In: *Warum ist Landschaft schön? Die Spaziergangswissenschaft*, Markus Ritter and Martin Schmitz (eds.), Berlin 2006, p. 327–335. – In: *Wieviel Garten braucht der Mensch?* Ingrid Greisenegger (ed.), Vienna 2003, p. 128–130, abridged under the title "Vom Mangel im Überfluss." – In: *Das kleine Gartenglück*, Munich 2004, p. 170–172, abridged under the title "Abstandsgrün."

On Movement And Vantage Points—The Strollologist's Experience (Bewegung und Standpunkt – Erfahrungen des Promenadologen). – In: *Über Denken – Ein Symposion über Gestalten und Denken*, Florian Aicher and Dagmar Rinker (eds.), Munich 1999, p. 98–113. – In: *Warum ist Landschaft schön? Die Spaziergangswissenschaft*, Markus Ritter and Martin Schmitz (eds.), Berlin 2006, p. 335–352. – In: *Lucius Burckhardt Writings. Rethinking Man-made Environments. Politics, Landscape & Design*, Jesko Fezer and Martin Schmitz (eds.) Vienna/New York 2012, p. 264–279.

Biography

Lucius Burckhardt (*Davos, 1925) gained a PhD in Basel then became a research assistant at the Social Research Center at Münster University in 1955. A guest lectureship at Ulm University of Applied Arts in 1959 was followed from 1961 to 1973 by several teaching assignments, including a guest lectureship in sociology at the Architecture Faculty of the Swiss Federal Institute of Technology (ETH Zurich). He worked simultaneously as editor-in-chief of the journal *Werk* from 1962 to 1973, was First President of the German *Werkbund* from 1976 to 1983, and professor of the socio-economics of urban systems at the University of Kassel as of 1973. He was also a correspondent member of the German Academy of Urban and Regional Spatial Planning, a Chevalier dans l'Ordre des Arts et des Lettres, from 1987 to 1989 a member of the Founding Committee of Saar University of Visual Arts, and from 1992 to 1994 the founding dean of the Design Faculty at the Bauhaus University Weimar. In recognition of his life's work, he was awarded the Hessian Culture Prize for Outstanding Achievements in the Realms of Science, Ecology and Aesthetics in 1994, the Federal Prize for Design Promoters in 1995, and the Swiss Design Prize in 2001. Lucius Burckhardt died in Basel in 2003.

Book publications: *Wir selber bauen unsre Stadt* (with Markus Kutter), Basel 1953; *Achtung: die Schweiz* (with Max Frisch and Markus Kutter), Basel 1955; *Die neue Stadt* (with Max Frisch and Markus Kutter), Basel 1956; *Reise ins Risorgimento*, Cologne/Berlin 1959; *Bauen ein Prozess* (with Walter Förderer), Teufen 1968; *Moderne Architektur in der Schweiz seit 1900* (with Annemarie Burckhardt and Diego Peverelli), Winterthur 1969; *Der Werkbund in Deutschland, Österreich und der Schweiz*, Stuttgart 1978 (translated into Italian, French, and English); *Für eine andere Architektur* (edited with Michael Andritzky and Ot Hoffmann), Frankfurt/Main 1981; *Die Kinder fressen ihre Revolution* (edited by Bazon Brock), Cologne 1985; *Le design au-delà du visible*, Paris 1991; *Design = unsichtbar*, Ostfildern 1995; *Wer plant die Planung?Architektur, Politik und Mensch*, Berlin 2004; *Warum ist Landschaft schön? Die Spaziergangswissenschaft*, Berlin 2006; *Design ist unsichtbar. Entwurf, Gesellschaft und Pädagogik*, Berlin 2012; *Lucius Burckhardt Writings. Rethinking Man-made Environments*, Vienna/NY 2012; *Der kleinstmögliche Eingriff*, Berlin 2013 and *Wir selber bauen unsre Stadt* (with Markus Kutter), reprint Berlin 2015.

Markus Ritter (* Basel, 1954) is a biologist. In 1986, he and Lucius and Annemarie Burckhardt founded the party "Grüne Alternative Basel" (Green Alternative Basel). From 1988 to 2001, Ritter was a Member of the Basel Canton Parliament, in the latter years also its President. He now works in the General Secretariat of the Presidential Department of Basel City Council. From 1987 onwards, he worked with Lucius Burckhardt on projects, seminars and articles regarding issues of the landscape, nature and the environment. He has published widely on the history of the environment and nature conservation as well as on ornithological and botanical themes. He has been engaged since 2012 in appraising the estate of Lucius and Annemarie Burckhardt, which is held in the archives of the University of Basel Library.

Martin Schmitz (* Hamm/Westf., 1956) studied under Lucius Burckhardt in Kassel and held lectureships to date in Saarbrücken, Weimar, and Kassel. He has been an independent publisher since 1989 and is the author of *Currywurst mit Fritten – Über die Kultur der Imbißbude* (1983). He was the curator of the movie program at documenta 8 in 1987, the "Dilettantism" conference in Görlitz in 1995, the *documenta urbana* symposium "Kunst plant die Planung" in Kassel in 2007, the international convention "Spaziergangswissenschaft: Sehen, erkennen und planen" in Frankfurt/Main in 2008, and the 1st Lucius Burckhardt Convention in Kassel in 2014. He is co-editor of several books by Lucius Burckhardt: *Wer plant die Planung?, Warum ist Landschaft schön?, Design ist unsichtbar, Der kleinstmögliche Eingriff, Wir bauen selber unsre Stadt* and *Lucius Burckhardt Writings*. Since being appointed Interim Chair in 2013, he teaches the theory and practice of design at Kassel University of the Arts. www.martin-schmitz.de

Also available at Birkhäuser:
Lucius Burckhardt Writings. Rethinking Man-made Environments. Politics, Landscape & Design, Jesko Fezer and Martin Schmitz (eds.) Vienna/New York 2012.

Index